AF792537

Committees and Commissions in India
1977

Concepts in Communication
Informatics & Librarianship-51

General Editor : **S.P. Agrawal**

Committees and Commissions in India 1977

Volume 15

PART D

A Concept's Project

Compiled by a team of professionals
guided by
VIRENDRA KUMAR

CONCEPT PUBLISHING COMPANY, NEW DELHI 110059

ISBN 81-7022-487-X (Vol. 15, Part D)

First Published 1993

Published and Printed by
Ashok Kumar Mittal
Concept Publishing Company
A/15-16, Commercial Block, Mohan Garden
NEW DELHI 110059 (India)

Lasertypeset by
Printing Express
H-13, Bali Nagar
NEW DELHI 110015

CONTENTS

PART B

PART C

PART D

43

NATIONAL POLICE COMMISSION, 1977 — FOURTH REPORT[1]

Chairman	Shri Dharma Vira, retired Governor
Members	Shri N.K. Reddy; Shri K.F. Rustamji; Shri N.S. Saksena; Prof. M.S. Gore
M. Secy.	Shri C.V. Narasimhan
Alterations	Shri C.V. Narasimhan, former Director of Central Bureau of Investigation, functioned as Member Secretary of the Commission from its inception till 19th April, 1980 when he left to take a posting in his parent cadre in Tamil Nadu on replacement of his services from the Central Government to the State Government. After the departure of Shri Narasimhan, Shri M.D. Dikshit, Principal Director of Research, functioned as the Secretary Incharge.

Appointment

Far-reaching changes have taken place in the country after the enactment of the Indian Police Act, 1861 and the setting up of the second Police Commission of 1902, particularly during the last thirty years of Independence. Though a number of States have appointed Police Commissions after Independence to study the problems of the Police in their respective States, there has been no comprehensive review at the national level of the police system after independence despite radical changes in the political, social and economic situation in the country. A fresh examination is necessary of the role and performance of the Police — both as a law enforcement agency, and as an institution to protect the rights of the citizens enshrined in the Constitution. The Government of India have, therefore, decided to appoint a National Police Commission. The National Police Commis-

---

1. Controller of Publications, Delhi, 1981, i + 81 p.

sion was appointed under the Government of India, Ministry of Home Affairs Resolution No. VI-24021/36/77-GPA.I, dated November 15, 1977.

Terms of Reference

The following will be the terms of reference of the Commission:

(1) Re-define the role, duties, powers and responsibilities of the police with special reference to prevention and control of crime and maintenance of public order.
(2) Examine the development of the principles underlying the present policing system, including the method of magisterial supervision, evaluate the performance of the system, identify the basic weaknesses of inadequacies, and suggest appropriate changes in the system and the basic laws governing the system.
(3) Examine, if any changes are necessary in the existing method of administration, disciplinary control and accountability.
(4) Inquire into the system of investigation and prosecution, the reasons for delay and failure; the use of improper methods, and the extent of their prevalence; and suggest how the system may be modified or changed, and made efficient;scientific and consistent with human dignity; and how the related laws may be suitably amended.
(5) Examine methods of maintaining crime records and statistics and suggest methods for making them uniform and systematic.
(6) Review policing in rural areas, evaluate any new arrangements that have been made, and recommend changes that are necessary.
(7) Examine the system of policing required in non-rural and urbanised areas including metropolitan areas, and suggest the pattern that would be the most suitable.
(8) Examine the steps taken for modernising law enforcement, evaluate the work of police communications, the computer net-work, scientific laboratories and agencies for research and development, and examine whether modernisation can be speeded up; examine to what extent, as a result of the modernisation of Police forces, streamlining of its functions and its re-structuring, it would be possible to economise in the manpower in the various areas of its activities.

(9) Examine the nature and extent of the special responsibilities of the Police towards the weaker sections of the community and suggest steps to ensure prompt action on their complaints for the safeguard of their rights and interests.

(10) Recommend measures and institutional arrangements: –

(i) to prevent misuse of powers by the police, and to examine whether police behaviour, outlook, responsiveness and impartiality are maintained at the correct level, and if not the steps such as recruitment and training which should be taken to improve them;

(ii) to prevent misuse of the Police by administrative or executive instructions, political or other pressure, or oral orders of any type, which are contrary to law;

(iii) for the quick and impartial inquiry of public complaints made against the police about any misuse of police powers;

(iv) for the quick redressal of grievances of police personnel and to look after their morale and welfare; and

(v) for a periodic objective evaluation of police performance in a metropolitan area/district/State in a manner which will carry credibility before the public.

(11) Examine the manner and extent to which police can enlist ready and willing co-operation of the public in the discharge of their social defence and law enforcement duties and suggest measures regarding the institutional arrangements to secure such cooperation and measures for the growth of healthy and friendly public-police relationship.

(12) Examine the methods of police training, development, and career-planning of officers and recommend any changes that are required at any time in their service, to modernise the outlook, and to make the leadership of the force effective and morally strong.

(13) Examine the nature of the problems that the police will have to face in the future, and suggest the measures necessary for dealing with them, and for keeping them under continuous study and appraisal.

(14) Consider and make recommendations and suggestions regarding any other matter which the Government may refer to the Commission; and

(15) Any other matter of relevance or importance having an impact

on the subject.

Contents

Investigation; Court trial; Prosecuting agency; Industrial disputes; Agrarian problems; Social legislation; Prohibition; Summary of observations and recommendations; Appendices I to XV.

Recommendations

Investigation

34.1 The major problems of reform as viewed by the Law Commission in its Thirty-seventh Report were:

(a) separation of the judiciary and the executive;
(b) abolition of the jury trial;
(c) simplification of the various categories of trials;
(d) Magistrates in Presidency Towns;
(e) abolition or retention of the ordinary original criminal jurisdiction of High Courts;
(f) the law of arrest; and
(g) the duty to give information about offences.

It, therefore, happened that in the above view of the matter, the report of the Law Commission did not adequately deal with several other aspects of procedure which created difficulties for the police while conducting investigations in the field. Compliance of certain provisions in law proved unrealistic and difficult in actual investigations and, therefore, led to the adoption of certain improper methods and practices by investigating officers to meet the requirements of case law as it developed over several years. In the course of our tours in States and discussions with judges, magistrates, lawyers, police officers, general administrations and representative sections of the public, we have identified some aspects of the present procedural law relating to investigations where there is urgent need and ample scope for meaningful reform to make investigations conform to the real situations in the field and help in the expeditious conduct of investigations with minimum inconvenience to persons who may be concerned in specific cases as complainants, witnesses or accused persons. (Para 27.2)

34.2 Section 154 Cr.P.C. may be amended to—

(i) enable the officer incharge of police station to ascertain adequate information from a complainant and incorporate it in the form prescribed for registering First Information Report;
(ii) make it clear that the registration of First Information Report is mandatory whether or not the alleged offence has taken place in the jurisdiction of the police station; and
(iii) facilitate the recording of First Information Report in constituent units attached to the police station—for example: police out post or such other reporting centres as may be evolved in due course. (Para 27.6)

34.3 The cadre of investigating officers has to be increased. The police hierarchy has to be re-structured to secure, *inter alia*, a larger number of officers to handle investigational work. (Para 27.7)

34.4 Provision of adequate transport, strengthening of Forensic Science Laboratory facilities and scientific aids to the detection of crime, the provision of mechanical aids like typewriter and tape recorders at the police station level, improved supply of printed forms and standardised stationery for documentation and scriptory work and the introduction of computers for the maintenance of crime records as suggested in Chapter XXIV of our Third Report would greatly improve the quality and quickness of investigations. (Para 27.8)

34.5 Section 37 Cr.P.C. may be amended to facilitate the conduct of identification parades by police themselves as an aid to investigation. (Para 27.9)

34.6 It would greatly help cordial police-public relationship if the examination of witnesses is conducted, as far as practicable, near the scene of offence or at the residence of the witnesses concerned or at some convenient place nearby. This arrangement might be secured by the issue of appropriate departmental instructions. (Para 27.10)

34.7 It is desirable to make a specific provision in law that when a person is examined by a police officer under Section 161 Cr.P.C. no other person shall, except in the exercise of powers under the law, have the right to be present during such examination. (Para 27.11)

34.8 The Code of Criminal Procedure, 1973 had done away with the procedure of preliminary enquiries by magistrates in cases exclusively triable by a Sessions Court. Before this Code came into force, the procedure envisaged the examination of material witnesses twice over, once by the Committing Magistrate and later by the Sessions Judge. Thus, for the same witness, we would have three sets of statements on record, one recorded by the police during investigation, the second recorded by the Committing Magistrate and the third recorded by the Sessions Judge. It is a basic principle of justice that the findings of the trying judge should be based on what the witnesses actually depose before him; but the availability of detailed statements from the same witnesses before another forum recorded on an earlier occasion provides scope for arguments based on *contradictions* however, trivial or natural they might be in the circumstances of any particular case. We consider it wholly improper, if not unjust, for the conclusions in judicial proceedings to be largely determined by contradictions in evidence by a mechanical or routine comparison of the statement made separately by the witness before different authorities instead of by probabilities flowing from the evidence. The Code of Criminal Procedure, 1973, has rightly eliminated on unnecessary stage of recording the detailed statement of a witness by the Committing Magistrate. A further step would be to do away with the detailed recording of statement as made by a witness in the course of investigation, and substitute in its place a revised arrangement in which the investigating officer can make a record of the facts as ascertained by him on examination of a witness. This shift in emphasis from the statement made by the witness to the statement of facts ascertained from the witness would imply that the statement could be in third person in the language of the investigating officer himself. This statement of facts as recorded by the investigating officer would be adequate to assess the evidentiary value of the different witnesses and accordingly cite them in the charge sheet, if and when it is laid in court on conclusion of investigation. (Para 27.14)

34.9 When the statement as described above becomes a statement of facts as ascertained and recorded by the investigating officer, it loses its significance to serve as an earlier statement made by the witness himself in his own language, and, therefore, the question of using that statement for contradiction or corroboration would not arise. The present provisions in Section 162 Cr.P.C. relating to the restricted use of the statements of witnesses would, therefore, become redundant. (Para 27.15)

34.10 A police malpractice brought to our notice is the habit of some police officers to be very cursory in their examination of certain witnesses and then proceed to make a detailed record of the witness's statement, assuming it to be what they would like it to be in the context of statements of other witnesses already recorded. It is imperative that we put down this malpractice to ensure the honesty and cleanliness of investigations. A great measure of credibility could be imparted to the statement of facts as recorded by the police officer after examination of a witness, if we provide in law that a copy of the statement so recorded shall, if desired by the witness, be handed over to him under acknowledgement. A similar arrangement already exists for the delivery of a search list prepared under Section 100 Cr.P.C. to the occupant of the place searched or the person searched. (Para 27.18)

34.11 For giving effect to the revised arrangements proposed above, Sections 161 and 162 Cr.P.C. may be amended on the lines recommended in the Report. (Para 27.19)

34.12 Section 172 Cr.P.C. relating to the case diary may be amended on the lines indicated in the Report. (Para 27.20)

34.13 Section 100 Cr.P.C. may be amended to facilitate the admission of search list as a piece of evidence without having to call search witnesses to depose in court, and further to facilitate public servants to function as search witnesses in certain situations. (Para 27.21)

34.14 Section 102 Cr.P.C. may be amended to give greater discretion to the police for releasing seized property. (Para 27.22)

34.15 The police may be required through departmental instructions to initiate appropriate steps immediately after the disposal of a case for the prompt return of the case properly to the person entitled to get it. (Para 27.23)

34.16 A new Section—50A—may be added to Chapter V of Cr.P.C. requiring the police to give intimation about the arrest of a person to anyone who may be reasonably named by him for sending such intimation, to avoid agonising suspense for the members of his family about his whereabouts. (Para 27.25)

34.17 It is most important for improving police image that the senior officers and the supervisory ranks in the police deem it their special responsibility to put down the practice of third degree methods at the operational level in police stations and elsewhere. Some remedial measures are indicated below:

(i) Surprise visits to police stations and similar units by the senior officers would help the immediate detection of persons held in unauthorised custody and subjected to ill-treatment. Malpractices, if any, noticed during such visits should be met by swift and deterrent punishment;

(ii) A Magistrate or Judge before whom an arrested person is produced by the police for remand to custody should be required by administrative rules of criminal practice to question the arrested person specifically if he has any complaint of ill-treatment by the police, and if he has any complaint the Magistrate or Judge should get him medically examined and take appropriate further action;

(iii) In Chapter X of our First Report, we have already recommended a scheme for mandatory judicial inquiries into complaints of death or grievous hurt caused while in police custody. Such an arrangement would itself act as an effective check against the continuance of third degree methods in police work;

(iv) Supervisory ranks, including the senior levels of command in the police and the Government, should strictly eschew a purely statistical approach while evaluating police performance. Any administrative review of a kind which is likely to induce the subordinate ranks to adopt *ad hoc* and short-cut methods to show results should be avoided. Adequate emphasis should be laid on the honesty and cleanliness of investigations and the adoption of proper methods while handling all the connected work; and

(v) Training institutions should pay special attention to the development of interrogation techniques and imparting effective instructions to trainees in this regard. (Para 27.26)

34.18 We are convinced that if the average police officer is assured of adequate time and facility for patiently examining an accused person and pursuing the examination from point to point through a process of simultaneous verification of facts mentioned by the accused, it would facilitate a proper examination of the accused person without resort to questionable methods involving pressure tactics. This would become possible if the police can secure the remand of an arrested person to police custody for a few days under orders from a Magistrate. When the accused remains in police custody under specific orders from a Magistrate, the scope for using third degree methods while interrogating him in such custody would get greatly reduced since he would be liable for production before Magistrate on expiry of the brief custody. In the light of the present phraseology of Section 167 Cr.P.C., some conventions and practices have developed in several States for the Magistrates not to grant police custody unless the Investigating Officer pleads that the accused has already made a confession and his continued custody with the police is necessary to take him from place to place and recover property. This peculiar requirement of convention and practice drives police officers to make false statements before the Magistrate while in fact the accused would not have made any such confession and they would merely be requiring to verify several facts mentioned by him and continue with his examination. Existing sub-sections (3) and (4) of Section 167 which imply that remand to police custody should be exceptional may, therefore, be deleted and a new sub-section (3) may be added to facilitate remand to police custody in the interest of investigation whenever required. (Para 27.27)

34.19 Section 167 Cr.P.C. may be amended on the lines suggested in the Report to facilitate remand by Executive Magistrate in certain specified situations. (Para 27.28)

34.20 Sections 2 Cr.P.C. may be amended on the lines indicated in the report to facilitate the establishment of special police stations to deal with particular cases or classes of cases. (Para 27.32)

34.21 Section 26 and 27 of the Evidence Act may be deleted and section 25 of the same Act may be substituted by a new section as recommended in the Report to facilitate the proof of a confession recorded by any person in authority (including the police) in the course of any judicial proceedings, against a person making the confession, not to be used as an evidence against him but to be taken into consideration by the court to aid it in an inquiry or trial in the manner provided in Section 30 of the same Act and section 172 Cr.P.C. (Para 27.33)

34.22 The comprehensive amendments in procedural law and Evidence Act as proposed above would not by themselves bring about noticeable improvement in the quality of investigations unless the supervisory ranks in the police hierarchy pay adequate attention to the detailed supervision over the progress of individual investigations. The quality and quantum of supervisory work done in regard to crime investigations as distinct from mere *ad hoc* maintenance of public order from day to day on a 'somehow' basis should be carefully assessed for each supervisory rank and taken due note of for his career advancement. (Para 27.35)

Court Trial

34.23 The disposal of cases in courts has not kept pace with the institution of fresh cases for trial year after year with the result that the entire judicial machinery has got clogged up and the protracted disposal of cases has diluted the desired deterrence on the criminal elements in society. (Para 28.1)

34.24 Protracted proceedings in courts followed by acquittal in heinous crimes tend to generate a feeling of confidence among the hardened criminals that they can continue to commit crimes with impunity and ultimately get away with it all at the end of leisurely and long drawn legal battles in courts which they can allow their defence counsel to take care of. Such a situation is hardly assuring to the law abiding citizens and needs to be immediately corrected by appropriate measures even if they should appear drastic and radical. (Para 28.3)

34.25 The Law Commission in its Seventy-seventh Report (November, 1978) has dealt with the problem of delays in court trials and made some recommendations to improve matters. These recommendations relate mostly to administrative measure including supervision and inspection by the judicial hierarchy. Some changes in law have also been suggested but they appear peripheral. The entire philosophy and procedural conduct that attend the present working of the legal system, particularly in regard to court trials, would need a detailed examination for revamping the system to make it conform to the expectations of the common people to secure speedy and inexpensive justice which would appear meaningful and effective in their daily lives. There is obvious scope and need for cutting down a lot of rituals and imparting a sense of commitment and urgency to the participants in judicial proceedings to secure the ultimate objectives of rendering justice to society as well as to the individuals concerned. We, as a Police Commission, are aware of some requirements of reform viewed from the angle of Investigating Officers and the prosecuting agency, but the sweep of reforms in the legal system has to be much wider and cover several other areas in which the lawyers and judges have a prominent role to play. It is beyond our present scope and competence as a Police Commission to go into the wider aspects of legal reform but we would urge and recommend that an appropriate body might be asked by the Government to go into this matter. We would further urge that functionaries from the police and Correctional Services might be associated with the deliberations of this body to ensure a comprehensive look at the entire scheme of things and identify the requirements of reform. (Para 28.4)

34.26 While the reforms that may emerge from the deliberations of a body as suggested above might meet the long term requirements of the current situation of judicial stagnation, we feel there is ample scope for some immediate changes in law which might relieve the present stagnation and help the judicial machinery to start rolling smoothly for the dispensation of justice. The reforms we have in mind are intended to:

(i) reduce the institution of fresh cases in courts year after year;
(ii) withdraw old cases from courts according to some accepted norms; and
(iii) expedite the disposal of pending cases by simplifying the procedures. (Para 28.5)

34.27 The institution of Gram Nyayalayas as proposed in Chapter XVI of our Second Report would be a positive step for reducing the input of fresh cases for trial in regular courts. (Para 28.6)

34.28 The adoption of a 'ticketing system' for on-the-spot disposal of traffic offences would also help in reducing the input of an appreciable volume of cases for trial in courts. (Para 28.7)

34.29 Section 173 Cr.P.C. may be amended to facilitate the compounding of certain types of cases even at the stage of investigation. (Para 28.8)

34.30 The decision to launch prosecution should be based on a proper assessment of the evidence available and generally speaking, prosecutions should not be launched unless the evidence warrants a reasonable expectation of conviction. (Para 28.9)

34.31 There should be a periodic review at the district level of every police case pending in court for more than one year from the date of filing chargesheet and a decision should be taken whether it would be in public interest or in the interest of justice to pursue the prosecution or whether the case may be withdrawn. Some possible criteria for deciding this matter are furnished in the Report. (Para 28.10)

34.32 There is need for establishing some norms for the disposal of criminal cases by Magistrates and Sessions Judges and increasing the number of courts accordingly. A Committee with members drawn from the judiciary and the prosecuting staff may be set up by the High Court in each State for evolving these norms, having regard to local conditions. (Para 28.12)

34.33 The progress of court trials gets blocked by a variety of reasons, some of which are correctible by administrative measures and some are relatable to the general attitude and approach shown by the prosecuting staff, defence counsel and the Presiding Magistrate/Judge. We have known of badly delayed trials arising from causes like non-appearance of witnesses, lack of preparedness of the prosecuting or defence counsel to get on with the day's work in court, frequent adjournments granted on the slightest move for adjournment, prolonged cross-examination without regard to its relevance or need, taking unduly long time for perusing records or otherwise getting prepared for the case at different stages of trial, etc. We feel that several of these causes may be eliminated, if the Presiding Magistrate/Judge adopts a positive approach to the daily proceedings in every case and adequately uses his powers under the Criminal Procedure Code and Section 165 of the Indian Evidence Act for expeditious disposal of the case. There is need for evolving a scheme of inspections at the level of High Court as well as Sessions Courts to ensure the business-like functioning of the subordinate courts. (Para 28.13)

34.34 A whole time functionary of the rank of a senior District and Sessions Judge who is qualified for appointment as High Court Judge may be attached to each High Court to inspect the district courts periodically. A similar functionary of the rank of Additional Sessions Judge may be entrusted with inspections at the district level. (Para 28.13)

34.35 The inspecting arrangement proposed above should also ensure the availability of adequate staying facilities for the witnesses and others who participate in court proceedings. The dissatisfaction of the public with the woeful lack of such facilities in court gets reflected in their hostile and critical attitude to the police whom they view as their first point of contact with the criminal justice system and whom they are in a position to criticise more freely and sharply than they can in regard to matters inside the court hall which, in their view, are protected by the legal rituals and formalities which pass of as part of the majesty of law. (Para 28.14)

34.36 The allowances payable to witnesses for their attendance in court should be fixed on a realistic basis and their payment should be effected through a simple procedure which would avoid delay and inconvenience. (Para 28.15)

34.37 There is obvious scope for appointing a larger number of Special Magistrates under Sections 13 and 18 Cr.P.C. specially for dealing with cases under local and special laws. (Para 28.16)

34.38 It would make for a much quicker disposal of several cases if the summary trial procedure is made mandatory for the offences specified in Section 260 Cr.P.C. and for this purpose we recommend that the words 'may, if he thinks fit', appearing in the aforesaid section be substituted by the word "Shall". (Para 28.17)

34.39 All First Class Magistrates, Special Judicial Magistrates and Special Metroplitan Magistrates may be empowered to act under the above mentioned sector, without necessarily having to be specially empowered by the High Court, as prescribed now. (Para 28.18)

34.40 It has been brought to our notice that in the system of reviewing the work done by Magistrates, the disposal of cases under the summary trial procedure is not given credit by the High Courts in certain States. We would recommend appropriate value being given to the volume of work handled under Section 260 Cr.P.C. also while assessing the performance of a Magistrate. (Para 28.19)

34.41 State Governments may avail the provisions of Section 206 Cr.P.C. as recently amended and notify all the Magistrates including Special Magistrates and Special Metropolitan Magistrate as empowered under this section. The maximum amount of fine that can be imposed under this section may be increased to Rs. 500 from the existing Rs. 100. (Para 28.20)

34.42 Section 294 Cr.P.C. requires the prosecution or the accused to admit or deny the genuineness of documents as and when they are filed in court. The same principle may be incorporated in a separate section in Chapter XIX of Cr.P.C. to enable the court to ask the accused before framing the charge as provided in Section 240 Cr.P.C. whether the accused accepts any part of the prosecution evidence as furnished in the documents supplied under section 207 Cr.P.C. (Para 28.21)

34.43 Sections 291, 293 and 296 Cr.P.C. may be amended on the lines indicated in the Report to facilitate easy proof of evidence of medical officers and other experts. (Para 28.23)

34.44 Section 256 Cr.P.C. may be amended to make it inapplicable to cases in which a public servant figures as the complainant in his capacity as public servant. (Para 28.24)

34.45 Section 321 Cr.P.C. relating to withdrawal of cases from Courts and Section 397 Cr.P.C. may be amended on the lines indicated in the Report to provide for the following:

(i) Having regard to the fact that the withdrawal of a case may have to be decided sometimes with reference to the appreciation of a local public order situation by the executive authority, it would be necessary to retain the power of the Government to initiate action for the withdrawal of a case. The Public Prosecutor should be empowered in law to act under directions from the Government for this purpose;

(ii) The application for withdrawal should mention in detail the reasons for the proposed withdrawal;

(iii) The court should be satisfied that the withdrawal would be in the interests of public order or justice;

(iv) The court's order should incorporate the reasons for according the permission for withdrawal; and

(v) Any member of the public should have the facility to go in appeal against an order passed by the court permitting withdrawal of the prosecution in any specific case. (Paras 28.29, 28.30 and 28.31)

34.46 Important cases, i.e., cases triable by a Court of Session, which are withdrawn during a year in accordance with the principles detailed above, shall be mentioned in the Annual Report on the performance of the State police presented to the Legislature by the State Security Commission as suggested in paragraph 15.48 of our Second Report. (Para 28.32)

34.47 The National Institute of Social Defence under the Ministry of Social Welfare at the Centre may take appropriate steps to evolve norms of workload for Probation Officers. They may also consider evolving a suitable model of career structure for the personnel in the probationary services which would help them rise to higher levels of responsibilities including appropriate positions in the administration of jails and other corectional homes. It should be possible to evolve a unified career structure to cover all such institutions within each State. (Para 28.34)

34.48 Section 13 of the Probation of Offenders Act enables even a private individual or a representative of a privately organised society to function as Probation Officer. It is seen that very few States have involved private agencies in this work. State Government's attention may be drawn to this aspect of the matter and they may be advised in involve volunteer social welfare agencies in a much greater measure in implementing the Act. (Para 28.35)

34.49 A procedure may be prescribed for the investigating police officer to collect some information and data relevant to probation work even at the stage of investigation of any specific case, and refer to them in appropriate columns in the charge-sheet prescribes under

Section 173 Cr.P.C. The actual headings of these columns may be determined in consultation with experts in the field of correctional services. Availability of this information in the charge-sheet itself would help the court to apply its mind to this aspect of the matter at a later stage during trial. (Para 28.36)

34.50 The Children Act provides for even private institutions to function as Children's Home, Observation Home, Special Schools and After-care Organisation, but the involvement of volunteer social welfare agencies in fulfilling this purpose appears insignificant now. The attention of State Governments may be drawn to this matter for appropriate corrective action. (Para 28.38)

34.51 Juvenile Crime Squads may be established in urban areas to handle investigational work in a much more substantial manner than at present so that the police officers working in these squads may function after proper orientation and briefing and deal with all crimes involving juveniles. Crimes in which juveniles figure along with adult criminals may have to be dealt with by the regular police in the normal course, but even in their cases the Juvenile Crime Squad may keep itself informed of the background and circumstances in which the juvenile criminal came to be involved in the case. (Para 28.39)

34.52 An adult who is proved to have organised a gang of juvenile criminals or otherwise abetted the commission of crime by a juvenile should be held punishable under a separate section to be added to Chapter V of the Indian Penal Code which should provide for a more severe punishment than that stipulated for the main crime by the juvenile. The new section may also provide for the mandatory award of a minimum punishment, except for special reasons to be recorded by the Court. (Para 28.40)

34.53 While the Advocates Act clearly specifies the role and responsibility of a lawyer towards his client, there does not appear appropriate emphasis on the lawyer's role for the overall dispensation of justice to society. A lawyer's responsibility towards his client has to be discharged within the framework of the overall requirements of justice to society. Any lawyer who deliberately adopts dilatory tactics to prolong the proceedings in court is doing something against the interest of quick dispensation of justice to society. Similarly the conduct of any lawyer in becoming a party to the initiation of vexatious or malicious prosecution has to be viewed blameworthy from the point of view of justice to society. (Para 28.41)

34.54 The Bar Council of India may get this aspect examined and evolve some norms for determining a lawyer's conduct towards achieving the ultimate objective of the criminal justice system, namely the quick dispensation of justice not only to individuals but also to the society at large. It may even be desirable to amend the Advocates Act to specify the lawyer's role more pointedly for this purpose. (Para 28.41)

34.55 In paragraph 14.14 of our Second Report we have already recommended the constitution of a Criminal Justice Commission at the Centre supported by a similar arrangement at the State level for monitoring and evaluating the performance of the criminal justice system as a whole. The arrangements for regular inspections of courts and the satisfactory functioning of the Correctional Services *vis-a-vis* the Probation of Offenders Act and the Children Act in particular could be appropriately overseen by the proposed Criminal Justice Commission. (Para 28.42)

Prosecuting Agency

34.56 The post of Assistant Public Prosecutors, Additional Public Prosecutors and Public Prosecutors should be so designed as to provide a regular career structure for the incumbents for the entire state as one unit. (Para 29.6)

34.57 The Public Prosecutor in a district should be made responsible for the efficient functioning of the subordinate prosecuting staff in the district and he should have the necessary supervisory control over them for this purpose. He should also be provided with appropriate office accommodation, library and a small ministerial staff to perform this supervisory role effectively. (Para 29.7)

34.58 The Public Prosecutor and the subordinate prosecuting staff should be made responsible not only for conducting prosecution in courts but also for giving legal advice to police in any matter, general or special, arising from investigations and trials. For the latter purpose, the role of the prosecuting staff will be that of a Legal Adviser. This also may be emphasised in departmental instructions governing the working of the prosecuting staff. If considered necessary from the legal point of view, a suitable section may also be incorporated in the Cr.P.C. to specify this role. (Para 29.8)

35.59 A supervisory structure over the district prosecuting staff should be developed with Deputy Directors of Prosecution at the regional level and a Director of Prosecution at the State level. While we consider it necessary to mesh the prosecuting agency set-up with the police set-up to ensure active cooperation and coordinated functioning in the field in day to day work, we also consider it important that the assessment of evidence collected during investigation and the handling of prosecution work at the district level should be as much detached and objective as possible and free from local departmental or other pressures which might arise from a variety of considerations. The meshing of the two hierarchies may be effected from the regional level upwards, with the Deputy Director of Prosecution placed under the administrative purview of the Range Deputy Inspector General of Police, and the Director of Prosecution at the State level functioning under the administrative control of the Inspector General of Police. In fact, the Director of Prosecution should function as the head of the legal wing of the State police set up. Such an arrangement is absolutely necessary to bring about close coordination and cooperation between the prosecuting staff and the investigating staff down the line and also enable a joint monitoring and evaluation of their performance from time to time. The arrangement as envisaged above would also ensure professional accountability at all levels. (Para 29.9)

34.60 To bring about an additional measure of objectivity and detachment in the functioning of the legal wing, it may be laid down that the post of Director of Prosecution shall be filled on deputation basis for a specified term by drawing officers of appropriate rank on deputation from the law department or the State judiciary. There can be an additional post at the State level called the Additional Director of Prosecution which will be the highest career post available for the regular prosecuting cadres to reach by promotion. (Para 29.10)

34.61 The posts of Assistant Public Prosecutor may be categorised under two grades, I and II. In the initial few years of the new scheme direct recruitment may have to be made at the levels of Assistant Public Prosecutor Grade II and Deputy Director of Prosecution. After the recruits gain experience in handling different types of prosecution and other legal work, direct recruitment may ultimately be confined to the level of Assistant Public Prosecutor Grade II, and thereafter postings will be by promotion to the ranks of Assistant Public Prosecutor Grade I, Public Prosecutor (including Additional Public Prosecutor), Deputy Director of Prosecution and Additional Director of Prosecution. (Para 29.11)

34.62 The minimum qualification and experience for recruitment to different categories of prosecuting staff and their pay scales and service conditions may be on the lines recommended in the Report.

(Para 29.12 and 29.13)

34.63 There would be need for a whole time functionary of the rank of Assistant Public Prosecutor Grade I free from prosecution work in courts to function as the Legal Adviser to the Superintendent of Police in each district for giving him legal advice in specific cases as also other general matters relating to criminal work in the district from time to time. The Deputy Director of Prosecution at the regional level and the Additional Director of Prosecution and the Director of Prosecution at the State level shall perform a similar role to aid and advice the Deputy Inspector General of Police and Inspector General of Police respectively. (Para 29.16)

34.64 Section 25 Cr.P.C. may be amended to enable the placement of the prosecuting cadres under the administrative purview of the Chief of Police. (Para 29.17)

Industrial Disputes

34.65 In a socialist democracy there has to be a proper balancing of the interests of labour, owners of industry and the consumer so that there can be quick economic growth accompanied by an even flow of benefits of such growth to all the three parties. It has, however, happened that the industrial development in the country has witnessed increasing number of conflict situations between the management and the labour, each tending to take a rigid stand to promote the interests of one to the exclusion of the other, instead of consensus situations which would promote the interests of both as well as the community at large. (Para 30.1)

34.66 The Industrial Disputes Act provides several agencies like Works Committees, Conciliation Officers, Boards of Conciliation, Courts of Inquiry, Labour Courts and Tribunals to resolve a variety of industrial disputes. But in the perception of the labour, the formal and legal exercises before such bodies are viewed as time consuming and cumbersome where the management is at an advantage with assistance and advice from legal experts and can also afford a prolonged legal battle without any financial difficulty. This circumstance makes the labour feel that they have a better alternative to secure their objectives quickly by coercive and pressure tactics in the form of strikes or other demonstrations and agitations supported by other demonstrations and agitations supported by their muscle power. The multiciplicity of trade unions also induces minority groups to adopt militant postures to secure bargaining powers which may not be available to them on the strength of their mere numbers. Industrial disputes have, therefore, increasingly tended to become focal points for trial of strength between the labour and management and also between the labour unions. When an industrial dispute crosses the limits of democratic and accepted legal forms and gets into areas of violence and breaches of public order, it immediately attracts police attention under the law, and the police are required to respond to the situation for effective maintenance of law and order. (Para 30.2)

34.67 Police response in an industrial dispute situation has to be very carefully determined and then put into operation in a manner which would command the confidence and trust of both parties to the dispute. While evolving norms for determining this response it has to be remembered that the ultimate objective of all the conciliation exercises envisaged in various labour laws is to promote industrial harmony. This harmony cannot be satisfactorily brought about by any action which makes one party feel that the other party has contrived to gain an undue advantage by adopting militant postures and resorting to coercive and pressure tactics. Maintenance of order accompanied by quick and effective prevention of crime, particularly crimes involving violence, in a conflict situation is very necessary for removing the elements of coercion and pressure from the conflict atmosphere. By the removal of such factors the ground would get cleared for the parties concerned to discuss the issues involved in a calm and free atmosphere where concern and consideration would replace anger and distrust. Police role and responsibility for maintaining law and order in labour dispute situations should be largely guided by the above objective to bring the agitated contending parties to normal levels of thinking in which they would be able to evolve a constructive approach for settlement of their disputes to mutual satisfaction. (Para 30.3)

34.68 A fundamental requirement for proper planning of police action in any industrial dispute situation is the availability of a variety of basic data at the district level relating to all industrial establishments in the district. Responsibility for compiling these basic data and information should be taken on by a special cell of the Intelligence wing at the district level under the Superintendent of Police. A similar cell in the Intelligence branch of the CID at State headquarters should cover major industrial establishments which may give rise to industrial disputes having ramifications over more than one district. Industrial establishments in the public sector, both Central and State, should also be covered by these cells for this purpose. The most important point in the working of these cells would be the constant updating of the information collected from time to time and their dissemination to the various operative units at the sub-division, circle and police station level at regular intervals. (Para 30.4)

34.69 Besides collecting the basic data and information as detailed above, these cells should also collect intelligence about matters that arise in the day-to-day working of the establishments which generate friction between the labour and management. Timely knowledge of such matters would help the police to anticipate crisis situations and be adequately prepared to deal with them. It is, however, important to note that collection of intelligence on such matters is not meant to secure police intervention as such in these disputes unless there is a distinct public order angle. Intelligence gathered in such matters from time to time should be passed on to the appropriate labour authorities to enable their timely intervention for sorting out the problems within the framework of various labour laws before they explode into violent confrontations. (Para 30.5)

34.70 When a specific labour dispute arises and tension begins to build up it would be necessary to augment the above-mentioned intelligence cells with special teams at the local level for collecting intelligence in depth about the likely agitationist plans of the organisers. (Para 30.6)

34.71 Police presence at gate meetings should be for the purpose of keeping themselves informed of the trends of ideas expressed and the measure of support extended by workers, and to prevent the commission of any cognizable offence on the spot. (Para 30.7)

34.72 When specific crimes are committed in the course of gate meetings or collection of subscriptions, the normal processes under the law should be set in motion immediately and the offenders should be brought to book. Police should take care that their action in such specific cases does not draw the criticism that they are soft towards one union and harsh towards another. A high degree of impartiality and objectivity should attend police action in all such cases. (Para 30.9)

34.73 While a situation within the precincts of a factory might be deemed to be directly connected with legitimate trade union activity and would, therefore, require to be treated on a special footing as far as police response in concerned, maintenance of order and a feeling of security among the residents in workers' colonies or the residences of individual members of the management should be treated as a public order problem as in any other locality and appropriate police action taken to deal with mischief makers. (Para 30.10)

34.74 While it is important to ensure the security of sensitive and vital installations within the establishment damage to which might eventually mean a big public loss, it is equally important to avoid unnecessary police presence in those areas of the establishment which are not sensitive from this angle, because it might give the impression of undue police proximity to the seat of management in the establishment. Posting of police personnel for providing security to specified installations in an industrial establishment in a strike situation should, therefore, be carefully determined by the police themselves on the basis of their own intelligence and appreciation of public interest. (Para 30.11)

34.75 Police are duty-bound to give protection to any worker who expresses the desire to work during a strike situation and seeks protection to do so. Police action in this regard should, however, be related to the desire expressed by the worker himself and not to his reported willingness as communicated to the police by the management. (Para 30.12)

34.76 While it is recognised that any person, whether a new recruit or old worker, has the right to seek opportunity for doing work of his choice, any action taken by the police to give protection to new recruits for exercising this right in a strike situation might operationally amount to undue police interference in favour of the management to break the strike. It is, therefore, our view that, when the management try to bring in new recruits, police action should not be in the nature of giving them individual protection to enter the factory but should be confined to action under the law if and when specific offences get committed in the confrontation that might ensue between the striking workers and the new recruits. (Para 30.13)

34.77 The management may sometimes attempt to remove finished or unfinished goods from the factory premises in a strike situation and this may be resisted by the striking workers. Police action in such a situation should ensure adequate protection for the removal of goods, provided one or the other of the following grounds is satisfied:

(a) The finished goods are required to be exported to fulfil contractual obligations and to keep up the export earnings of the industry and the country;

(b) The goods sought to be removed are essential either by themselves or as inputs for the defence needs of the country;

(c) The goods are of a perishable nature and unless they are taken out and disposed of they would be damaged, causing considerable loss to the industry; and

(d) If some goods which are essential inputs for other industries are not removed from the factory and are not made available to other units, then those establishments would also cease to function and thus create problems for the workers of such establishments. (Para 30.14)

34.78 If, however, under the cover of removal of goods, the management attempt to remove substantial parts of the machinery or other equipment in order to revive their activity elsewhere, it would be beyond the norms mentioned above and, therefore, police action in such a situation should not be in the nature of preventive or protective action but should be related to specific offences, if and when they occur in the course of removal of such machinery or other equipment and the obstruction thereto by the striking workers. (Para 30.15)

34.79 Sometimes workers indulge in wild-cat strike and peremptorily lay down tools while actually working during a shift inside the factory. While their continued presence within the factory premises during their shift period may not by itself provide ground for police action in the strike situation, the refusal of such workers to leave the factory premises even after their shift period is over should be deemed as criminal trespass and they should be dealt with by the police accordingly under the law. (Para 30.16)

34.80 Several cognizable offences like wrongful restraint, wrongful confinement, etc., are committed in the course of a gherao and, therefore, a gherao should be deemed a cognizable crime. (Para 30.18)

34.81 Police action in respect of gheraos or sit-in strikes would consist of the following two parts:

(i) Registering a First Information Report in respect of the cognizable crimes committed and documenting the investigation thereon; and

(ii) Lifting the gherao by the physical removal of persons doing the gherao or eviction of the sit-in strikers as the case may be.

The first part would present no difficulty, but the second part would require careful operation in the field. In exercise of their powers under section 149 Cr.P.C. for preventing the commission of any cognizable offence, the police may physically remove the persons doing the gherao. They may even arrest the persons who have committed specific offences in the gherao situation and remove them for production before a Magistrate. In some cases, when faced with violent defiance, it may even become necessary for the police to declare the gathering of persons doing the gherao as unlawful and proceed to disperse them as members of an unlawful assembly. Before embarking on the operation of removal, arrest or dispersal of unlawful assembly as might be warranted by the situation, the police should, subject to the exigencies on the spot, satisfy themselves that all other processes of persuasion, appeal and conciliatory measures have been tried and exhausted. (Para 30.19)

34.82 Specific cognizable crimes committed in the course of an industrial dispute may later get prosecuted in court on conclusion of investigation by police. It has become a practice with the administrators to withdraw such cases from court after the industrial dispute is settled. In fact, in many instances the very agreement to withdraw cases would form part of the settlement. In paragraph 28.29 of this Report, a revised arrangement in law has been recommended for the withdrawal of a criminal case to be sought only on grounds of justice or public interest and not on a mere executive desire for compromise in any particular case. The revised procedure would help to ensure that criminal cases arising from industrial disputes are not light-heartedly withdrawn from court on extraneous considerations. There is urgent need to stop the growing feeling among the agitating sections of the public that they can commit crimes with impunity and later get away without any punishment by seeking executive interference on their behalf. (Para 30.20)

34.83 It is important that police officers, particularly the senior officers at the commanding levels, avoid doing anything which may give the impression to the labour that the officers are unduly obliged to the management on account of facilities like transport, guest house and other entertainment freely provided by the management and readily accepted and enjoyed by the officers. (Para 30.21)

34.84 When the maintenance of an essential service like communications, transport or supply of electricity/water is threatened by an impending strike by the workers concerned, Government usually resorts to a special law of Ordinance for totally prohibiting a strike in the service concerned. While once the strike in a service gets totally prohibited under the law, the police role and responsibility for dealing with the strikers will have to conform to special norms different from what may be applicable to a normal industrial dispute. Police action while dealing with strikers in an essential service in which strikes are totally banned would include:

(i) preventive action against organisers of the strike;
(ii) prompt registration of cases arising from cognizable crimes and the arrest of offenders concerned;
(iii) given protection to loyal workers; and
(iv) giving protection to fresh recruits or the personnel drawn from other units like the territorial army, home guards, etc., for the performance of essential jobs.

The primary objective before the police in such situations should be to keep the essential services going and they should not hesitate to take whatever action is permissible under the law to secure this objective. (Para 30.22)

34.85 The norms for determining police response in an industrial dispute situation should be the same whether it relates to the public sector or private sector. (Para 30.23)

34.86 The Central Industrial Security Force (CISF) has a statutory role and responsibility for the security of the machinery and other equipment and property in certain public sector undertakings which are covered by this force. In a labour dispute situation in such a public undertaking, the police may, in the normal course, be able to take the assistance of the CISF personnel to provide guards for the sensitive vital installations in the establishment. Where, however, the personnel of the CISF themselves become a party to a strike situation or are likely to be want only negligent or indifferent in the performance of their duties because of their sympathy with the other striking workers, the police will have an additional responsibility to provide security to the sensitive and vital installations of the establishment. The nature and extent of security cover to be provided by the police in replacement of the CISF should be decided sufficiently in advance by mutual consultations between the police and the management of the undertaking, also taking into account the intelligence gathered by the police themselves regarding the attitude and involvement of the CISF in this regard. (Para 30.24)

34.87 While laying down norms for police response in industrial dispute situations, it has to be remembered that the formation and functioning of Policemen's Associations in the recent years are likely to influence and condition the attitude of police personnel towards striking workers. A general feeling of sympathy might be generated among the policemen towards the striking workers and a feeling might get induced that nothing should be done to weaken the power of strike as a weapon for collective bargaining. To secure uniformity and effectiveness of police approach to the problem of handling labour dispute situations, it would be necessary for the senior officers at commanding levels to apprise the police personnel individually and also collectively through their Associations wherever they exist about the norms as suggested in this Report and ensure their understanding by the police system as a whole for maintaining their position and prestige as a law enforcement agency. Any attempt made to involve the police personnel in an *ad hoc* disposal of a labour dispute situation in an illegal or irregular manner without conforming to accepted norms is likely to complicate matters and weaken the command structure of the police. (Para 30.25)

Agrarian Problems

34.88 Agrarian problems have increasingly tended to draw police attention from the angle of maintenance of public order, particularly from the sixties. Persistence of serious social and economic inequities in the rural areas has frequently generated tensions between different classes and posed problems for the police. (Para 31.1)

34.89 In the actual implementation of land reform legislation several loopholes were taken advantage of by vested interests to perpetuate the existing inequities. The land owning community retained large tracts of land under their effective control under the guise of resuming land for self cultivation which was permissible in law. The law of ceiling on land holdings by individuals was effectively circumvented by the partitioning of landed property among members of the same family and dependent relatives, with the result that no land emerged as surplus for disposal outside the family domain. According to the Twenty-sixth Round of National Sample Survey (July 1971—September 1972), 54.91 per cent of households in the country owned land of area less than 1 acre per household, and the total area owned by them constituted 2.21 per cent of the total area of holdings in the country while 4.38 per cent of households held area of more than 15 acres each and the total area held by them amounted to 39.43 per cent of the total area of holdings in the country. (Para 31.4)

34.90 The land reform measures so far spelt out and implemented have not had the desired impact for the removal of inequalities and injustice on the agrarian front. This is mainly because those administering the reforms had no interest in doing so and were very much in favour of maintaining the *status quo*. The reforms were only lip-service to an ideology which had to be professed for political purposes. (Para 31.4)

34.91 The Scheduled Castes do not form a resident majority group in any part of the country but live interspersed with other sections of the population. They constitute more than 20 per cent of the population in 666 talukas. On the other hand, the Scheduled Tribes live as majority groups in 329 talukas. While a large number of Scheduled Castes earn their livelihood by working as agricultural labourers, the Scheduled Tribes are by and large a self cultivating class. Agrarian problems of the Scheduled Castes are related to insecurity of employment, low wages and grossly unjust treatment at the hand of the land owning community in a variety of ways. The problems of the Scheduled Tribes arise from the intrusion and exploitation by non-tribals for expropriating lands from the possession of tribals, and the economic hold over the tribals by non-tribal money-lenders and the like. (Para 31.5)

34.92 The proportion of agricultural workers from Scheduled Castes and Scheduled Tribes varies from State to State. Scheduled Caste workers preponderate in Punjab, Rajasthan, Tamil Nadu, Uttar Pradesh and West Bengal. Animosities and tensions arising from the inter-play of caste prejudices have also tended to foul the relationship between land-owners and the agricultural labourers owing to the latter's caste composition as indicated above. (Para 31.6)

34.93 The economic distress of the landless agricultural labourer is further accentuated by the growing pressure on land in rural areas owing to rise in population without a corresponding increase in the area available for cultivation. Compared to the position in 1951, the population in 1976 had increased by 61.3 per cent while the net area of land sown increased by 19.8 per cent only. (Para 31.8)

34.94 From the All India Debt and Investment Survey 1971-72 conducted by the Reserve Bank of India it is seen that the borrowings of an average cultivator/agricultural labourer was very much more from sources like professional money-lender/agriculturist money-lender/trader/landlord than from Government or Co-operative Societies/ bank. This analysis highlights the economic hold the landlord and other richer sections of the village continue to have on the cultivator and the agricultural labourers. (Para 31.9)

34.95 It has already been recommended in Chapter XIX of the Third Report that the allotment of land to the landless poor, particularly the Scheduled Castes and Scheduled Tribes, should be effected through a separate comprehensive legislation which should have provision for effectively handing over possession of the land to the allottee and for promptly evicting the unauthorised occupants or trespassers who may subsequently try to nullify the allotment order. It has also been recommended that the police should collect intelligence about forcible dispossession of the poor from lands allotted to them, and get the matter set right with the help of the revenue authorities concerned. This arrangement would help in giving some effective relief to the landless poor and to that extent reduce agrarian distress and tension. However, this by itself may not take us far since there is not sufficient land in any case to meet the entire requirements of the rural poor with our steeply rising population. There is, therefore, side by side with land reforms, urgent need for providing alternative sources of employment in rural areas for the rapidly growing rural population. For this purpose measures have to be taken in hand early for bringing about the requisite infrastructure of communications, power and water in the rural areas. The danger of fragmentation of holdings as a result of the operation of the inheritance laws of the country, should also not be lost sight of. (Para 31.12)

34.96 Under the Industrial Disputes Act, several agencies like Conciliation Officer, Board of Conciliation and Tribunal exist for adjudicating disputes between the labour and management in an industrial establishment. But there is no special agency in a district to adjudicate on a matter arising from agrarian disputes. It is usually dealt within the normal course by the revenue authorities. It would make for speedier settlement of such disputes if the District Civil Rights Cell recommended in paragraph 19.14 of the Third Report could be given some staff support to perform this role. It would also help the police to secure relevant information through this cell, while dealing with criminal cases arising from such disputes. (Para 31.13)

34.97 The existing arrangements in States for the maintenance of the basic record of rights in villages or groups of villages may be checked and revised to ensure their factual accuracy, besides making them proof against *mala fide* manipulation and interpolation. (Para 31.14)

34.98 When disputes arise and tensions build up between two groups of the land owning community in a village regarding ownership or right of use of any land or irrigation facility, police should not hesitate to take effective preventive action against the leaders on both sides by resorting to section 107 Cr.P.C. and also making preventive arrests where called for. (Para 31.14)

34.99 Recent years have witnessed another type of agitation on the agrarian front in which farmers organise themselves to protest against the Government and allied agencies on such issues like charges for power supply for pump sets, grant of loans and subsidies, writing off arrears of loans, etc. Since these agitations are primarily directed against the Government and do not involve two opposing groups among the public themselves, it becomes easier for the organisers to whip up emotions and instigate violence. Police should handle this type of agitations as a matter of maintenance of public order and take all permissible steps under the law including preventive arrests to contain the situation in public interest. (Para 31.16)

34.100 A fundamental requirement for planning police action in any public order situation is the timely collection of intelligence on the growing developments. Apart from the intelligence wing of the police at the district level, the village police as organised on the lines recommended in Chapter XX of the Third Report should be actively involved in gathering advance intelligence in this matter which would be of great help to the local police in effectively anticipating local situations in time. (Para 31.17)

34.101 The re-organisation and strengthening of rural police calls for immediate attention from the Government in the context of present developments. (Para 31.19)

Social Legislation

34.102 Social legislation may be broadly classified into two categories for appreciating the problems that arise in the enforcement of the legislation. The first category is the permissive type in which the reformative law merely seeks to enlarge the freedom of social action and interaction in certain fields and protect the person so acting from any disability that might fall on him but for the law. Legislation concerning inter-caste marriages and divorce proceedings is of this type. The second category is the proscriptive type which seeks to restrict certain social practices and penalise any conduct that is specifically prohibited in law. Laws relating to suttee, child marriage, polygamy, dowry and untouchability are examples of this category. Enforcement of this category of social legislation meets with resistance from groups which are interested in the continuance of the old practices. (Para 32.2)

34.103 Any attempt to legislate a social change without a prior value change in society amounts to the use of authority and the coercive power of the State to enforce a new value framework. Unless there is a measure of consensus among the generality of people about the desirability of the change that law seeks to achieve, it would result in our seeking a social change in a manner which might simultaneously generate social hatred and hostility. Social legislation of this kind, that is the proscriptive type, has, therefore, to be preceded by a measure of debate, discussion and propaganda which would convince the people in general and prepare them to accept the proposed change. If legislation goes far in advance of the preparedness of the people for the proposed change, enforcement of such a legislation will lack people's support and therefore will generate a situation of conflict between the people and the enforcement agency. (Para 32.6)

34.104 The police, as the premier law enforcement agency in the country, are frequently involved in the enforcement of a variety of laws aimed at social reforms. The normal role of the police as expected by the people is in the field of laws relating to the protection of life and security of property. The Indian Penal Code is the basic criminal law of the country for the police to perform this role. Public understand this role well and willingly cooperate with the police in individual cases but the position becomes different when the police are involved in the enforcement of a social reform law which the public at large are not yet prepared to accept. The timing of enactment of a law of social reform and the degree of involvement of police in its enforcement have to be finely adjusted and regulated so that public support for its enforcement will not be prejudiced. Legislation by itself would not be effective for bringing about a change in the social value system and, therefore, the police may not be looked upon as a primary instrument for effecting a social change. (Para 32.7)

34.105 Investigational power and responsibility of the police are now confined to cognizable offences which are specified as such in law. In their anxiety to secure effective enforcement of a new social law, social reformers and legislators are inclined to declare all offences under such a law as cognizable and leave the matter there in the belief that strict and severe enforcement thereof by the police would achieve their purpose. It is at this stage that there is scope for introducing some refinements in law which would greatly reduce the scope for malpractices when the offences are taken cognizance of by the police. Even now there are several cognizable offences in which, after completion of investigation by the police, there are restrictions at the stage of the court taking cognizance of the case for commencing trial. All offences under Chapter VI of the Indian Penal Code and offences under Sections 153A, 153B, 188, 295A, 471 and 505 of the same Code are examples of this kind where the court can take cognizance only on a complaint from a specified individual or on sanction from a specified authority. There is scope for extending this concept of conditional cognizability even at the earlier stage when the police register the case and commence their investigation. The conditions can be suitably determined to reduce the scope for harassment and corruption. (Para 32.11)

34.106 Social legislation may be categorised under five groups as indicated in the following paragraphs and the nature and extent of police involvement in the enforcement of each group may be as indicated therein. (Para 32.12)

34.107 *First Group*

(i) This group would cover laws regulating social institutions like marriage, divorce, adoption, inheritance, etc.; and
(ii) Police should have no role at all in the enforcement of these laws. It should be left to the affected parted to take matters direct to courts and get their disputes resolved through judicial adjudication. (Para 32.13)

34.108 *Second Group*

(i) This would cover laws dealing with some social problems like prevalence of dowry, discrimination against women, begging, vagrancy, etc.; and
(ii) Police should not have any role to play in the enforcement of these laws, excepting some which may have a public order or crime prevention aspect. For example, if there is a law prohibiting begging in specified public places, police should have the powers to enforce the relevant provision, solely from the point of view of maintaining public order at the specified place. Police should not be involved in rounding up individual beggars and marching them to a rehabilitative home or any

such institution. That job should be left to the Municipal agencies. (Para 32.14)

34.109 *Third Group*

(i) This group would cover laws aimed at promoting the health of the people in general and, in particular, prohibiting the consumption of intoxicating drinks and of drugs which are injurious to health; and

(ii) Offences under these laws which involve commercially organised activity (for example : trafficking in drugs) or disturbance to public order should be made fully cognizable by the police. Offences which do not have any such angle but involve individual behaviour and conduct without creating any public order situation may be made cognizable by the police only on a specific complaint from a person alleging annoyance or injury caused to him by such behaviour and conduct, and not on any intelligence gathered by the police themselves. (Para 32.15)

34.110 *Fourth Group*

(i) This would cover laws aimed at prohibiting or regulating certain pastimes which are likely to operate to the detriment of the earnings of poor families and result in the drain of their meagre financial resources; and

(ii) Laws which regulate gambling horse racing, lotteries, crossword puzzles, etc, fall under this category. Police cognizability of offences under these laws should be limited to those which have a public order aspect. For example, gambling in a public place is like to promote disorderly behaviour an disturbance to public order and should therefore be made fully cognizable by the police. Offences which do not involve this public order aspect may be made cognizable only on a specific complaint from an affected party. (Para 32.16)

34.111 *Fifth Group*

(i) This group would cover laws which are meant for protecting and rehabilitating the handicapped and weaker sections of society, and preventing exploitation of their economic weakness or otherwise distressed situation; and

(ii) Police should be fully involved in the enforcement of these laws. Protection of Civil Rights Act and the Suppression of Immoral Traffic Act are examples of laws under this group. Offences under these laws should be made cognizable and the general police should have full powers of enforcing them. (Para 32.17)

34.112 In the investigation of offences which are made conditionally cognizable as recommended above, the police need not have the power of arrest. They may, on conclusion of investigation, put the matter before a court if evidence warrants such a course of action, and take from the accused person a bond for his appearance in court when summoned. (Para 32.18)

34.113 Appropriate amendments to several pieces of social legislation would be required to implement the above recommendations regarding conditional cognizability by the police and the restriction on their powers of arrest in certain cases. The various social laws may be individually examined from this angle and appropriate amendments evolved by the Social Welfare Departments of the State Governments in consultation with the State Police agencies. (Para 32.19)

Prohibition

34.114 Over six lakh prohibition cases have been registered annually in the recent years all over the country and a similar number of persons arrested in such cases every year. 25,692 juveniles were arrested under the Prohibition Act in 1977. The arrest of such a large number of persons year after year and their passing through police custody for their involvement in prohibition offences alone would tend to 'criminalise' persons who are not perceived as criminals in the normal sense of the term by the society at large. (Para 33.9)

34.115 Some aspects of the actual field situation and the practical difficulties in the enforcement of prohibition are enumerated below:

(1) Illicit distillation is mostly carried on in remote areas or densely populated slums which offer safe hideouts for the distillers. Detection of distillation activities in such circumstances becomes extremely difficult, particularly in the absence of public cooperation which seldom comes forth in the cause of prohibition.

(2) The easy availability of a variety of sources for preparation of illicit liquor encourages illicit distillation and brewing.

(3) Any amount of severe punishment by way of imprisonment or fine for the prohibition offenders does not seem to deter them since the economics of illicit distillation is in their favour and they find the business of illicit liquor quite profitable, even after making allowances for the temporary immobilization of the personnel concerned by the processes of trial and punishment.

(4) Illicit liquor trade provides big business, and those who organise it from behind the scene exploit the poverty of weaker sections in society and draw them into this business to function as intermediaries for transport and sale of liquor. In this process it is these poor people who ultimately get caught by the enforcement agency and subsequently languish in jail. Very rarely does one come across prohibition convicts in jails drawn from the rich and business sections of the community. It is indeed tragic that the prohibition law which was conceived as a legislation primarily meant to benefit the ill-informed and poorer sections of the community ultimately results in a large number of persons of this very category getting into prison for their involvement in illicit liquor trade.

(5) Corruption spreads quickly and widely as a result of persistent influence from illicit liquor business on the police force, making it more and more inefficient in dealing with professional bootleggers and big organisers of illicit liquor trade.

(6) The mounting pendency of prohibition cases in courts has clogged up all property rooms and storage space in police stations and their compounds. (Para 33.10)

34.116 From the standpoint of enforcement the following broad amendments in prohibition law are urgently necessary to eliminate some of the serious evils noticed in the existing scheme of enforcement:

(i) Cognizable offences under the prohibition law should be limited to those relating to manufacture, transport and sale of liquor;

(ii) Offences relating to possession of liquor or drinking of liquor or being found in a state of drunkenness should be made non-cognizable. They may, however, be taken notice of by the police while they investigate any other accompanying cognizable offence;

(iii) In regard to the above category of non-cognizable offences police should, however, have the power to seize any illicit liquor that may be connected with the non-cognizable offence if it comes to their notice and they may send the seized liquor to court for further disposal;

(iv) The procedure for conducting searches under the prohibition law should be separately laid down without drawing a close parallel from the Code of Criminal Procedure; and

(v) There should be legal provisions to enable the enforcement agency destroy on-the-spot any illicit liquor or any other material connected with its manufacture when the liquor and such material are found in a public place without being claimed by anybody. The destruction may be documented in the presence of witnesses. (Para 33.11)

34.117 As regards arrangements within the police for detection of prohibition offences mobile parties may be constituted at the sub-division level to concentrate on the more serious offences of illicit manufacture, transport and sale of liquor which alone would be cognizable in the revised prohibition law. The functioning of these mobile parties can be on the lines indicated by the Tamil Nadu Police Commission. (Para 33.12)

34.118 Unless there is a measure of consensus among the generality of people about the desirability of the change that a law of social reform seeks to achieve, its enforcement would lack people's support and might even generate hostility between the people and the enforcement agency. From the long experience of States like Tamil Nadu, Gujarat and Maharashtra in the enforcement of prohibition it is clear that the prohibition law does not enjoy acceptance and support from the public at large. Their cooperation, therefore, is totally lacking for the police to enforce the law. In fact, its enforcement brings the police into situations of conflict with substantial sections of the public who do not view drinking liquor as an act to be held criminal and made punishable under the law. In the light of the realities and difficulties in enforcement work as detailed in this Report, it emerges that the prohibition law, as presently enacted with emphasis on total prohibition, is practically non-enforceable. The Government may review their prohibition policy in general and the structure of prohibition law in particular and evolve a revised practical measure for dealing with the problem of economic distress among the low income groups of our populations, owing to the evil of drinking. (Para 33.13)

NATIONAL POLICE COMMISSION, 1977 – FIFTH REPORT[1]

Chairman Shri Dharma Vira, retired Governor

Member Shri N.K. Reddy; Shri K.F. Rustamji; Shri N.S. Saksena; Prof. M.S. Gore

Secretary Shri. C.V. Narasimhan

Alterations Shri V. Narasimhan, former Director of Central Bureau of Investigation, functioned as Member Secretary of the Commission from its inception till 19th April, 1980 when he left to take a posting in his parent cadre in Tamil Nadu on replacement of his services from the Central Government to the State Government. After the departure of Shri Narasimhan, Shri M.D. Dikshit, Principal Director of Research, functioned as the Secretary Incharge.

Appointment

Far-reaching changes have taken place in the country after the enactment of the Indian Police Act, 1861 and the setting up of the second Police Commission of 1902, particularly during the last thirty years of Independence. Though a number of States have appointed Police Commissions after Independence to study the problems of the Police in their respective States, there has been no comprehensive review at the national level of the police system after Independence despite radical changes in the political, social and economic situation in the country. A fresh examination is necessary of the role and performance of the Police—both as a law enforcement agency, and as an institution to protect the rights of the citizens enshrined in the Constitution. The Government of India have, therefore, decided to appoint a National Police Commission. The National Police

---

1. Controller of Publication, Delhi, 1983, i + 85 p.

Commission appointed under the Government of India, Ministry of Home Affairs Resolution No. VI-24021/36/77-GPA.I, dated November 15, 1977.

Terms of Reference

The following will be the terms of reference of the Commission :

(1) Re-define the role, duties, powers and responsibilities of the police with special reference to prevention and control of crime and maintenance of public order.

(2) Examine the development of the principles underlying the present policing system, including the method of magisterial supervision, evaluate the performance of the system, identify the basic weaknesses of inadequacies, and suggest appropriate changes in the system and the basic laws governing the system.

(3) Examine, if any changes are necessary in the existing method of administration, disciplinary control and accountability.

(4) Inquire into the system of investigation and prosecution, the reasons for delay and failure; the use of improper methods, and the extent of their prevalence; and suggest how the system may be modified or changed, and made efficient, scientific and consistent with human dignity; and how the related laws may be suitably amended.

(5) Examine methods of maintaining crime records and statistics and suggest methods for making them uniform and systematic.

(6) Review policing in rural areas evaluate any new arrangements that have been made, and recommend changes that are necessary.

(7) Examine the system of policing required in non-rural and urbanised areas including metropolitan areas, and suggest the pattern that would be the most suitable.

(8) Examine the steps taken for modernising law enforcement, evaluate the work of police communications, the computer network, scientific laboratories and agencies for research and development, and examine whether modernisation can be speeded up; examine to what extent, as a result of the modernisation of Police forces, streamlining of its functions and its re-structuring, it would be possible to economise in the manpower in the various areas of its activities.

(9) Examine the nature and extent of the special responsibilities of the Police towards the weaker sections of the community and suggest steps to ensure prompt action on their complaints for the safeguard of their rights and interests.

(10) Recommend measures and institutional arrangements:

(i) to prevent misuse of powers by the police, and to examine whether police behaviour, out-look, responsiveness and impartiality are maintained at the correct level, and if not the steps such as recruitment and training which should be taken to improve them;

(ii) to prevent misuse of the Police by administrative or executive instructions, political or other pressure, or oral order of any type, which are contrary to law;

(iii) for the quick and impartial inquiry of public complaints made against the police about any misuse of police powers;

(iv) for the quick redressal of grievances of police personnel and to look after their morale and welfare; and

(v) for a periodic objective evaluation of police performance in a metropolitan area/District/State in a manner which will carry credibility before the public.

(11) Examine the manner and extent to which police can enlist ready and willing co-operation of the public in the discharge of their social defence and law enforcement duties and suggest measures regarding the institutional arrangements to secure such co-operation and measures for the growth of healthy and friendly public-police relationship.

(12) Examine the methods of police training, development, and career-planning of officers and recommend any changes that are required at any time in their service, to modernise the outlook, and to make the leadership of the force effective and morally strong.

(13) Examine the nature of the problems that the police will have to face in the future, and suggest the measures necessary for dealing with them, and for keeping them under continuous study and appraisal.

(14) Consider and make recommendations and suggestions regarding any other matter which the Government may refer to the Commission; and

(15) Any other matter of relevance or importance having an impact on the subject.

Contents

Recruitment of constables and sub-inspectors; Training of personnel in the civil police in the rank of Constables, Sub-Inspectors, Inspectors and Deputy Superintendents of Police with focus on implementation of the Committee on Police Training's Report, 1973; Dacoities; Arms Act; District police and the executive magistracy; Code of behaviour for police officers; Police-public relations; Women police; Summary of observations and recommendations; Appendices I to IV.

Recommendations

43.1 In future it would be necessary to limit recruitment to the police to two levels only, namely (i) Constables and (ii) Indian Police Service. The recruitment to the other levels should be eliminated by a phased programme. (Para 35.5)

43.2 Properly developed psychological tests are an important ingredient of a proper recruitment procedure. Despite the recommendations of the Committee on Police Training, nothing much has been done for developing these tests. A start should be made immediately by introducing these tests during training to weed out those who are not likely to shape into good policemen. (Para 35.6)

43.3 There is need for creating interest among the youth in police work as a part of the school and college curriculum. This should be supplemented by establishment of a Police Cadet Corps at develop the necessary interest in the work of the police. Healthy Student-Police interaction in an understanding atmosphere should be encouraged. (Para 35.7)

43.4 The minimum educational qualification for recruitment as Constables in the armed as well as civil police should be High School pass uniformly throughout the country. This should not operate against attracting candidates of higher educational qualifications and some weightage in the form of bonus marks may be given to candidates with higher qualifications. (Para 35.8)

43.5 There is no dearth of candidates with minimum educational and physical qualifications available from among the Scheduled Castes, Scheduled Tribes and backward classes. No relaxation, therefore, need be made in the prescribed educational qualifications and physical standards for recruiting candidates from these reserved classes. (Para 35.9)

43.6 The minimum age for recruitment should be 17 years and the maximum 21 years with normal relaxation of upper age limit in the case of Scheduled Castes/Tribes and Backward Classes. (Para 35.10)

43.7 The recommendations of the Committee of Police Training, 1973, in respect of height, chest and standard age-height-weight correlation are endorsed. The effectiveness of the policemen is directly proportionate to a large extent, to his physical fitness, stamina and appearance. Any relaxation in the physical qualifications will have an adverse impact on the performance of the policemen and the force as a whole. There should be no compromise, therefore, in regard to physical qualifications except where regional factors as in the case of hill tribes call for the same. No relaxation is required for the reserved classes either. (Paras 35.11 and 35.12)

43.8 Physical efficiency Test should form an essential criterion for recruitment. While one star standard is minimum for entry, appropriate weightage should be given to those with two and three star standard of physical efficiency. (Para 35.13)

43.9 Recruitment to the constabulary shall be done at the district level to ensure adequate representation for every district in the police. But recruitment should be based on uniform standards of objectivity and impartiality throughout the State. (Para 35.16)

43.10 Wide publicity is essential to ensure that sufficient number of suitable candidates come forward from all parts of the district and from the various cross-sections of the people. Predictability regarding the dates of recruitment should be introduced by fixing some dates on some months uniformly by the State Governments every year. (Para 35.17)

43.11 All police stations, police lines and other police units and offices like offices of SDPO, SSP and DIG should make it a point to be courteous and helpful to young men and women coming to make enquiries about the recruitment or about police as career. This would include helping them to know if they would qualify in physical standards. This public relations exercise could be supported by suitable incentives to those units or offices who have been specially helpful to applicants. The publicity should make it clear that the recruitment is subject to fulfilment of minimum educational qualifications and physical efficiency standards. (Para 35.18)

43.12 Recruitment involves two stages (i) elimination of the unfit and (ii) selection of the suitable. In the elimination process the District SP should scrutinise the application and exclude candidates who do not fulfil the minimum educational qualifications and physical standards on the basis of the applications. A list should be prepared of the applicants who satisfy the minimum qualifications with details of their qualifications and physical standards. The list should be published. Another list consisting of those found not eligible should also be published. This process will inspire confidence and promote objectivity. The Superintendent of Police may call any of the applicants if he thinks it necessary to check the contents of the applications. (Para 35.19)

43.13 In the selection process equal weightage should be given to the following 3 factors:

	Marks
(a) The percentage of marks in the High School Examination	100
(b) The marks awarded by the Selection Board	100
(c) Physical standards including Medical fitness category	100
	300 (Para 35.19)

43.14 The Selection Board should consist of the DIG as the Chairman, assisted by a Superintendent of Police from one of the district and a Superintendent of Police incharge of an armed police battalion. The Board should also include a Sociologist or head of a local school and wherever possible the Head of the Police Training School or one of its senior Instructors. The Selection Board should interview each candidate and award marks out of 100 broadly on the following criterion:

(i) Personality		80
(ii) Comprehension		
(iii) Oral expression		
(iv) Temperament and Response		
(v) Social Consciousness		
(vi) Bonus for higher qualifications		20
(a) 1st Division in Higher Secondary	10	

	or Intermediate	
(b)	Second Division in Higher Secondary or Intermediate	5
(c)	First Division in Graduation	10
(d)	Second Division in Graduation	5 (Para 35.20)

43.15 The same Selection Board of another Board with the Medical Officer, the physical instructor and the District SP, Dy. SP should evaluate the physical standard of candidates and award marks as follows out of 100:

(i)	Physical efficiency test		50
(ii)	(a) One Star standard	10	
	(b) Two Star standard	30	
	(c) Three Star standard	50	
(iii)	Medical fitness in all respect		20
(iv)	Additional weightage of height, chest, eye-sight, muscular powers and sports.		30
	Total		100 (Para 35.21)

43.16 There is no need for any written examination and the percentage of marks in the High School Examination should form the basis in the final merit list. (Para 35.22)

43.17 The minimum educational qualifications for recruitment to the post of Sub-Inspectors shall be a Graduate Degree from a recognised University. No special weightage need be given to post-Graduates. This should be uniform throughout the country for both armed and unarmed branches of the police. The minimum age limit for recruitment should be 20 years and the maximum 23 years. This is subject to usual relaxations in the case of Scheduled Castes and Scheduled Tribes. The physical standards as are applicable to the constabulary shall apply to the recruitment of the Sub-Inspectors also. (Para 35.24)

43.18 The recruitment to the rank of Sub-Inspectors be made through a competitive examination by the State Public Service Commission. Due weightage should be given for performance in an interview and physical efficiency test in the screening scheme for recruitment. The percentage of weightage of a candidate for performance in the three areas of test shall be as follows: –

(Actual marks can be correspondingly more).

Written test	65	
Interview	25	
Physical efficiency	10	
Total	100	(Para 35.30)

43.19 The interview shall be carried out on a Service Selection Board model as in the Defence Forces but adopted for police needs. The Chairman of the Selection Board shall be a Member of the State Service Commission assisted by (i) Inspector General of Police or his representative (ii) a senior Police Office-incharge of training or the head of the State Training College (iii) a Sociologist or an academician and (iv) a personnel management expert or behavioural scientist, if available, or an officer from another Department. (Para 35.31)

Training of personnel in the Civil Police in the rank of Constables, Sub-Inspectors, Inspectors and Deputy Superintendents of Police with focus on implementation of the Committee on Police Training's Report, 1973.

43.20 There is an urgent need for a change and improvement in police attitudes and performance. Without this they will be unable to discharge the additional responsibilities and challenges in law enforcement that they have to face in present times. While prevention and detection of crime and maintenance of law and order will remain the core responsibility, they also have to fact a new range of problems emerging from a wide spectrum of social welfare laws enacted in the last five decades. (Para 36.1)

43.21 A qualitative change in police perspective and approach demands a total change in the police culture and much greater effort in training and education to develop greater professional competence. Being aware of the above need, the Government of India appointed a Committee on Police Training in the year 1973. (Para 36.4)

43.22 The Committee found that in general with the exception of some of the Central Police Organisation professional training was in a state of neglect qualitatively and inadequate quantitatively. The main reason for the same was the lack of genuine interest on the part of the Government and higher ranks in the police in the value of training. The Committee made a compact set of recommendations on all aspects of training and other allied areas in the police system:

(i) To ensure maximum level of professional competence;
(ii) To ensure an optimum level of managerial competence in police work; and
(iii) To ensure a higher level of personality competence which would include education and development of leadership qualities. (Paras 36.11 and 36.14)

43.23 Training, though an essential input, is not the only input for a total transformation. The whole organisational climate, environment in which the police has to function, official attitude, etc., have to be simultaneously tackled to make training effective as an integral part of the total system. For this the co-operation of the State Governments. Inspectors General of Police and other senior police officers is very essential. The State Governments should take due note and correct the existing defects in the system. (Paras 36.15 and 36.16)

43.24 Training cannot be a substitute to intelligent supervision, purposeful inspection, favourable environmental conditions, mutual trust and willingness to delegate. A good training can at best support, enhance and optimise performance provided the other factors are taken care of. (Para 36.17)

43.25 Time bound implementation of the committee of Police Training, 1973's recommendations both on the core aspect of training and other important complementary factors will provide the neccessary training support for realising the objectives of our recommendations on other aspects of police working. The task of implementation must be supplemented by reforms in structure, organisation and climate work. (Para 36 19)

43.26 The implementation of the recommendations of the Committee of Police Training, 1973, despite the lapse of more than five years is disappointing and frustratingly slow. There appears to have been no sustained effort either by the Centre or the States to implement the recommendations. While the syllabi and training format have been adopted fully by all States, in other areas like recruitment, organisation of training, training of trainers, motivation of trainers, preparation of training material, etc., no perceptible improvement has been made. Lack of finance and adequate guidance and assistance from the Centre has prevented the State Governments from making such progress. The Centre has not spelt out a time-frame and the process of implementation. The role of the Centre and States has not been defined clearly. (Paras 36.21, 36.22, 36.24 and 36.26)

43.27 The main reasons for the tardy implementation of the recommendations can be listed as follows:

(i) Lack of constructive contribution by the Central Government in the implementation process specially in matters of financial resources, both capital and recurring;
(ii) Non-development of psychological tests due to lack of expertise and guidance;
(iii) Continued lack of commitment to the concept of training in the police system, resulting in poor image of police training institutions and the role of training in police work;
(iv) Non-availability of training material and basic instructional literature;
(v) Poor planning of trainee man power release; and
(vi) Lack of rational staffing patter in the training institutes without providing necessary motivators and career planning, etc. (Para 36.27)

43.28 In order to correct these shortcomings:

(i) The Central Government must undertake a leading role in the implementation process, after assessing the existing facilities and gaps in the State Training Institutions, the Central Government should undertake to provide the full capital cost for establishing the new training institutions and for improving the existing ones;
(ii) The Central Government should bear the recurring cost initially for a period of five years, starting with the first year at 75 per cent to be reduced annually by 10 per cent;
(iii) The Centre should develop the parameters of psychological tests with the help of Ministry of Defence and recruit the necessary staff;
(iv) A spell as Principal or a directing staff in the PTC should be made a very desirable requirement for consideration for

promotion in the hierarchy;

(v) Adequate incentives and other facilities must be provided to the staff selected for serving in Training Institutions;

(vi) To remove the complaint that officers due for training are not relieved for the courses, a roster for attending in-service training and refresher courses, should be prepared at the Police Headquarters; and

(vii) Sufficient training reserves be provided to fill the posts of the officers deputed for training. The officer deputed for training should as far as possible be posted to the place from where he had proceeded on training. A training roster should be kept and strict compliance ensured. (Para 36.28)

43.29 The posting in training institutions should carry attractive pay and other amenities. It will be desirable to select the staff by competition and on merit. They should be given training before they take over as trainers. Working in Training Institutions should be made one of the desirable qualifications for promotion to higher ranks up to IG. (Paras 36.31 and 36.32)

43.30 The training will be meaningful and purposeful if the health of the other components of the police system is good. The factors that are essential to make the other components function optimally have to be simultaneously attended to. In the absence of a climate which supports performance and innovation and trust in the officers, training can have only a limited impact. (Para 36.33)

43.31 The maximum visibility of the police to the people as an organisation centres round the Constables. His interactions are not persons to person but with groups of people as well. He is the only limb of the Government who comes more in contact with the common man in his every day life than the personnel in any other wing of the Government. The Constable will be required to perform a variety of tasks in future and thereby derive career/job satisfaction instead of being dehumanised under the monotony of being a mechanical lathi-weilding robot. (Paras 36.34 and 36.35)

43.32 The Committee on Police Training, 1973's recommendations cover all aspects of training essential for induction to the new role of the constabulary. The implementations of the recommendations of the Committee will ensure necessary training support to the police in their enlarged role as envisaged. However, the training format prescribed by the Committee on Police Training, 1973 needs some addition for the new role of the Constable. In view of the fact it is envisaged that the Constables should be a potential investigating officer who can, with the experience, handle investigational work independently. It would be appropriate to provide for adequate training in the basic principle of investigational work and allow interaction with the public at this stage as a part of the promotional course for a period of about four months before the Constable becomes an Assistant Sub-Inspector. (Para 36.39)

43.33 On the job training plays an important role for this level. It will condition the recruit to the culture of the police force. This involves responsibility at higher levels for the subordinate's development. This should be an essential ingredient in the system. (Para 36.40)

43.34 The nature of the Constables interaction with the public needs greater attention. Hence, his attitudes, conduct and response, even how he addresses the fellow citizens, his politeness and courtesy, all those needs greater attention as part of the training and should be indoctrinated on the job by the personal example of superior officers. No amount of theoretical training will achieve this result unless the constables see their superiors act and behave in the same way. (Para 36.41)

43.35 The training institutions should make the Constable aware of his prospects for promotion in the career structure within the police system. The training institutions should help in identifying constables who show some real merit and aptitude and possess the potential to reach high ranks with necessary support. They should encourage such deserving candidates by guidance and other means. (Para 36.42)

43.36 The Constables like sub-Inspectors should be attached to some social service organisations. The initial on the job training should concentrate on exposing the Constable to several emergencies other than routine crime prevention, detection and law and order. This will create the proper attitudes in sensitive areas like dealing with weaker sections, women and children and the other lower strata of society. Such civil emergencies can be stimulated for role play at regular intervals. This will help the growth of the correct attitudes and perceptions. (Para 36.43)

43.37 The Sub-Inspector/Inspector occupies the most important functional area in the police hierarchy. He has enormous powers whose impact on citizens' rights is far-reaching. He combines in himself the preventive, detective, regulatory and control functions of law enforcement. Much depends upon his capacity to get the cooperation and assistance of the staff under his and the goodwill of the people whom he serves. (Para 36.44)

43.38 His periodical exposure by way of refresher courses to increase his sensitivity and understanding of psychology and to enlighten him on management techniques and behavioural sciences will be desirable. He should be made an agent of change and develop the necessary attitude to accept change as a necessary factor in the developing society. He should also be periodically exposed to a change in technology and science pertaining to his profession by way of refresher courses. (Para 36.48)

43.39 The course content for the promoted Sub-Inspector should be so designed that on the passing of the departmental examination, the candidate could be awarded a degree/diploma/ certificate in police sciences. For this purpose each Academy may be declared as a centre of education in police sciences just as IIT's, Institute of Management, Institute of Chartered Accountants, etc. This will ensure that he will be able to feel a sense of equality and parity with the directly recruited Sub-Inspector and can hope to catch up with the IPS Officers as well. As a measures of incentive those who pass in first class should be given an award of Rs. 3,000 and those who pass in the 2nd Class with over 50 per cent should be given Rs. 1,500. (Para 36.52)

43.40 A special course may be organised in the State Training Institutions for those Sub-Inspectors who are selected for promotion as Inspectors. The duration of this course may be 6 weeks. Its objective would be to serve as a gap between the 2 ranks and be a refresher course which could blend knowledge of work with problem solving skills. (Para 36.53)

43.41 A special course for Inspectors who have worked as SHO for a period of 3 years be conducted at the National Police Academy. Only outstanding and exceptional Inspectors should be nominated by the IG for this Course and it would be one of the very prestigious courses conducted by the NPA. Those who pass the course with credit should be given a merit certificate plus cash awards ranging from Rs. 1,000 to Rs. 5,000 depending upon the percentage of marks obtained by them in the future examination. (Paras 36.54 to 36.57)

43.42 The post of Deputy Superintendent of Police is a continuing historical reality. An experienced Deputy Superintendent of Police has years of working experience in all aspects of police functioning with the results that the system has to rely on him for bulk of the police work. He does the bulk of supervisory work in the field and also makes personality a large number of enquiries. The rank of the Deputy Superintendent of Police will have to continue as he has become an important functionary with a distinct role to play. This rank also provides a promotionary level. (Paras 36.58 and 36.59)

43.43 The directly recruited Deputy Superintendent of police should receive the training imparted to IPS trainees, during short interregnum till direct recruitment is stopped. (Para 36.61)

43.44 In future, the rank of the Deputy Superintendent of Police will be filled by promotion from the level of Inspectors. A refresher course of about 3 months to equip them to understand and undertake the additional responsibilities is sufficient. The training format needs to be modified to give necessary exposure to the Administrative Side of the police work as the trainees will be experienced officers on the professional side. The focus should be on administration, supervision and leadership and other managerial techniques. A sensitivity training of a short duration is also recommended to orient them to the new role. (Paras 36.62 and 36.63)

43.45 In future the training for officers promoted as Deputy Superintendents of Police should be conducted at the National Police Academy. Suitable course design will have to be evolved by the National Police Academy and the candidates would be required to be proficient in English so that some of them who later promoted to IPS are not handicapped. This will also reduce the gap between the Deputy Superintendent of Police and Assistant Superintendent of Police and bring them together in the same Institution. (Paras 36.62 and 36.64)

Dacoities

43.46 The present recorded incidence of dacoities, 1.8 per lakh of population is considerably less than the actual figure. (Para 37.3)

43.47 Dacoities should, for purposes of statistics and handling be classified into three categories:

(1) Technical dacoity, that is, a dacoity committee by persons who do not make a habit of it but on account of a dispute they happen to have committed and offence which falls within the ambit of Section 391 of the IPC. This may be called *simple dacoity.*
(2) Dacoity committed by persons who treat it as a source of profit but who remain part of the society from which they

assemble to commit it and into which they merge after they have committed it. These people may have normal avocations also. This may be called *professional dacoity.*

(3) Dacoity committed by a gang of dacoits which lives outside the society as a separate cohesive group. The members of such gangs live only by a life of crime. Often their names and descriptive rolls are known. This may be called *gang dacoity.* (Para 37.4)

43.48 The first type of dacoity is just as bad as any other crime. The second type of dacoity is a menace because it is indiscriminate and corrodes the vitals of a society. The seriousness of the third type of dacoity has been acknowledged for a long time. It is open and blatant defiance of law and society. The use of firearm makes any offence serious and, as things are, the type of firearm used, breach loading muzzle loading, country made, licensed, unlicensed should also be a statistically recognizable fact. (Para 37.5)

43.49 When the police come upon a dacoit gang in any way, the resistance on the part of the dacoits to evade arrest leads to use of force by both the dacoits and the police and this exchange – normally there is an exchange of fire because both the groups are armed – is commonly referred to as an encounter. (Para 37.7)

43.50 There is a general public feeling in some areas that often encounters are stage-managed by the police in which the dacoits are killed in order to avoid going through the process of a trial which may or may not result in their conviction and a deterrent sentence. It has been alleged that even after being arrested, some notorious dacoits are done away with by documenting a fake encounter. We are aware of the various difficulties in collecting evidence against dangerous dacoits to prove their crimes to the satisfaction of a court. We are also aware that witnesses would not be forthcoming into trails against dacoits because of fear. An incident in which a large number of witnesses – more than thirty – were murdered when a trial against a notorious dacoit was going on in a court of laws was in fact brought to our notice. In spite of all these practical difficulties, we strongly disapprove of any action on the part of the police which exceeds the limits imposed by law. The law demands that no person shall be considered a criminal unless pronounced to be so after a due and proper trial by a court of law. (Para 37.8)

43.51 In order to strengthen the law against those who commit heinous crimes such as dacoity, Section 82 of the Code of Criminal

Procedure, 1973, should be amended and a new Section 174-A added to the Indian Penal Code. The following may be added as sub-section (4) and (5) to Section 82 Cr. P.C.

Proclamation for Person Absconding

82. (1) *** *** ***
(2) *** *** ***
(3) *** *** ***

(4) In a case where the proclamation published under sub-section (1) is in respect of a person accused of an offence punishable under any of the following sections of the Indian Penal Code, namely, 302, 304, 364, 365, 367, 368, 382, 392 to 400 (both inclusive), 402, 436, 449, 439 and 460, if that person fails to appear at the specified place and specified time mentioned in the proclamation, may thereupon, after making such inquires as it things fit, declare him a proclaimed offender and make a declaration to that effect.

(5) The provisions of sub-sections (2) and (3) shall also apply to declaration made by the Court under sub-section (4).

The new Section 174A—to be added to the Indian Penal Code may be on the following lines :

Non-attendance in obedience to a proclamation published by Court

174A Whoever, being legally bound to attend in person at a certain place and time in obedience to a proclamation published under sub-section (1) of Section 82 of the Code of Criminal Procedure, 1973, intentionally omits to attend at that place or time or departs from the place where he is found to attend before the time at which it is lawful for him to depart, shall be punished with imprisonment of either description for a term which may extend upto three years; and in a case where, in addition to the aforesaid proclamation, a declaration has also been published under the provision of sub-section (4) of Section 82 of the aforesaid Code, shall be punished with imprisonment of either description for a term which may extend to seven years. (Para 37.9)

43.52 The concept of a proclaimed offender should then be included in Section 46(3) of the Code of Criminal procedure as below:

Arrest how made

46. *** *** ***
*** *** ***

(3) Nothing in this section gives a right to cause the death of a person who is not accused of an offence punishable with death of with imprisonment for life or is not a proclaimed offender as declared by a court under the provisions of sub-section (4) of Section 82. (Para 37.10)

43.53 Simple dacoities should be handled like any other crime, that is, investigated thoroughly and prosecuted competently in a court of law. Professional dacoities call for meticulous building up of police station records on the basis of continuous collection of intelligence, and preventing inflow of arms and ammunition into the hands of the criminal elements. Gang dacoities need to be handled in the same manner as insurgency: location, isolation and eradication. As all the five processes mentioned above, building up police station records, preventing inflow of arms and ammunition, location of gangs of dacoits including identification of membership, isolation of the gangs from their supporters and harbourers and their eradication through operations efficiently planned and mounted, require intelligence the first task is to collect information and process it. In a dacoity-infested area, the task of collecting intelligence should not be confined to a special group like the CID. Each armed police unit and each police station must help in gathering information and it should be a specific task of the officer in command to set targets and to see whether the uniform side is participating in the collection of intelligence in the correct manner. (Para 37.11)

43.54 On the basis of continuous collection of intelligence, police station records that are normally neglected in areas in which the crime of dacoity is endemic, should be built up, particularly those relating to crime and criminals, suspected or otherwise, and gang history sheets should be prepared with comprehensive data on organisation of the dacoit gangs, membership, castes and relationships of members of the gangs, weapons in possession, the areas of depredation, helpers, harbourers, receivers, places from where food is obtained, sources of medical aid, etc. (Para 37.12)

43.55 For sustained and expert investigation, particularly of professional dacoities, special investigation squads should be set up at the level of the range DIG. In the affected Ranges, there should be an officer of the rank of Superintendent of Police, attached to the office of the DIG, to supervise the work of this squad. All men posted in the dacoity area, whether in the armed police or the civil police, should be trained in fieldcraft and tactics and in all must be inculcated some degree of self-control. Many operations have failed because one man started smoking and the wind gave away the position of the party. (Para 37.13)

43.56 In dacoity areas an important requirement is dedicated leadership. The police officer in command, whether of a section, platoon, company or a mixed group, should be able to bear privations, face hazards and enforce discipline among the men. At all times he must manifestly be concerned about the welfare of his men. During operations, he should eat same food as his men. It is for him to decide the right time to strike. The most important leadership quality required is faithful reporting to the media and the government because false reports about an operation not only damage that operations but also do serious disservice to future operations. (Para 37.14)

43.57 The police strength in a dacoity area needs to be much more than usual. A heavy police presence is very essential. It has been the experience of the Chambal Valley that when after the surrenders in 1972-73 the presence of armed police battalions was reduced, crimes of dacoity and kidnapping shot up within a couple of years. Further, the affected area must have a good network of roads and a wireless network connecting every police station and every fixed police picket. Mobile police patrols should also be in communication with similar mobile patrols in the area and the concerned police station and supervisory officers in order to convey information and seek assistance. This would involve not onlv point to point communication but also inter-communication between groups patrolling the area. (Para 37.15)

43.58 The village defence parties in selected dacoity-prone areas should be equipped with firearms, if they are to play an important role in dealing with dacoities. Village defence parties in dacoity-prone areas, which are earmarked for the purpose of playing a role in control of dacoities, should be properly trained in the care and use of firearms. For this purpose, a police officer of suitable rank should be earmarked in each district of such areas. It should be the function of this officer not only to train the members of the village defence parties in the care and use of firearms, but also to go round the villages and ensure that the firearms are kept in proper custody and in a safe place. By moving round the villages, the officer should also constantly update the expertise of the members of the village defence parties in collection of intelligence and any other activities connected with anti-dacoity operations. (Para 37.16)

43.59 Something special should be done for the victims of the offence of dacoity. Often encounters take place between villagers and dacoits in which several villagers are either killed or injured. The valour and courage of those killed or injured, from among the villagers, are hardly recognised. In some States a very meager pension is given to the dependents of those killed. Those villagers, who defend themselves and other against notorious dacoits, should be recognised as performing a very important public function in the face of serious hazards. In order to boost the morale of the villagers and as a matter of recognition of the courage and determination of these villagers, it is recommended that generous grants and pensions should be paid to the dependents of those villagers who are killed in encounters. Those, who are injured in encounters, should also be paid generous grants and disability pensions. Further, thc dcath or the permanent maiming of the bread winner of a family in a dacoity is a matter of perpetual misery to that family. The Government should sanction suitable compensation to the dependents of a persons who is killed in the course of a dacoity. Government should also pay suitable compensation by way of pension to a person who is permanently maimed due to injuries received during the commission of a dacoity. Such an action on the part of the government would go a long way in mobilising public support in the fight against dacoities. (Para 37.17)

43.60 The police personnel who come to harm in areas ravaged by armed gangs of desperadoes may be given financial compensation and benefits on an enhanced scale, as compared to those applicable to police personnel in other areas not so infested. Depending on the crime situation operational areas, which would entitle police personnel to enhanced benefits under this arrangement, may be notified by the Government from time to time. (Para 37.18)

43.61 Kidnapping for ransom, as a criminal activity, is increasingly being preferred to the commission of a regular dacoity by dacoit gangs. A new kind of crime a coming to notice, particularly in the towns and cities situated in the dacoity-infested area. Small time criminals and anti-social elements kidnap persons and sell them to regular gang of dacoits for a price. The gang then negotiates release with the relatives of the kidnapped and extorts a much higher price. In other words, the powerful gangs kidnap people through agents living in society to whom only a commission is paid. It is, therefore, necessary that this emerging activity is studied carefully from now onwards and intelligence built up to put it down ruthlessly because this could otherwise become the crime of the next decade producing a more devastating impact upon the people than the heinous dacoities of the present times. (Para 37.19)

43.62 One method of dealing with the problem of dacoity has been to accept conditional surrender by dacoits. As any criminal can always surrender to the police or the law court there can be no objection to a policy of accepting surrenders. As a dacoit would not surrender in order to be hanged this minimum condition that he will not be hanged has to be more or less accepted by the State. But beyond this no other condition should be accepted by the State. Dacoits surrender because of the mounting pressure of living the life of an outlaw, the pressure from police, the desire to enjoy the gains of the life of crime and now and then a change of heart. (Para 37.23)

43.63 In order to check the flow of arms and ammunition to criminals it is recommended that the appropriate Departments should be directed to reexamine their procedures and practices to eliminate loopholes so that the weapons and ammunition held by them do not fall into undesirable hands. (Para 37.24)

43.64 For a durable solution of the problem, it is vital that the administration in these areas is made highly responsive to local needs and also keep itself in constant touch with the people so that their problems, grievances and disputes can be perceived and solved quickly. It is recommended that, in addition to the strengthening of the police, the entire civil administrative machinery in these areas should also be considerably strengthened and its capability increased. It is found that films have been made glamourising dacoits. Recently some crimes were committed particularly a kidnapping for ransom, on the basis of an incident depicted in a film. The politicisation and glamourisation of dacoits who, under the law, arc nothing more than dangerous criminals is strongly condemned. It is recommended that the Government should tighten the censorship of films to ensure that dacoits are not glamourised. Well planned and well-executed administrative and police efforts can only contain and perhaps eliminate the depredations of dacoits over brief spans of time, but they cannot root out the problem. There were some dacoity-infested areas in this country in the past, e.g., PEPSU, northern Punjab, Saurashtra where now there is no trace of organised gangs of dacoits. The reason is economic development and that and an effectively functioning criminal justice system are the real remedies. (Para 37.26)

Arms Act

43.65 The Arms Act 1959, which came into force from 1st October, 1962 brought in liberalisation of the licensing provisions. In the last two decades, there have been disturbing indications of easy availability of firearms to criminals, anti-social elements and extremists and their frequent use in commission of offences, armed hold-ups, elimination of rivals and even against policemen engaged in lawful discharge of duties. The threat posed by easy availability of firearms and ammunitions necessitates reforms to make the Arms Act stringent. (Para 38.1)

43.66 In commission of offences, unlicensed weapons are being used in greater numbers and this has been predominant in States like Uttar Pradesh, Bihar and West Bengal although a number of other States have also shown an increasing accessibility of unlicensed firearms to anti-social elements. There is clandestine trade in the illegal manufacture, repair and conversion of firearms. (Para 38.2)

43.67 Various considerations operate in the issue of firearms licences and only a few cases are decided on merits. An individual who has necessary resources and influence acquires any number of firearms as the act does not specifically limit the number of firearms to be held by an individual. Possession and display of firearms has become more a status symbol and in some parts of the country they are displayed on various occasions. (Para 38.4)

43.68 There has been considerable increase in the number of firearm licences issued in the country. The bulk of ammunitions used in unlicensed weapons comes from licensed weapons. (Para 38.5 and 38.6)

43.69 The number of offences registered for violation of the provisions of Arms Act has also been steadily mounting and in 1977, Uttar Pradesh showed the highest volume of Arms Act violations per lakh of population followed by Punjab. (Para 38.7)

43.70 The existing conditions in the country warrant strict

measures—both executive and legislative—to control the proliferation of legal and illegal firearms and ammunitions. (Para 38.8)

43.71 A stricter control should be exercised over issue and renewal of licences. While there should not be any objection to issue of licences to law-abiding citizens for bona fide purposes, in a matter such as this, we feel, that private rights have to yield place to public interest. Holding of arms by individuals should be drastically reduced and maintained at a much lower level than now to ensure the use of arm only for bonafide purposes such as self defence. Sale of arms and specially ammunition should be carried out through government agencies instead of through private dealers as is presently being done. A stricter supervision and screening of those who have licensed firearms at present is also necessary in order to reduce arms traffic. It is our view that this will in practice be possible only if licences are reduced to the barest minimum. This really means that a new Arms Act is needed which provides for stricter conditions for issue of a licence and on the part of the licensee enhanced responsibility for security and accountability of ammunition. (Para 38.9)

43.72 Under the new Act, the antecedents and proclivities of the intending licensee should be required to be thoroughly verified before grant of licence. The drive for recovery of unlicensed arms will become easier once strict control is introduced and licensed arms have been reduced in number. (Para 38.10)

43.73 The new Arms Act and its operation should be the exclusive responsibility of the Central Government. The State Governments and authorities at the district can be delegated with the necessary powers by the Central Government. The working of the Arms Act/Rules should be entrusted to a Central Board who should review the issue of arms and other licences and exercise check on the manufacture, sale, purchase and distribution of arms, ammunition and explosives. (Para 38.11)

43.74 The provision contained in sub-section (3) of Section 13 is very liberal and the licensing authority has practically no discretion to refuse licence and needs to be changed in the new Act. (Para 38.12)

43.75 Not only a condition should be imposed that arms and ammunitions shall be kept in safe places to avoid falling into unauthorised hands but it should also be ascertained whether the intending licences is in a position to ensure the safety of the weapons and account for the ammunition taken by him. (Para 38.13)

43.76 Ordinarily an individual should not be allowed to hold more than one firearm. The amount of ammunition that can be bought by him should be limited in the course of a year with attendant obligation to maintain a strict account of the expenditure of ammunition purchased. Both shall be open to inspection in the normal course at least once a year along with the licence by the licensing and police authorities. These inspections should be carried out with great care and not as mere rituals and it should be made obligatory for the licensee to obtain an endorsement annually from the authorities concerned of having undergone such a scrutiny. (Para 38.14)

43.77 The words "shall grant" appearing in Section 13(3) should be substituted by the words "may grant" and it should further be stipulated in the new Act that besides having good reasons to obtain a licence for a firearm the applicant should be in a position to ensure the safe custody of the arms and ammunitions and accept responsibility to account for the ammunition used. (Para 38.15)

43.78 In Section 22 officers-in-charge of Police Stations should be invested with powers also to conduct or cause a search of premises or recovery of arms, etc. All police officers not below the rank of Sub-Inspector should be empowered to check gun licences for purposes of annual verification and when suspicion arises. (Para 38.16)

43.79 Special task forces should be constituted to unearth illicit arms. (Para 38.17)

43.80 The present Act does not make a distinction between inadvertent violation of law and rules and deliberate disregard or breach of law. Offences committed with firearms which are unlicensed or have been illegally or unauthorisedly acquired should be taken serious not of and visited with the award of much more deterrent punishment than at present prescribed. The Act should provide for a minimum sentence of one year being imposed on an accused on his conviction of offences which are serious. (Paras 38.18 and 38.20)

43.81 Possession, etc., of illicit firearms and other offences should be met by deterrent punishment. The punishment of 3 years prescribed in clauses (b), (c), (d), (e), (g), (i) and (j) of sub-section (1) of Section 25 should be enhanced to 7 years and these together should constitute a new Section 25A. (Para 38.21)

43.82 The punishments of 6 months and 3 months imprisonment prescribed in Sections 29 and 30 should be enhanced to 7 years and one year respectively, with fine. (Paras 38.22 and 38.23)

District Police and the Executive Magistracy

43.83 The district police is an integral part of the State-wide police set-up, which is hierarchically structured and held together by bonds of strong discipline. Over a period of time, the District Magistrate has come to assume a role of authority, command and control over the discharge of police functions within the district. The district police and the Superintendent of Police are thus subjected to two kinds of control—a hierarchical control exercised by the officers in the police and an operational control exercised by the Chief Executive of the district. (Paras 39.1, 39.2 and 39.3)

43.84 The evolution of the police system in India was closely linked with the objectives of the Government in power and the need for maintaining a tight control over the people of this country so that the stability and growth of British rule was not threatened. The conditions prevailing immediately after 1857 and the growth of the national movement in India appear to have significantly conditioned the views of the British rulers on police reform. (Paras 39.6 and 39.7)

43.85 The arrangement contemplated in law for the administration of the police in the district is set forth in paragraph 2 of Section 4 of the Police Act 1861. The "general control and direction" of the District Magistrate mentioned in Section 4 governs the relationship between the police and the magistracy in most parts of the country. (Paras 39.9 and 39.12)

43.86 The words "general control and direction" have been left undefined in law. (Para 39.13)

43.87 Even in the existing legal set up considerable amount of operational independence in matters relating to the internal management of the force is vested in the Superintendent of Police. The general control and direction of the District Magistrate cannot be construed as warranting any interference in the internal management of the police force. This control should be restricted to selective and individual situations and should be exercised more as an exception than as a rule. The present position, in several States far exceeds this legal stipulation. This is untenable and needs to be corrected. (Para 39.16)

43.88 If the police function of prevention and control of crime is to have a social purpose, then the police objective should be positive and should involve the soliciting of public cooperation in the fight against criminality, and the functioning with public support in the fight against the criminal. The enlarged duties and responsibilities with a shift from the restricted 'holding' function to a much larger service function makes it necessary to think in terms of a new organisational structure. (Para 39.18)

43.89 Police functions fall under two broad categories — investigative and preventive. The maintenance of public order is in a way part of preventive function. The manner in which the investigative functions of the police are to be performed is described in detail in the Criminal Procedure Code. Most aspects of preventive action initiated by the police are justiciable and should not be considered as left to unfettered executive discretion. (Paras 39.20 and 39.21)

43.90 After the adoption of our Constitution, matters affecting such rights will be tested against their Constitutional validity. Preventive action by the Police could also be questioned in a court of law and the police will have to account for its action before such a court. (Para 39.22)

43.91 All aspects of police work are now subject to judicial scrutiny. Executive interference by an authority, not empowered in the law governing police functions, would be improper and untenable. The police should functions under the law and be accountable for all the actions to the law and hence to impinge upon the police another executive direction could only lead to distortion of police performance and dilution of police accountability to the law of the land. (Para 39.23)

43.92 A careful reading of the present police manuals leads to the conclusion that the only areas in which the DM is not expected to control the activities of the SP are drill, arms and accoutrements and discipline of the police force. The DM has come to acquire considerable authority to interfere with the internal management of the district police organisation. The positioning of personnel in the organisation, exercise of disciplinary control, providing of housing and other infrastructural facilities for the growth and well-being of the organisation, reporting on the competence of the members of the organisation and utilising the resources of the organisation in an optimum manner to achieve goals, are matters entirely within the purview of the internal management of police organisation. (Paras 39.25 and 39.26)

43.93 The position on the ground today is one of total subordination of the police to the executive magistracy. This subordination is not contemplated even under the present law which vests the administration of the police force in a district solely in the Superintendent of Police, subject only to "the general control and direction" of the District Magistrate. (Para 39.29)

43.94 The separation of the judiciary from the executive is now more or less complete in a few remote parts of the country. Prior to the separation even if there might have been some justification for subjecting the police to the control of the DM, such justification no longer exists. There are no reasons to subject the district police administration to any control other than that exercised by officers in the departmental hierarchy itself, and subject to only such coordination by the Chief Executive of the district as may be essential for the purpose of maintenance of public order, services and supplies essential to the community in certain specified situations and administrative effectiveness. (Paras 39.35, 39.37 and 39.39)

43.95 The new police which is hoped to be created should have a self-contained organisational structure where there is no distortion of command and no dilution of accountability. The police should perform with full accountability to the law of the land. The activities of the police organisation require a high degree of interactive and multi-directional communicative skills with the community. Hence the police should have direct contact with the people whom they profess to serve. (Para 39.40)

43.96 The police is a vital adjunct of the district administrative set up and its performance affects all aspects of public activity and public welfare. In this context the district officer and the SP have to work in close association with each other and cannot afford to assume postures which would tend to promote individualism and destroy collective performance. A positive approach would consist in identifying and removing all irritants and prescribing a clear procedure for effective and active coordination at the district level. (Para 39.41)

43.97 Any police rule or regulation which unnecessarily or without purpose subordinates the police to the DM should be removed or amended in such a way that the requirements of administrative and public interest alone are kept in view. The list below includes some of the major ares which, subordinate the police and the SP to the DM. They serve no administrative purpose and should be done away with.

(a) The DM initiating the Annual Character Roll of the SP;
(b) The DM commenting on ACRs of subordinate police officers particularly officers in charge of the police stations;
(c) Posting and removal of officers with the prior approval of the DM;
(d) The disposition of the police force within the district and its movement outside the district with the DM's approval;

(e) DM's authority to countersign TA bills, grant of casual leave to SP and insistence on the SP taking prior approval before leaving the headquarters;

(f) Proposals of building programmes, opening of new police stations, creation of additional strength of police force to be routed through the DM;

(g) The inspection of police stations by the DM and subordinate magistrates; and

(h) Submission of a number of periodic reports about crimes in the district to the DM. (Para 39.42)

43.98 While the police should have a district identify and adequate competence and operational independence to play an effective role in the administration, it cannot exist in isolation and away from other areas of administration affecting the people. While the police should belong to a sound centralised organisation which flow out of a sound organisational structure it should also have a high degree of interactive capability with other areas of administration, particularly at the grass root levels. The district officer can play an important role as an effective interface in dealing with the different administrative system, including the district police system in his area. (Paras 39.43 and 39.44)

43.99 There are a number of areas which would require the active cooperation of different departments and in such matters coordination by the District Officer would be necessary. The activities of the police in maintaining public order and controlling crime to the extent to which such action is essential to lay a foundation for orderly development is a matter which should concern the authorities charged with development processes. In this regard a measure of local coordination of police activity with other departments and by the District Officer is essential. In the existing set-up the only authority which has some degree of influence with different agencies is the district officer and as such he should be entrusted with these coordinating functions. (Para 39.45)

43.100 The role of the district Officer as the Chief Coordinating Authority in the district be recognised and respected by the police. The District Officer should have the capability to generally advise the police regarding the extent and quantum of performance for the purpose of achieving development targets and to maintain administrative standards. (Para 39.46)

43.101 There should be frequent and intimate contact and consultation between the District Officer and Chief of the District Police. It should be obligatory for the SP to give the utmost consideration and attention to a communication from the District Officer. The SP should take prompt steps to look into and deal with any situation brought to his notice by the District Officer. (Para 39.47)

43.102 Subordination of one agency to another is not essential for healthy cooperation between two agencies. On the contrary we feel that subordination is an extremely unsuitable factor to generate satisfactory coordination. Subordination pre-supposes the carrying out of orders and hence instead of there being a dialogue, discussion and thereafter a decision, there is only implicit compliance where one party performs under resentment and the other under apprehension. Therefore, it is recommended that subordination of the police to the District Officer should be removed. (Para 39.48)

43.103 The SP should be adequately armed under the law to deal with situations independently and without recourse to detailed consultation and advice from any other authority. All powers which are required for regulation and control and for the promotion of order should vest in the SP and other appropriate ranks in the police. (Para 39.50)

43.104 All powers relating to the removal of nuisances, the regulation and control of processions and other public activity, and powers of appointing special police officers should vest in police officers. In respect of powers of licensing, in any matter where the licensing will affect public order in a substantial manner, such as the Indian Arms Act, the Indian Explosives Act, the Motor Vehicles Act, should also vest in police, as is the case even now in areas where the Police Commissioner system is in force. Other powers particularly those which involve the judicial evaluation of a right, and which is not of an urgent nature need not vest in police officers. (Para 39.52)

43.105 Powers under Section 144 Cr. P. C. powers of disposing of cases under Section 107 Cr. P. C., powers of externment of certain categories of persons, which at present already vest in some cities in the police, should be vested in police officers of similar status, in other areas also. (Para 39.53)

43.106 The following amendments to Section 4 or the Police Act 1861 be incorporated in the Police Act:

Section: *Administration of District Police*

The administration of the Police throughout a district, or part thereof shall be vested in the Superintendent of Police appointed under Section XXX.

Section: *Coordination in District Administration*

(i) For the purpose of efficiency in the general administration of the district it shall be lawful for the district officer, by whatever name he is called in the different States, to coordinate the functioning of the police with other agencies of the district administration in respect of the following:

(a) In matters relating to the promotion of land reforms and the settlement of land disputes;
(b) In matters relating to the extensive disturbance of the public peace and tranquillity in the district;
(c) In matters relating to the conduct of elections to any public duty;
(d) In matters relating to the handling of natural calamities, and the rehabilitation of the persons affected thereby;
(e) In matters relating to situations arising out of any external aggression; and
(f) In any similar matter not within the purview of any one department, and affecting the general welfare of the people of the district.

(ii) For the purpose of such coordination, the district officer, by whatever name he is called, may:

(a) call for information of a general or special nature, as and when required, from the police, and any other agency connected with the general administration of the district;
(b) call for a report regarding the steps taken by the police or other agency to deal with the situation; and
(c) give such directions in respect of the matter, as are considered necessary by him to the police and the concerned agency.

(iii) The Superintendent of Police or the head of the agency mentioned in the sub-section above, shall render assistance to the authority specified in sub-section (i) for the purpose of coordination, as specified above.

Explanation

For the purpose of this section, coordination means to combine, or integrate harmoniously.

All the provisions in the State Police Acts which would be contrary to the proposed amended sections of the Police Act would need to be deleted. For instance, some Sections like 16, 17 and 18 of the Bombay Police Act, 1951 would be contrary to the amendment proposed and hence would need to be deleted. (Para 39.54)

Code of Behaviour for Police Officers

43.107 All officers irrespective of their rank should submit themselves to the requirements of the following code of behaviour which would supplement the organizational principles and codes. It would be the special responsibility of all police training institutions and the National Police Academy to ensure that all police personnel imbibe the code of behaviour in both letter and spirit:

(1) *Neglect of Duty*

No police officer without good and sufficient cause shall—

(a) neglect or omit to attend to or carry out with due promptitude and diligence anything which it is his duty as a member of a police force to attend to or carry out, or
(b) fail to work his beat in accordance with orders, or leave the place of duty to which he has been ordered, or having left his place of duty for a *bona fide* purpose fail to return thereto without undue delay, or
(c) be absent without leave from or be late for any duty, or
(d) fail properly to account for, or to make a prompt and true return of, any money or property received by him in the course of his duty.

(2) *Disobedience to Orders*

No police officer shall, without good and sufficient cause, disobey or omit or neglect to carry out any lawful order, written or otherwise, or contravene any provision of the police regulations containing restrictions on the private lives of members of police forces or requiring him to notify the chief officer of police that he, or a relation included in his family has a business interest in his jurisdiction within the meaning of those regulations.

(3) *Discreditable Conduct*

No police officer shall act in any manner prejudicial to discipline or conduct himself in such a manner which is reasonably likely to bring discredit on the reputation of the police force or of the police service.

(4) *Misconduct Towards a Member of Police Force*

(i) A police officer shall be deemed to have committed misconduct towards a member of a police force, if—

(a) his conduct towards another such member is oppressive or abusive, or
(b) he assaults or misbehaves with him.

(ii) No police officer shall, without good and sufficient cause, commit misconduct, as aforesaid.

(5) *Falsehood or Prefabrication*

No police officer shall—

(a) knowingly or through neglect make any false, misleading or inaccurate oral or written statement or entry in any record or document made, kept or required for police purposes, or
(b) either wilfully and without proper authority or through lack of due care destroy or mutilate any record or document made, kept or required or police purposes, or
(c) without good and sufficient cause alter or erase or add to any entry in such a record or document, or
(d) knowingly or through neglect make any false, misleading or inaccurate statement in connection with his appointment to the police force.

(6) *Corrupt or Improper Practices*

No police officer shall—

(a) in his capacity as a member of the force and without the consent of the chief officer of police or the police authority, directly or indirectly solicit or accept any gratuity, present or subscription, or
(b) place himself under a pecuniary obligation to any person in such a manner as might affect his properly carrying out his duties as a member of the force, or
(c) improperly use, or attempt so to use, his position as a member of the force for his private advantage, or
(d) in his capacity as a member of the force and without the consent of the chief officer of police, write, sign or give a testimonial of character or other recommendation with the object of obtaining employment for any person or of supporting any application for the grant of a licence of any kind.

(7) *Abuse of Authority*

(i) A police officer shall be deemed to have committed abuse of authority if he—

(a) without good and sufficient cause makes an arrest, or
(b) uses any unnecessary violence towards any prisoner or other persons with whom he may be brought into contact in the execution of his duty, or
(c) is uncivil to any members of the public.

(ii) No police officer shall commit abuse of authority as aforesaid.

(8) *Neglect to Health*

No police officer shall neglect his health or without good and sufficient reasons neglect to carry out any instructions of a medical officer appointed by the police authority or, while absent from duty on account of sickness, commit any act or adopt any conduct calculated to retard his return to duty. It is essential and desirable that every officer takes special care to maintain and improve his health by proper exercises, etc.

(9) *Improper Dress and Untidiness*

No police officer shall, without good and sufficient cause, while on duty, or while off duty but wearing uniform in a public place, be improperly dressed or be untidy in his appearance.

(10) *Drunkenness*

No police officer shall be in a state of drunkenness which renders him unfit for duties which he is or will be required to perform or which he may reasonably foresee having to perform.

(11) *Being an Accessory to a Disciplinary Offence*

No police officer shall be an accessory to a disciplinary offence either by conniving at it or knowingly becoming accessory to any offence against discipline.

(12) *Damaging the Unity of the Force*

No police officer shall by commission or omission do or fail to do anything, which creates or is likely to create divisions in the police force on grounds of religion, caste or community or affect the reputation and effectiveness of the force as an unbiased and impartial agency.

(13) *Anti-national Conduct*

No police officer shall do anything which affects or is likely to affect the security and integrity of the national or lowers or is likely to lower the repute of the country. (Paras 40.1, 40.2 and 40.3)

Police-public Relation

43.108 A healthy police-public relationship on a continuing day-to-day basis is vital to secure the desired measure of public involvement and cooperation in police work to make it meaningful and acceptable to society and to further the cause of law enforcement. (Paras 41.1 and 41.2)

43.109 One objective of the police-public relations should be the direct involvement of the people in the prevention and detection of crime and in the maintenance of order. (Para 41.4)

43.110 The conclusions, on the present state of police-public relations, are as under:

(1) Police-public relations at present are in a very unsatisfactory state. While there are several reasons for it, police partiality, corruption, brutality and failure to register cognisable offences are the most important factors which contribute to this sad state of affairs.

(2) Police do in fact harass even those people who try to help them.

(3) There is a certain degree of ambivalence in people's views about police efficiency; by and large they do not think the police are inefficient. A change in the style of police functioning is what they desire foremost.

(4) Due to lack of even the basic amenities, bullying cross-examinations and inadequate financial compensation, both in coverage and quantum, people who appear in courts as witnesses have to undergo considerable inconvenience and hardship, and for this they blame the police more than the law courts because their appearance in a court of law is a consequence of their involvement in a police investigation. Therefore, very often the people, in order to avoid going to courts of law, try to avoid police.

(5) Those who have interacted with the police have a slightly better opinion of it than those whose opinions are based on what they have heard.

(6) Even though criminogenic factors are not under the control of police, and the forces which generate disorder the confused with normal dissent, the press and the political leaders generally blame the police for rise in crime and spread of disorder.

(7) The Indian Police Commission of 1902-03 had after discussing police corruption 'practices of extortion and oppression', their 'unnecessary severity' and harassment of people, concluded (Para 26) : "What wonder is it that the people are said to dread the police, and to do all they can to avoid any connection with a police investigation". Those observations can very well apply to the conditions obtaining even today. People now may not dread the police but they certainly dead getting involved with it in any capacity.

(8) Policemen, in general, do not believe that they are very much at fault. They believe that the 'system' is like that. The more cynical among them believe that no improvement is possible. It is considered basic and fundamental for promoting healthy

police-public relationship that every police officer develops in attitude of utmost courtesy and consideration combined with sympathy and understanding towards any member of the public who comes to him seeking help. The manner in which the police officers at the lower level behave towards individual member of the public who approach them is largely conditioned by the manner in which these police officers are themselves treated by their own higher officers within the force. Therefore, there is a simultaneous need for reform in inter-departmental behaviour and conduct of police officers towards one another. (Para 41.10)

43.111 The idea of a special Crime Prevention 'Week' should be given up; instead the police should perform the activities that form part of this week throughout the year in accordance with a schedule drawn up at the beginning of every calendar year. In any dialogue with the people through lectures, seminars, or through the media, the emphasis should be not so much on advising the people about their responsibilities as on making them aware of the genuine difficulties of police and what help the people can render to mitigate them. On good citizenship and police a number of short films have been made, particularly by the Films Division of the Government of India. Such films should continue to be made and be shown throughout the year, in all parts of the country, at regular intervals. (Para 41.12)

43.112 A suggestion has been made that the scheme of special police officers should be extended by way of time and functions, that is such appointments should not be confined to occasions of law and order requirements only but should be an ongoing affair and the functions of the special police officers should not merely be to protect life and property during riots but also, once it becomes an ongoing institution, to investigate ordinary crimes. The suggestion is endorsed. (Para 41.15)

43.113 The substantive message of training programmes in police should be:

(1) That the police is a service dedicated to the protection of the common citizen and it is a force against the elements of lawlessness and disorder.
(2) That they are part of a democratic society and that citizens have a right to organize and express themselves; dissent on the part of the citizen is not be construed as a threat to law and

order unless there is a breach of apprehensions of breach of the peace.

(3) That policemen are in the 'business' of extending help and affording satisfaction to the people so that when they are approached for help their attitude should be to decide how best they can render the help sought and not how, through subterfuge of law and regulation, they can evade their legitimate responsibility. (Para 41.7)

43.114 While the content of training is important in all orientation programmes, the process of imparting the training is even more important where attitudinal changes are sought to be brought about. One cannot teach people to be polite through curt orders and threats of disciplinary action. The existing attitudes are a result of a complex of factors including service conditions, actual behaviour of senior officials, the conduct of public men in power, etc. Training is one, though an important factor, among these. The recommendations on the need for improved training and on special reorientation programmes must, therefore, be read and taken together with the recommendations on other aspects of the police organisation. (Para 41.18)

43.115 The police function in the context of a punishment-oriented judicial system. No matter what the offence, the objective of the criminal justice system is to catch the culprit and, if found guilty in a court of law, punish him with fine and/or imprisonment of death. As there is no concern for the victim of crime at any stage, the system does not offer any satisfaction to anyone except, perhaps, those who live off it. As a sub-system of the criminal justice system, the role of the police also becomes punitive and, therefore, negative. On paper this situation is balanced by the right of every victim of a crime to claim damages in a civil court but it is common knowledge that very few of us can afford the excessively lengthy processes of civil courts the end results of which are often uncertain and unsatisfactory. Given this situation, there is little even for the victim of a crime to motivate him to cooperate with the police except a wish to impose retribution. The legislation of a criminal injuries compensation act is recommended. (Para 41.20)

43.116 While the in-built constraints of a negative role will remain, the police could place greater emphasis, wherever and whenever possible, on the service-oriented functions outlined in paras 14.49 and 14.50 of the Second Report. (Para 41.22)

43.117 One service-oriented function, youth counselling, needs to be made a regular feature of police work. The police must concentrate on the young, particularly the youth in slum areas of cities. A positive relationship established with this section can prove an effective preventive service. Introduction of the Junior Police Call (JPC) scheme of the Hong Kong police is recommended to involve the young in community service, including prevention and detection of crime. (Para 41.23)

43.118 The introduction of the scheme like Junior Police Call here should be feasible. Already there is a tradition of boys clubs, traffic patrole and police-sponsored games and competitions. These need to be strengthened and built upon. In all large cities, this scheme should be tried out by expanding the activities and facilities of existing clubs. It is hoped that ultimately every district headquarters will provide a club-house for young members of such clubs. But if police are only going to impart traffic training and harangue the young people on their duties and if the right kind of policemen and policewomen are not involved in it the scheme will become unsuccessful and counterproductive. (Para 41.26)

43.119 In addition to the negative and punitive role of police arising out of the similar character of our criminal justice system, there is the historical change in the role performance of police which has yet to work itself through. Policemen now have to depend exclusively on law, but legal provisions cannot elicit public cooperation. In our democratic polity, the police must win public cooperation; in fact there is no other way. While there are several hindrances to securing such willing cooperation of the people, the police must remove those that are within their sphere of activity. To begin with, people should be able to come to police with information without fear of harassment by way of repeated summonses to police station and the ordeal of a court attendance and cross-examination. With respect to people who sometimes bring a road accident victim to a public hospital, the Delhi Police have issued written instructions that such persons should under no circumstances be detained in the hospital for interrogation and that there should be no insistence on knowing their personal particulars. It is recommended that this should be the practice not merely in regard to traffic offences but in all cases where people volunteer information to police. (Para 41.27)

43.120 The remedies for the organisational constraints on police performance lie in proper living and working conditions for policemen and reform of the police organisation. Some of the constraints have been examined in earlier Reports. During tours to the various States, it was found that, in general, police station buildings have a forbidding aspect and the condition of lock-ups a dreadful. Further, hardly any police station has a visitors' room. So even if a well-meaning policemen were to try to be polite and courteous he has hardly anything to be courteous with. As the objective is to create a new climate in the police organisation and thereby change the style of police work it is recommended that police station buildings should be properly furnished, well lit and should have a separate reception room for visitors. Large police stations should have facilities for drinking water, tea and coffee. (Para 41.31)

43.121 In view of the very high visibility profile of policemen on traffic duty special attention should be paid to this activity. A similar visible activity is patrolling which has, in recent years, fallen into considerable disuse. The system of patrolling needs to be revived. As the West Bengal Police Commission had observed : "The sight of patrolling policemen is welcome to all and is regarded as a visible sign that the police are at work in preventing crime and keeping a watch over their localities. Patrols are, in our opinion, one of the best means of establishing good relations with the public (p. 255)". This view is endorsed. Beat patrolling should be revived and, in urban areas, combined with the system of neighbourhood policing. (Para 41.32)

43.122 For better communication with the people, police will have to give up, to a considerable extent, the secrecy which surrounds their functioning. Just as structurally the police is accountable only to the executive and not to the immediate community it is supposed to serve, the information that is generated in and by police is also meant exclusively for the government. This matter has been considered very carefully and the conclusion is that all police activities, to the extent possible, should be open except for four specific areas. These four areas are (1) operations, (2) the intelligence on the basis of which operations are planned and conducted, (3) privacy of the individual citizen, and (4) judicial requirements. Barring these four considerations a change from the present practice of withholding every information to sharing as much information as possible is recommended. The exercise of discretion should be in favour of giving as much information as can be given. (Para 41.33)

43.123 News of crime and disorder is of considerable interest to the people and, therefore, the press is interested in it. The police should establish a system of communication through which the authentic facts relating to crime and disorder can quickly be given to the press. If the police will not do it then the journalists will tend to depend on whatever they can gather. In several States the SP cannot hold a press conference and the SHO is not permitted to provide any information to the press. The present failure of police towards the press has thus been denial of prompt factual information to it either on the pretext of secrecy or because no regular facility exists for it. Every district Superintendent of Police should be permitted to deal directly with the Press. The police stations should also be permitted to give the statistical details of number of crimes registered, under investigation, arrests made, cases convicted, etc. When important or sensational cases occur, brief details can be given by police stations, subject to the four considerations for secrecy pointed out before. (Paras 41.35 and 41.36)

Women Police

43.124 The change in social situation due to increased juvenile delinquency and female deviancy have necessitated the employment of women police officers in policing. At present women police form an integral part of police forces in almost all countries of the world. (Para 42.1)

43.125 In the Indian system of police organisation, women police are of comparatively recent origin. After the partition of the country in 1947 and the large-scale violence that followed, the need was felt to look after the abandoned women and children. As a response to this, slowly women police got to be added to the police force during the last 30 years and at present women police form a part in the police force in all States and the Union Territories barring a few. Yet the total number of women in the police forces all over India is a little over 3,000 and is hardly 0.4 per cent of the entire police force of the country. (Para 42.7)

43.126 Women police have proved very useful in performing specialised task of dealing with women and children and specially women victims of crimes. They are now attached to city police stations, Juvenile Aid Police Units (JAPU) and other specialised units in different States. They have, however, until now not been given an equal share in other areas of police work and as such the full extent of their role is yet to be developed. (Para 42.8)

43.127 They should handle investigational work in much greater measure than at present. They should be entrusted with investigation of cases especially relating to women and children and employed in intelligence work connected with said crimes. Women police should become an integral part of the police organisations, with a special role in juvenile crime squads to be set up in urban areas. (Para 42.9)

43.128 Delinquency among girls is a more serious problem than delinquency in boys as women play a vital role in the upbringing of the child and maintenance of some norms in the family. Women police should play a very constructive role in re-establishing and reforming delinquent girls. Young girls in danger of exploitation get some measure of protection under the Children Act as well as Suppression of Immoral Traffic Act, 1956. Women police can play a very useful role, both preventing and investigative, in this sphere. Day time patrolling of slums, labour colonies, bus stands, railway stations should be undertaken by them to locate deviant children and women and help and guide women and children passengers. They should also be utilised in traffic control operations near schools, market places, fairs, festivals and similar situations attended by women and children in large numbers. (Para 42.10)

43.129 In order to deal effectively with women and children demonstrators in the universities, college campus, in the industrial belts and in the streets, a sizeable contingent of women police would need to be deployed. Therefore, women police need to be fully trained and well-equipped to deal with such agitations in close coordination and fully supported by their counter-parts in the male police. (Para 42.11)

43.130 Women police have great potential to cool, defuse and de-escalate many situations and, therefore, greater use should be made of them than at present. In non-combative roles requiring restraint, patience and endurance they can be employed with advantage. They are specially needed in areas where police come in contact with women, so as to obviate complaints of indignity and misbehaviour towards women. The presence of women police in police stations will greatly help in creating confidence and trust in the police. Women police can also help in giving better attention to service aspects of police work. (Para 42.12)

43.131 The basic training course for different ranks of women police should be imparted at the same police training institute where policemen are trained. The duration and the content of the training should be the same as for the male counterparts. This will ensure uniformity in recruitment and training standards. However, certain modifications are suggested in the physical training programme for the women recruits. Besides adequate physical training, arrangements should be made for them to acquire mastery over tactics of unarmed combat such as "judo" and "karate". In addition they have to be given special training in the handling of women demonstrators and mob upsurges in a humane and sensitive manner. (Para 42.13)

43.132 Women recruits, in addition to being trained like men should be put through special courses in schools of social work so as to be able to perform their special role in relation to women and children. Intensive training should be imparted to them in the matter of enforcement of special Act relating to children and vice and also in the technique of search of women and their belongings. They should, in due course, share all the duties now performed by their male counterparts especially the following which are now performed by women police in other countries of the world as reported by the International Criminal Police Organisation (ICPO):

(i) Road traffic regulations and road traffic control duties in large towns involving guarding of pedestrian crossings and the approaches to schools;
(ii) Dealing with women including search, arrest, questioning women suspects who have or are suspected of having committed an offence;
(iii) Crime investigation in general;
(iv) Handling and investigating cases involving view or sexual offences, such as rape, trafficking in women and sexual offences against children;
(v) General foot and/or vehicular patrol duty;
(vi) Social work and child welfare such as handling cases involving missing or badly treated children, liaison work with social welfare organisations and agencies, and assisting women and children in distress;
(vii) Juvenile delinquency case work;
(viii) Clerical work;
(ix) Telecommunications equipment operators switchboard operators and related work;
(x) Prosecution duties in cases involving minor offences committed by young persons brought before Magistrates or juvenile courts;
(xi) Immigration duties and check on travellers, especially female travellers, at airports and other points of entry into the country;
(xii) Guarding female prisoners;

(xiii) Fingerprinting work in CID;
(xiv) Public relations work in order to help create better image of police;
(xv) Instructors in police training institutes;
(xvi) Crime prevention work such as giving talks in Secondary Schools on police work and, in particular, on roads safety regulations;
(xvii) Crowd control duties at special events;
(xviii) Special branch and security work;
(xix) Protection of female VIPs;
(xx) Drug related case work;
(xxi) Administration and guard duties at prisons for women;
(xxii) Technical and document examination work;
(xxiii) Police drivers; and
(xxiv) Police social welfare activities. (Para 42.14)

43.133 Women police need to be recruited in much larger numbers than at present, preferably in the ranks of Assistant Sub-Inspectors or Sub-Inspectors of Police rather than in the rank of constables. Assistant sub-inspectors and sub-inspectors should be graduates preferably with diploma in social work. Provision should be made for recruiting the widows of police men killed in action provided they are otherwise fit and qualified for the appropriate grade of Constable, Assistant Sub-Inspector or Sub-Inspector. Residential accommodation and rest and retiring rooms for them should, as far as possible, be located near the place of work. (Para 42.15)

43.134 In order to have a greater involvement of women police in police administration as well as to provide equal opportunities to them, they should be recruited in vacancies in general duty posts after careful estimation of requirements of women police in the force on the basis of analysis of factors such as population, incidence of crime by women and Juveniles, etc. Women police should not constitute a separate branch of the police with recruitment and promotion confined to women in that branch only. Women police is considered essential for cities, the urban police stations and thickly populated areas. (Para 42.17)

45

NATIONAL POLICE COMMISSION, 1977 – SIXTH REPORT[1]

Chairman Shri Dharma Vira, retired Governor

Members Shri N.K. Reddy; Shri K.F. Rustamji; Shri N.S. Saksena; Prof. M.S. Gore

M. Secy. Shri C.V. Narasimhan

Alterations Shri C.V. Narasimhan, former Director of Central Bureau of Investigation, functioned as Member Secretary of the Commission from its inception till 19th April, 1980 when he left to take a posting in his parent cadre in Tamil Nadu on replacement of his services from the Central Government to the State Government. After the departure of Shri Narasimhan, Shri M.D. Dikshit, Principal Director of Research, functioned as the Secretary Incharge.

Appointment

Far-reaching changes have taken place in the country after the enactment of the Indian Police Act, 1861 and the setting up of the Second Police Commission of 1902, particularly during the last thirty years of Independence. Though a number of States have appointed Police Commissions after Independence to study the problems of the Police in their respective States, there has been no comprehensive review at the national level of the police system after independence despite radical changes in the political, social and economic situation in the country. A fresh examination is necessary of the role and performance of the Police — both as a law enforcement agency, and as an institution to protect the rights of the citizens enshrined in the Constitution. The Government of India have, therefore, decided to appoint a National Police Commission. The National Police Com-

---

1. Controller of Publications, Delhi, 1982, 67 p.

mission was appointed under the Government of India, Ministry of Home Affairs Resolution No. VI-24021/36/77-GPAI, dated November 15, 1977.

Terms of Reference

The following will be the terms of reference of the Commission:

(1) Re-define the role, duties, powers and responsibilities of the police with special reference to prevention and control of crime and maintenance of public order.
(2) Examine the development of the principles underlying the present policing system, including the method of magisterial supervision, evaluate the performance of the system, identify the basic weaknesses of inadequacies, and suggest appropriate changes in the system and the basic laws governing the system.
(3) Examine, if any changes are necessary in the existing method of administration, disciplinary control and accountability.
(4) Inquire into the system of investigation and prosecution, the reasons for delay and failure; the use of improper methods, and the extent of their prevalence; and suggest how the system may be modified or changed, and made efficient; scientific and consistent with human dignity; and how the related laws may be suitably amended.
(5) Examine methods of maintaining crime records and statistics and suggest methods for making them uniform and systematic.
(6) Review policing in rural areas, evaluate any new arrangements that have been made, and recommend changes that are necessary.
(7) Examine the system of policing required in non-rural and urbanised areas including metropolitan areas, and suggest the pattern that would be the most suitable.
(8) Examine the steps taken for modernising law enforcement, evaluate the work of police communications, the computer net-work, scientific laboratories and agencies for research and development, and examine whether modernisation can be speeded up; examine to what extent, as a result of the modernisation of Police forces, streamlining of its functions and its restructuring, it would be possible to economise in the manpower in the various areas of its activities.

(9) Examine the nature and extent of the special responsibilities of the Police towards the weaker sections of the community and suggest steps to ensure prompt action on their complaints for the safeguard of their rights and interests.

(10) Recommend measures and institutions arrangements:

(i) to prevent misuse of powers by the police, and to examine whether police behaviour, out-look, responsiveness and impartiality are maintained at the correct level, and if not the steps such as recruitment and training which should be taken to improve them;

(ii) to prevent misuse of the Police by administrative or executive instructions, political or other pressure, or oral orders of any type, which are contrary to law;

(iii) for the quick and impartial inquiry of public complaints made against the police about any misuse of police powers;

(iv) for the quick redressal of grievances of police personnel and to look after their morale and welfare; and

(v) for a periodic objective evaluation of police performance in a metropolitan area/District/State in a manner which will carry credibility before the public.

(11) Examine the manner and extent to which police can enlist ready and willing co-operation of the public in the discharge of their social defence and law enforcement duties and suggest measures regarding the institutional arrangements to secure such co-operation and measures for the growth of healthy and friendly public-police relationship.

(12) Examine the methods of police training, development, and career-planning of officers and recommend any changes that are required at any time in their service, to modernise the outlook, and to make the leadership of the force effective and morally strong.

(13) Examine the nature of the problems that the police will have to face in the future, and suggest the measures necessary for dealing with them, and for keeping them under continuous study and appraisal.

(14) Consider and make recommendations and suggestions regarding any other matter which the Government may refer to the Commission; and

(15) Any other matter of relevance or importance having an impact

on the subject.

Contents

Police leadership—the Indian Police Service; Training and career development of Indian Police Service Officers; Police and students; Communal riots; Urban policing; Summary of observations and recommendations; Appendices I to IV.

Recommendations

Police Leadership—the Indian Police Service

49.1 The police service can have no future unless it earns the respect and confidence of its men and the public, and therefore the standards for the conduct and performance of the IPS officers should be set at an appropriately high level. (Para 44.10)

49.2 As the functions of the IPS officers have not only multiplied manifold, but are becoming more complex, hard and hazardous, calling for higher professional and technical skills and competence, special measures to attract some of the ablest officers from the lower echelons and also from the outside world are required. This means that the terms and conditions of this service should be comparable with those of the best services. There appears, therefore, no justification for the emoluments and prospects of the IPS being in any way inferior to those of the IAS. The minor improvements in the various pay scales of the IPS did not adequately improve the career value of the service because the yawning gap with the IAS has remained. At present the country is facing such serious dangers that its very integrity and unity are threatened. Needed in the IPS are men whose calibre is not only equal to that of the IAS officers, but who also profess certain mental qualities, courage and higher physical standards, that are specially needed for effective police work. Therefore, the present differentials are counter-productive and it would be cost-effective for the Government to improve the quality of recruitment, emoluments and career prospects of the IPS by bringing them on par with those of the IAS. This recommendation is made because of the importance of stability in society and, therefore, to improve the calibre and performance of this most essential service. This recommendation also flows logically from the recommendations of the Kothari Committee which should be implemented in full. (Paras

44.14, 44.15 and 44.16)

There is persistent public criticism of the police and its role in society which is in contradiction to the glamour associated with some other services. A service which is thus associated with a high degree of personal risk and professional hazards, which suffers from lack of status because of the very nature of its work and which does not have within its pay structure and service conditions an adequate element of compensation cannot be expected to be popular with young men while choosing a career from among a number of avenues open to them specially when, in some services, the hazards and risks are negligible, conditions of work are not so exacting, emoluments and benefits are greater and social status and recognition better. While the handicaps and drawbacks inherent in police work cannot be removed they can partially be compensated for, by putting them on par with officers of other services. That is why the equality in the pay scales and parity in prospects of the IPS with the IAS is recommended. (Paras 44.20, 44.21 and 44.22)

49.3 The Kothari Committee had suggested that officers be assigned to the various Services on the basis of aptitude and suitability, after the completion of the foundational course, a subsequent examination and more specialised interview to provide for individual psychological and aptitude tests. These recommendations of the Kothari Committee and more particularly that part which suggests allotment of officers to various Services on the basis of aptitude are endorsed. (Para 44.23)

49.4 To allow greater avenues for promotion to the various lower ranks in police direct recruitment to the IPS should be reduced to 50 per cent of the vacancies and this should continue to be made from the Civil Services Examination introduced from the year 1970, but the age limit for the IPS should be restricted to 21 to 24 years on account of the long training period of five years which is recommended later. Appointment of a candidate to the IPS after he has been selected for it should be held in abeyance if he wishes to compete again for other Services. It should be open to the candidate to accept the offer, after a year, should he so desire. In that case he would be given a place in the next batch of the IPS and he would thus lose one year of service and pay. This would save the Government from wastage of the training effort at the National Police Academy, Hyderabad and ensure that any officer who joins the IPS continues in the service and devotes his full attention to training. (Para 44.24)

49.5 The 16-2/3 per cent of the total vacancies may be filled by a Limited Competitive Examination to be conducted by the Union Public Service Commission which should be open to any police officer, including those in the CPOs, in the age group of 30 to 35 with a minimum service of 8 years. The remaining 33-1/3 per cent promotion quota should continue to be reserved for serving police officers in the rank of Deputy Superintendent of Police, as at present. The written examination for the Limited Competitive Examination should be designed to include subject relevant to police work such as law, Criminology, Police organisation, Sociology, Psychology besides the usual General Knowledge and English. Those, who qualify, should be required to appear for a personality test of 300 marks and their ACRs should be evaluated for which 200 marks be allotted. Thereafter, the successful competitors be required to appear before a Board for physical fitness test carrying 200 marks. Candidates successful at the Limited Competitive Examination should be allotted to State other than those in which they were serving before appearing for the Limited Competitive Examination. (Paras 44.25 and 44.26)

49.6 Promotion of Deputy Superintendents of Police with 8 years of service in the grade whose age does not exceed 52 years in the year of selection may be recommended for inclusion in the IPS Cadres by the UPSC. This selection would, however, be based upon the following:

(i)	A Qualifying written examination to assess professional knowledge, ability to comprehend and solve practical problems and the officers' efforts to keep abreast of changes and developments	200 marks
(ii)	Evaluation of ACRs by the UPSC assisted by Police Advisers including a serving IGP	500 marks
(iii)	Interview by the UPSC Board	200 marks
(iv)	Physical fitness to be assessed by a Selection Board through some tests	100 marks
	Total :	1000 marks

The list of those who qualify shall be prepared Statewise and the officers who are promoted to IPS after 45 years of age will continue to be allotted to their respective States and given, on promotion to the IPS due credit for their service in the lower ranks, as at present. Those who are promoted to IPS before they have crossed the age of

45 will be allotted to other States. (Para 44.27)

49.7 There is a strong case for rationalising and improving the internal structure of the Indian Police Service and bringing it on par with the IAS in pay structure and promotion prospects. It is recommended that the pay of the DIG should be the same as that of a Commissioner, of the IG the same as that of an Additional Secretary in the Government of India and of the Director General the same as that of a Secretary in the Government of India. Much higher standards of selection to the higher ranks in the police would be needed. All-India selection panels for those posts should be drawn up, based upon performance in various courses, evaluation of ACRs, interview by a UPSC Board an assessment of physical fitness. This will prevent the promotion of mediocre officers to higher levels and thereby assure the police of able and competent leadership. (Para 44.31)

49.8 There is a wide variation in the promotion prospects to the levels of DIG and IG of IPS officers from cadre to cadre and in comparison to the Central Police Organisations. This position, is quite unsatisfactory. There is need for uniformity of prospects within the IPS irrespective of cadres. This necessitates the creation of Central selection panels for the ranks of DIG and IG. [Para 44.33(1)]

49.9 In the interest of clean and impartial administration, every direct recruit taken through either the Civil Services Examination, or the Limited Competitive Examination should be posted outside his own State. This will promote the interest of national integration and clean and impartial administration, matters which have become of great concern to everybody in this country. Simultaneously with the adoption of this system of posting directly recruited officers, to States other than their home States, should be provided enhanced TA facilities on the same lines as in the case of commissioned officers in the Armed Forces. This would enable these officers to reach their homes on occasions of emergency without much expenditure and inconvenience. [Para 44.33(3)]

49.10 Each and every officer promoted from the State Police Service should work in the Central Government also unless he is promoted after the age of 48 years, i.e., he has less than 10 years to retire. State Service Officers promoted to the IPS before the age of 48 must do a minimum of one deputation at the Centre of 3 to 5 years. IPS officer should be exposed to a variety of jobs in and outside the police organisation in order to broaden their outlook. There are certain jobs outside the police organisation that require the special knowledge that police officers acquire. [Paras 44.33(4) and

44.33(5)]

49.11 The management of the IPS cadre should be by police officers, at the Centre, through the Central Police Establishment Board and in the States by similar Boards set up under the State Security Commissions. The High Powered Cadre Review Committee has no IPS officer on it and operates more or less mechanically with little scope for going deep into the cadre increase proposals. For purposes of expert advice, two heads of CPOs should by rotation be included in this Committee, in addition to its present membership. The Triennial Cadre Review must involve, in addition to the representatives of the State concerned, the IGP/DG also and go into the following matters:

(i) Review the performance of the State police against its IPS strength and the relative management by the IPS officers of the Civil and Armed Police;
(ii) Analyse with reference to the current needs and problems of the cadre structure of the State, the Central Deputation Reserve, the Deputation Reserve, the Training Reserve, the Leave Reserve and the number of junior posts; and
(iii) Formulate plans for the pattern growth in the light of the future needs of the State police, the challenges it will have to face and its pattern of growth. To begin with the first stage plan should be made or at least a decade on the basis of the recommendations made from time to time in the Triennial Review.

[Paras 44.33(7) and 44.33(8)]

49.12 Two Central IPS cadres should be constituted—one for the para-military organisations like the BSF, CRPF, ITBP and the other for such organisations as the IB, CBI and RAW. Such Central cadres can be constituted within the framework of Article 312 of the Constitution. The Constitution says that the Parliament may be law provide for the creation of one or more All India Services *common to the Union and the States*. The essential constitutional requirement that the All India Services should be common to the Union and the States can, not only be met but would also be desirable in respect of these two Central cadres. As already said, each and every IPS officer of these cadres should be sent to various States for spells of duty on the basis of a roster while IPS officers from the States would continue to come to these organisations on mandatory deputations. Rule 3(1) of the Indian Police Service (Cadre) Rules, 1954 will, however, need to be modified. It says that, "there shall be constituted for each State or group of State an Indian Police Service Cadre". The two Central cadres will have to be added in this Rule. There shall be three sources of recruitment in these Central cadres. The first would be direct intake of IPS officers through the Civil Services Examinations. This means the CPOs will no longer directly recruit any officer other than IPS officers coming through the U.P.S.C. The second source would be army officers and specialists such as engineers, doctors, computer specialists, etc., who would enter laterally as considered necessary from time to time. These officers will have the option to join the IPS through a process of selection. The third source would be IPS officers on deputation from the various States. (Para 44.35)

49.13 The creation of two Central cadres would throw up a large number of vacancies. It is recommended that the non-IPS officers, who are at present working in these organisations, be considered for filling up the new vacancies through a special recruitment to IPS to be conducted by the Union Public Service Commission. (Para 44.36)

Training and Career Development of Indian Police Service Officers

49.14 The police performance at the cutting edge level of constable and middle operational and supervisory levels of sub-inspector and inspector largely depends on the quality of leadership and professional competence of the officers of the IPS. New knowledge and skills have to be imparted to IPS officers to effectively deal with the new problems and requirements. The basic approach in stressing the importance of training and education in police at all levels is to build a new organisational and performance culture based on greater professional competence, enriched job content, improved interpersonnel as well as police-public relations. (Para 45.3)

49.15 The Committee on Police Training had restructured the curriculum of the probationers' course by changing the emphasis and without reducing either the indoor or outdoor contents of the existing programme. While both the perspective and the changes suggested by that Committee are endorsed it is suggested that instead of packing the entire knowledge and skill in one basic course it should be spread over the first five years of service and should alternate between training in the National Police Academy and training on the job. Accordingly, the following pattern of training and career development for directly recruited IPS officers is recommended:

Sl. No.	Course	Duration in months
1.	Foundational Course of LBSNAA	4
2.	Civil Defence and handling of explosives	1
3.	Basic course at SVPNPA	6
4.	Army attachment	1/2
5.	State PTC including a 12-day fleet Management Course at the Central School of Motor Transport, Sagar (M.P.) and 15-day course at the Central School of Weapons and Tactics at Indore (M.P.)	2
6.	Working in a P.S. as Constable and Head Constable	1
7.	Working as Sub-Inspector in a Police Station	2
8.	Attachments to Prosecution Branch, CID, Headquarters Lines and at District Police Office	2
9.	SHO rural police station	6
10.	Review Course at SVPNPA	2
11.	SHO urban police station	6
12.	SDPO	24
13.	Junior Management course at SVPNPA	3
	Total :	59½

(Paras 45.7 and 45.10)

49.16 It is proposed that before promotion to the ranks of Superintendent of Police, DIG and IG, all IPS officers should undergo specifically designed prepromotion courses followed by an examination and an objective selection process. (Para 45.13)

49.17 After an officer has completed 2 years in a Sub-Division he should go to the SVP National Police Academy for a Junior Management Course. At the end of the course there should be evaluation by the Ministry of Home Affairs through five papers of 100 marks each and 100 marks by the Head of the Academy on the officer's general development, efficiency, fitness, suitability, etc. On successful completion of this course, the officer can be posted as Superintendent of Police incharge of a district. It is suggested that this posting should have a minimum tenure of two years. Those officers who get more than 60 per cent marks in the evaluation should be given Rs. 2,000 as incentive, and those who get over 50 per cent but less than 60 per cent marks should be given Rs. 1,000. Of course to cater for inflation these amounts can be increased from time to time. Those who secure less than 50 per cent marks should be required to repeat the examination at their own expense until such time as they obtain at least 50 per cent marks and thus qualify in the course. (Para 45.14)

49.18 After the completion of 15 years of service and up to 18 years of service an IPS officer will be sent to attend a five-month

Senior Management Course at the SVP National Police Academy. The main emphasis in this course will be on coordinated thinking in facing the major problems confronting the police and each officer will be required to submit a thesis on a selected subject relating to the practical problems of police, law and order, economic crimes, intelligence and investigation. The Chief of the State Police will nominate officers for this course in accordance with seniority and ensure that all IPS officers who are, in the rank of Superintendent of Police/Commandant are, in rotation, sent for this course. Successful completion of this course would be an essential qualification for promotion to the rank of DIG. (Para 45.15)

49.19 All those who have worked in the rank of DIG for a period of 5 years and over and are between the 23rd and 25th year of service shall be sent to the SVP National Police Academy for a three-month Top Management Course. The main emphasis in this course would be on decision making, problem solving skills, and organisational development. This examination should be conducted by the UPSC and this body should appoint examiners and get the answer-books marked. For promotion to the rank of Inspector General, an all-India panel will be formed of all the officers who are successful in this course as also in the selection board before which they will have to appear at the end of this course. This selection board will be presided over by the Chairman of the UPSC, the other members will be a couple of distinguished police officers, sociologists, management experts and the Union Home Secretary. All those who are brought on this all-India Panel of Inspectors General shall be given the pay scale of Inspector General while their actual posting would only be a matter of deployment. (Para 45.16)

49.20 Those who join the IPS through the Limited Competitive Examination should be sent for the Basic Course for IPS officers in the SVPNPA together with other directly recruited IPS officers. If they have actually worked earlier as SHOs they need not, after the Basic Course, work at that level they should straightaway be posted as Sub-Divisional Officers of Police in rural and urban areas. As they should preferably be allotted to other States they must learn the language of the State to which they are allotted. The Junior Management Course which will prepare IPS officers for holding charge of a district is of special importance to these officers and they should attend it together with other directly recruited IPS officers. (Para 45.17)

49.21 For officers who are promoted to the IPS is suggested the development by the SVPNPA of a special six-month course. The course should equip them to assume higher administrative responsibilities as Superintendents of Police and above. After this six-month course they need not be posted as SHO and Sub-Divisional Police Officers if they have already acquired thi· xperience before. Otherwise they should go through the same job experience of one year as SHO and at least 2 years as a Sub-Divisional Police Officer. They should also attend, with the other IPS officers, the Junior Management Course. (Para 45.18)

49.22 Those officers who are not able to get selected for promotion to the rank of Deputy Inspector-General shall be permitted to make two more attempts within the next five years at the examination and if they fail in these also then their cases shall be reviewed with an inference that they are unfit for further retention in service. Those who are retired shall for pension purposes, be given a five year credit of service. Those who do not qualify for promotion to the rank of IG shall be given two more chances, and if they fail, they should be retired with a five year credit or credit till their normal date of superannuation, whichever is earlier, for purposes of pension. (Para 45.19)

49.23 For the three management courses, Junior Management Course, Senior Management Course and the Top Management Course the SVPNPA shall have to be strengthened. It will have to be in a position to meet the enhanced training requirements we have outlined in the foregoing paragraphs. The present SVPNPA will not be able to meet these needs without expansion and organisation. It would, therefore, be best if within the SVPNPA is opened a Centre of Higher Police Studies. This Centre will prepare for an run the three crucial management courses and a number of specialised courses on organised crime, terrorism, economic crimes, etc. Entry into specialised courses must be by competitive selection to test the preparation and interest of the officer. It is further recommended that completion of each such course should result in a lump sum award of Rs. 3,000 to Rs. 5,000 to serve as an incentive. Selection and performance at these courses should also be given due recognition by the Selection Boards at the time of consideration of an officer for promotion. The staffing of this Centre should not be confined to police officers but should include academicians and other specialists. For various courses, the Centre may also have to draw on the talent available in our Universities and Institutes of Management who could come on deputation for short periods on attractive terms. It is recommended that such a Centre be created as a part of the

SVPNPA. (Para 45.20)

49.24 It is recommended that an essential part of the career management of the IPS officers allotted to States should be their postings at the level of Superintendent of Police so organised that they serve on field jobs like District Superintendent of Police/Deputy Commissioner of Police/Additional Superintendent of Police for a period of five years or so. (Para 45.21)

49.25 It is, however, emphasised that these improvement require the prior acceptance of the basic principle that the scales of pay and the prospects of the IPS should be at par with those of the IAS. Intensive training and rigorous selection procedures for promotion to higher ranks have been recommended on the basis of that parity. (Para 45.1)

Police and Students

49.26 Sympathetic response to the problems of the students, elimination of the existing communication gaps and participative strategies in the administration of the Universities and Colleges deserve consideration in promoting a healthy and congenial atmosphere within the institutions to prevent agitations before they become uncontrollable. (Para 46.8)

49.27 The primary responsibility for resolving and mitigating campus problems of indiscipline involving students shall be that of the academic authorities. The police should not be unnecessarily brought into situations which do not involve problems of crime or of law and order. It is essential for the system to be shaped in such a fashion that police intervention is minimal but prompt and effective when situations so warrant. Institutions dealing with discipline and control within the campus have to be strengthened to ensure minimal police intervention. (Para 46.9)

49.28 The proctorial system does not obtain in all institutions and where it obtains, it can become ineffective if the Proctors do not assert themselves or abdicate their authority. The Proctors should keep close and constant liaison with the police authorities so that whenever there is possibility of a situation getting out of control, effective preventive intervention by police can be ensured. A sound information base will enable the Proctors to deal with situations more effectively and nip the agitations in the bud. Despite its limitations, the Proctor system holds a promise if properly developed and implemented. It is recommended that the system should be adopted at least in Universities and Colleges which have large campuses and many hundred students in residence. (Paras 46.11 and 46.12)

49.29 Police intervention should be avoided for preventing cases of group indiscipline and sporadic violence which can otherwise be regulated and controlled by the educational authorities. For this purpose and for security and safety problems, the creation of a separate Protection Force for residential Universities and bigger Colleges in non-residential/affiliated ones as part of the proctorial system is recommended. (Paras 46.13 and 46.14)

49.30 The Protection Force shall be responsible for the prevention of vandalism, pilferage, theft, sabotage and arson. It will also help the Proctors in the maintenance of internal discipline. The Protection Force should, among other things, undertake the following functions:

(i) Protection of the property of departments, faculties and laboratories and person of the University officers;
(ii) Providing a guard to residential areas of Universities;
(iii) Dealing with localised demonstrations by employees, students and teachers under instructions of the competent authority;
(iv) Providing adequate information base for ensuring security of person and property;
(v) Carrying out searches in University premises whenever necessary at the instance of the Proctor/University authorities; and
(vi) Assisting the University authorities during examinations, VIP visits and other bandobust arrangements. (Para 46.15)

The Protection Force should not be militant in character but should try to accomplish its role normally by persuasion and conciliation in its interaction with the students. Orientation of a non-para-military nature for the Force is, therefore, recommended. The Protection Force should be properly trained in civil defence, collection of intelligence, regarding unlawful activities among students and *Karamcharis*, identification of students, trespassers, i.e., non-students and other anti-social elements entering the campus, first-aid, traffic control, laws of arrest, use of minimal force, unarmed combat, etc. (Para 46.16)

The Protection Force would be required to intervene and contain developing situations under the direction of the Proctor till police presence becomes imperative. (Para 46.17)

The members of the Protection Force and other authorities concerned with discipline within the campus may be declared "public servants" under Section 21 IPC. (Para 46.18)

49.31 Police intervention should be restricted to situations of grave disorder or criminal activity or where such situations are apprehended. Police intervention in student agitations while being cautious, restrained and firm should be without any preferential treatment. It is recommended that force, when it is used, should be timely but within maximum restraint especially in the use of lethal weapons. (Paras 46.19, 46.20 and 46.21)

49.32 The University authorities and other academicians consider the portals of educational institutions as sacrosanct and inviolable. The Police also wait for requests from the University authorities before intervention. The delay caused by these indecisive attitudes has been responsible for the situations getting out of control, resulting in considerable damage to property and person. The law does not give an academic campus immunity against due enforcement of law by the police. On the contrary law makes it the duty of police to enter any premises when a situation so warrants and take such action as is necessary. It is, however, recommended that as a rule, the police may inform, if possible, the head of the institution or the competent academic authority before entering the campus. (Paras 46.22 and 46.23)

The necessity for the police to enter an academic campus and take action arisen in the normal discharge of duties:

(i) in the prevention of crime and other unlawful activities;
(ii) in the detection and investigation of crime; and
(iii) in cases where the authorities request for police intervention.

In category (iii) above where the educational authorities request for police help and intervention, the police should intervene provided they are satisfied that the situation is serious and is likely to result in a breach of law and order. The police should assess the situation and satisfy themselves whether the situation is serious enough to warrant their intervention. Routine disposal of requests for assistance from academic authorities is not justified. The presence of a senior police officer is an essential requirement in all campus interventions. This is intended to ensure that the force is firmly and fully under control and there is no vindictive action on the part of individual policemen. The police should have sufficient knowledge about the happenings on the campuses within their jurisdiction if they are to effectively deal with problems there. They should maintain close touch with educational institutions and exchange intelligence to facilitate timely action to prevent troubles. To achieve this objective, wherever there is a large concentration of students, the police should constitute a Special Cell comprising of carefully selected officers to deal with such situations. (Paras 46.24 and 46.25)

49.33 The police should also have adequate intelligence regarding collection of illegal arms, explosives and other lethal weapons within the campus. For this purpose, the right of police to enter the premises to search and seize firearms and ammunition cannot be circumscribed by any conditions. The institutional authorities concerned should, however, be informed at the time any search is carried out. The primary responsibility of the police to carry out searches and seize firearms does not absolve the academic authorities of their responsibility to keep a constant vigil and to prevent students from acquiring and storing firearms and explosive. On receipt of any such information or on reasonable suspicion, it shall be the duty of the academic authorities to inform the police forthwith and seek their help. (Para 46.26)

49.34 Student agitations when they spill out of campus, often erupt in acts of violence. In off-campus situations the question of disciplinary action by the University authority does not arise. The police should take action as per law against the offenders. No special preference or consideration be shown mainly for the reason that the party committing the offence happens to be students. (Para 46.27)

49.35 In Para 28.29 of our Fourth Report a revised arrangement in law has been recommended for the withdrawal of criminal cases to be entertained only on grounds of justice or public interest and not on a mere executive desire for compromise in any particular case. This arrangement should equally apply to the cases involving students. (Para 46.28)

49.36 Police interaction in non-conflict situations, needs encouragement as it will remove the impression among the students that the police are generally hostile to them. Students should be kept in police lock-ups and indiscriminate arrests or handcuffing should be avoided. Release on bail should be a rule rather than an exception. Wherever students are apprehended or arrested, their parents should be informed forthwith of the place of detention of the student and reasons for the apprehension and arrests. The general approach of the police in conflict situations with the students should be to project themselves as a neutral catalyst willing to help the students, wherever necessary. (Para 46.29)

Communal Riots

49.37 The examination reveals a pattern in the failures to deal effectively with some of the riots that have taken place recently. Invariably the district administration failed to anticipate the trouble and to make adequate planning on the ground. Either the intelligence of the impending trouble was not available or the administration failed to take notice of all the minor incidents and tensions. (Para 47.6)

49.38 In several instances police forces were deployed without any briefing whatsoever. In some cases, the armed police was collected at very short notice from different units wherever they could be made available from. Such a body not under the command of their own officers cannot be expected to operate in a disciplined and concerted manner. It is recommended that the armed police should move only in proper formation, along with full complement of their officers. (Para 47.7)

49.39 It is noticed with concern the growing tendency on part of the district authorities to seek instructions from higher quarters, where none are necessary. (Para 47.10)

There is a tendency among the officers to avoid taking responsibility for dealing with communal situations. They either avoid to go to the troubled spot or when they happen to be present there they try not to order the use of force when the situation so demands or better still slip away from the scene leaving the force leaderless. (Para 47.11)

It is unfortunate that after such riots, it is only those officer who had taken some action in dealing with the situation, are accused of all sorts of allegations and they have to face harassment and humiliations in the inquiries that follow. (Para 47.11)

The officer who allows the situation to deteriorate by not taking firm action in the initial stages to control the situation, manages to go scot free. The force gets the impression that their senior officers are not going to give any order for their protection and they go on helplessly watching the beating of their colleagues. The demoralised force, lacking confidence in their senior officers, often retaliates in anger and fear to settle score with the rioters. (Para 47.11)

The failure of the leadership coupled with the low morale of the force leads to many serious allegations of high handedness and other atrocities including criminal activity such as arson and looting, molestation of women, etc., from the force. (Para 47.11)

49.40 The training of police force leaves much to be desired. (Para 47.12)

49.41 There are frequent instances of friction between armed forces and the district administration in a communal situation. The aim and objective in a communal situation should be to strengthen the hands of the local administration and they should refrain from any dissemination of news to the media to give the impression that they have replaced the local administration. (Para 47.15)

49.42 Data pertaining to an area should be collected with great care. It should also be constantly updated. Changes in population and the distribution of population in the various towns and other significant areas in the district should be carefully observed and the reasons for such migration should be ascertained and analysed. (Para 47.17)

Records maintained at district and village level should be properly maintained by the police authorities in-charge of districts and police stations. It is also desirable to maintain such records at the State level. (Para 47.19)

A separate cell in the intelligence agencies available at the district level and at the State level should be earmarked whose only function should be to look for significant data which would indicate an imbalance in any particular area. The State level agency should interpret this data on a total basis for the whole State. (Para 47.20)

49.43 A strict vigilance is to be kept on day to day living problems as well as on the problems creating tension between the two communities. Whenever stresses are observed in any given area the police and the administration should identify them quickly and take prompt steps to defuse them. (Para 47.18)

49.44 Dependence on the intelligence collected by the plain-clothed staff alone is not desirable. Collection of intelligence by uniformed units needs to be reactivised. (Para 47.20)

49.45 There should be rehearsals to coordinate the law and order arrangements with the army and the para-military forces during the peace time as well so that there is no misunderstanding or lack of coordination with the army and para-military forces when they come to the aid of the civil authorities during riot situations. (Para 47.22)

49.46 Preventive action is not restricted to arrest and launching of cases under Section 107 Cr.P.C. Prevention can be brought about by regulation, restraint, constraint and control. In place where there is tension developing, if the policemen perform their normal tasks such as beat patrols which they send out during peak hours, the usual regulation of crowds, the normal control and direction of traffic, etc., normalcy is not only kept in the area but is also seen and felt by the people. Normalcy always acts as an anti-dote to tension and hence prevents it from growing beyond breaking point. Even if there is some risk in the relaxation of restrictive measures, for the restoration of normalcy, the risk is worth taking. (Para 47.23)

49.47 Restraint can be brought out by increasing police presence and by arresting those who are likely to indulge in acts prejudicial to public order. But restraint has to be imposed only upon those who are potential law breakers. (Para 47.24)

49.48 It is very important for the police to have an up-to-date and correct list of anti-social elements and to be able to identify and arrest them in a moment of crisis. (Para 47.25)

Mere identification of the mischief makers will not be enough. There is need for constant vigilance and action against such persons, even at times other than during the communal riots. (Para 47.26)

49.49 A developing situation can be defused effectively by enlisting public cooperation. The role of Peace Committees in this regard has been stressed by several Commissions in the past. It should be ensured that important publicmen with considerable local influence, and who are acceptable to both the communities because of their proven impartiality, are included as members of these committees. (Para 47.27)

49.50 In a riot situation, the administration should, take steps to disseminate correct and proper information to the public through all available means. In this connection we would emphasise the use of the radio and loudspeakers as an effective communication media. If correct and frank reports of the incidents occurring, and the steps taken by the authority are broadcast frequently, the morale of the people would be kept high and this itself allay feelings of fear and insecurity in the population. (Para 47.28)

In the case of mischievous reporting in the press which is likely to be prejudicial to national integration and public order, the State Government and local administrations should act impartially and use every weapon in their legal armoury to fight obnoxious propaganda which may be prejudicial to the maintenance of communal harmony. (Para 47.29)

49.51 Even a small quarrel or a minor incident involving members of the two communities should be attended to and dealt with by a responsible senior police officer and the dispute nipped in the bud so that it does not escalate into a major riot. The quality, quantum and timing of police response in such situations are important. (Para 47.31)

49.52 In dealing with processions likely to generate communal trouble there is such greater scope for the police to be prepared in advance. The police should, to the extent possible, collect information about the mood and intentions of the processionists and the attitude and preparedness of those who oppose the processions. Trouble spots should be identified and places of worship should be protected and cordoned off. Processions which are likely to generate tensions and riotous situations should be properly regulated and controlled under the law. In extreme cases, if the situation so demands, such processions should even be prohibited under the law. (Para 47.32)

While no hard and fast rules can be laid down for the regulation of a procession, the senior-most officer present and in-charge of arrangements must appreciate the local problems and after applying his mind, lay out the arrangements in such a way as to demonstrate to the local population that the police would act impartially, effectively and firmly. (Para 47.33)

As recommended by the Reghubar Dayal Commission the places of worship should be searched by the police to find out if brickbats or other offensive materials are stored in these places. In doing so, the police should go strictly by the intelligence available to them and not at the behest of one group or the other. (Para 47.32)

49.53 The authorities in dealing with communal riots should not be inhibited, by any consideration, to adopt luke-warm measures at the early stages of any communal trouble which may push the situation beyond a point of no return. A communal riot is different from any other law and order situation because it has its origin in deep seated passions and jealousies. The authorities should recognise the distinction and should show extreme firmness from the very beginning. (Para 47.34)

49.54 Immediate and exemplary action should be taken against the officers who wilfully fail to go to the trouble spot or slip away from there after trouble has erupted. Officers who have successfully controlled the situation at the initial stages with firm action should be suitably rewarded. (Para 47.35)

49.55 Only specially selected experienced officers with an image of impartiality and fair play should be posted to the communally sensitive districts. They should not normally be transferred before the completion of their tenure and in any case all district and police officers should not be transferred at the same time. (Para 47.36)

49.56 There should be a control room at least in all those places which have been identified as prone to communal trouble. These control rooms should function on an on-going basis and should be kept under the charge of officers who are polite and responsive and who are also professionally competent to assess the information passed on to them and indicate action to be taken on such information. (Para 47.37)

The control room should have an adequate team of well-briefed police officers who can be expeditiously despatched to a scene of trouble and who can be expected to deal with it effectively. (Para 47.38)

49.57 Most riot schemes are prepared in a routine manner and they are said to be impracticable because they are designed for a given area in total isolation of the surrounding areas. Many schemes cannot be implemented because the man-power contemplated in these schemes is not worked out in a realistic basis. (Para 47.39)

The riot schemes may be rehearsed from time to time and in this connection "Sand model" exercises could be useful. (Para 47.41)

49.58 The imposition of curfew in any area should be resorted to after careful thought and in such a manner that the least amount of inconvenience is caused to law abiding citizens. (Para 47.42)

Curfew should be restricted to those areas where curtailment of the movement of the people is absolutely necessary for the purpose of suppression of large scale illegal activity. Once a curfew is imposed, it should be enforced very strictly. Even before the imposition of the curfew or immediately thereafter, adequate police and security forces should be moved into the area bound by the curfew. Anybody found violating the curfew should be arrested and prosecuted. (Para 47.43)

49.59 The police party dealing with riots should be accompanied by ambulance and first-aid services. (Para 47.46)

49.60 Unless crimes committed during the riots are registered, investigated and the criminal identified and prosecuted, police would not have completely fulfilled its role as a law enforcement agency. This important legal function is presently being given a low priority by the police. If stringent judicial action is taken against a criminal and well publicised, it would impose a high degree of constraint upon others from indulging in criminal activities. (Para 47.47)

In a riot situation registration of offences becomes major casualty. It is futile to expect the victim of a crime to reach a police station risking his own life and report a crime to the police. The police should open several reporting centres at different points in a riot torn area. These reporting centres should be placed under the charge of competent police officers who should be firmly instructed to record all crimes reported to them. (Para 47.48)

Special investigation squads should be set up to investigate crimes committed in course of serious riots. Such squads should be set up under the State investigating agency [State CID (Crime)] to investigate all crimes committed in the course of a riot. (Para 47.49)

The investigation of reported crimes in serious riot situations should be done thoroughly, competently, quickly and impartially by special teams of competent officers working under the supervision of senior officers. Any interference in this process by any group, however, powerful it may be and whatever may be the reasons, should be strongly condemned. (Para 47.51)

Special courts with special procedure prescribed in the Disturbed Areas (Criminal Law Amendment) Act as recommended in the Third Report would be useful in the investigation and prosecution of offences committed during violent public disorder situations. (Para 47.53)

49.61 In a major riot it is the duty of the administration to compensate the unfortunate sufferers for the loss and suffering undergone by them and to assist them in their rehabilitation. (Para 47.55)

The police should play a very active and positive role in the rehabilitation of the people affected in the riots. They should record the extent of damage in the course of their investigations and enquiries in the cases reported to them and furnish copies of these documents to the appropriate authorities. (Para 47.56)

49.62 It is not desirable to reserve any fixed percentage as such among the vacancies in the police for the minority groups, since that would go against the fundamentals of police philosophy that the police as a system has to function impartially as an agent of the law and cannot have any caste or communal approach to the problem dealt with by it. (Para 47.57)

The police forces of the various States in the country should truly represent the social structure in the respective States. Such a situation should be brought about by a competitive, fair, impartial recruitment and training process and not by a protective process like the reservation of vacancies for members of the minority communities, in this sensitive wing of Government administration. (Para 47.58)

49.63 It is recommended that whenever allegations of personal aggrandisement are made, such allegations should be carefully examined and if specific instances of misbehaviour on the part of any policemen are found to be true, such policemen should be punished in an exemplary manner so that the credibility of the police organisation, as such, with the people, is not impaired. (Para 47.59)

49.64 The availability and capability of Home Guards in districts should be fully made use of by the police. In an emergent situation the local authorities themselves should be empowered to requisition the services of Home Guards, by framing appropriate rules for this purpose. (Para 47.60)

Urban Policing

49.65 While the problems of urban policing are very complex, the existence of an informed and vocal public which is willing to cooperate with the police by giving information can go a long way in helping the police to tackle these problems. (Para 48.5)

49.66 It is obvious that in urban areas police should be fully equipped to act promptly and effectively, should have an intelligence organisation to collect information on crime, criminals and other related matters, should have the capacity to undertake various duties relating to security and should have the means to take effective preventive and regulatory action to ensure order in the urban society. (Para 48.6)

49.67 In terms of manpower it is noticed that while additional duties are constantly given to police, generally through enactment of new laws, there seldom is a similar increase in police manpower. It is recommended that for every city a triennial assessment of manpower should be made. (Para 48.7)

49.68 The police need adequate transport to reach a scene of crime quickly and to mobilise manpower to deal with a law and order problem. Preventive work calls for patrol cars and flying squads. (Para 48.8(1))

49.69 Communication facilities for the police must serve two objective: facilitating communication with the public and facilitating intra-departmental communication for exchange of information and mobilisation of manpower to respond to a crime or a disorder situation. To meet the requirement of accessibility to the general public, the police require the general P&T telephone link, in addition to their own internal communication network. It is, therefore, essential that all police station and outposts should have a regular P&T telephone and all operational officers in the city police should be equipped with telephones both in their offices and residences. However, even in a city, not all members of the public have easy access to a telephone despite the fact that the P&T authorities do make arrangements to make available a large number of public call offices. In some countries this difficulty is overcome by placing police telephone booths in strategic places in the city. These booths can be used for dialling, free of cost, any police number or an emergency service such as the fire brigade or the ambulance. These police call booths could also be fitted with a light indicator which would indicate to the beat constable in the area when he is required by his police station. In the larger cities this facility should be provided to the people. For intra-departmental communication such as between control room, police stations, patrol vehicles, and patrol parties on the streets a VHF network of radio telephones is vital. The police in Indian cities have been given these facilities to some extent under the Police Modernisation Scheme. Their continuance and expansion would be a step in the right direction. In addition it is found that in a few cities the police have the systems of an internal PBX. This proves very useful when the P&T telephones fail to work or get congested. The P&T telephones in addition carry the risk of vulnerability of interception by undesirable elements. It is felt that these facilities should be set up in all the larger cities in India. Where possible, underground cables should be used to prevent sabotage. (Para 48.8(2))

49.70 It is recommended that all cities with a population of 5 lakhs or more should be provided with an exclusive Scene of Crime Vehicle and the larger cities should have more such vehicles. Similarly, all police stations should be provided with Investigation Boxes and particular care should be taken to ensure that police officers posted for investigation work are trained in the appreciation, collection and utilisation of scientific evidence. (Para 48.8(3))

49.71 Cities with 5 lakhs and above population should have a Single Digit Bureau. [Para 48.8(4)]

49.72 In urban areas, criminals have the advantage of mobility and police response would be adequate only if records are speedily available to them. This is possible only with the help of computers. The creation of a National Crime Records Bureau with a spread down to police station level has already been recommended in the

Second Report. The use of computers for registration of all motor vehicles and the antecedents of persons of doubtful character is also envisaged. [Para 48.8(5)]

49.73 The importance of a Control Room in urban areas cannot be over-emphasised and its role as the centre of all police operations, a centre for receipt of calls for police aid, a coordinator of all police mobiles and as the place from where all police activity is directed to meet a public disorder situation or a natural calamity, requires no reiteration. It is recommended that Control Rooms should be located within the Office of the Chief of City Police. [Para 48.8(6)]

49.74 Policemen in urban areas should have adequate supply of law and order equipment, such as helmets, visors, body-guards, shields, tear gas masks and ammunition to meet their full requirements. When policemen do not have proper equipment to face a barrage of stones they tend to react in panic and use firearms. [Para 48.8(7)]

49.75 All over the country the condition of police station building is distressing. A police station building should have adequate space for its staff as well as reception facilities for members of the public. It should have conveniences for the staff and visitors. Ideally, there should be provision for staff quarters within the police station precincts to ensure availability of police manpower round the clock. Besides, in large cities a great deal of time is spent on commuting from home to police station and back leaving the men, on account of their long hours of duty, little or no time for their personal affairs. Police station buildings in urban areas should be developed on these lines. [Para 48.8(8)]

49.76 At present all policemen whether they have to work in a rural or an urban areas are trained in identical fashion. Urban policemen at present learn through experience. It is recommended that policemen in urban areas should be specifically trained to handle (1) sophisticated equipment; (2) withstand stress; and (3) respond quickly to directions received. This response training is very important. In the gazetted ranks there should be a free inter-change of officers between urban and rural areas while in the subordinate ranks officers should be given a longer tenure, something like ten years, to specialise in either rural or urban policing without ruling out the need for inter-change of expertise and talent for the healthy development of police in both the areas. In a city the subordinate ranks of policemen, are under close and continuous supervision of higher, officers and, therefore, the one key professional requirement from them is quick response to directions given. In the rural areas a Sub-Inspector posted as SHO in a remote corner with poor communication facilities may be able to manage with a slow response to difficult situations but cannot manage without taking decisions, the decision-making requires ability. It is, therefore, wrong to consider that those posted in urban areas are in any way superior to their counterparts in the rural areas. (Para 48.9)

49.77 A higher status for the constable and his association in the investigation of minor offences has already been recommended in the First Report. A beginning in this regard could be made in the urban areas as constables would have the benefit of close supervision from their superior officers. Full utilization of every policemen is essential to meet the resource constraint that we envisage. (Para 48.10)

49.78 In large urban areas several problems arising out of social tensions, more opportunities for crime, and the occasionally spontaneous explosion of law and order situations called for an extremely quick response from the police at the operational levels and precise, comprehensive and prompt directions from the superior levels. There is seldom any time for discussion and debate and assessments and agreements. Quick action springing from purposeful direction is called for. This can be achieved only when the police are organised in a unitary chain of command which embraces the two basic functions of decision-making and implementation. Particularly in large cities these two functions have to go together. It is, therefore, recommended that in large cities that is those with a population of 5 lakhs and above and even in places where there may be special reasons like speedy urbanisation, industrialisation et cetera the system of Police Commissionerates as it exists in Bombay, Calcutta, Delhi, Madras, Nagpur, Poona, Hyderabad, Ahmedabad and Bangalore should be introduced. In view of the complexity and enormous dimensions of police problems that frequently arise in large cities the Commissioner should be a police officer of adequate maturity, seniority and expertise. This is important because an advantage of this system is the direct, and not supervisory, involvement of a senior and mature police officer in the day to day policing of the city. It is this that operationally distinguishes a Police Commissioner from a Superintendent of Police in a district. The Police Commissioner should have complete authority over his force and should be functionally autonomous. (Para 48.12)

49.79 It is felt that the Inspector General or the Director General of Police, since he is responsible for the policing of the State, should have control over the police forces in the major cities of his State. For this reason it is felt that while the Commissioner of Police should be delegated all financial and disciplinary powers of a head of department to facilitate his working he should remain subordinate to the Police Chief of the State. (Para 48.13)

49.80 For cities below five lakhs and above one lakh population is visualised a separate city police force exclusively earmarked for the urban areas, working under the direct supervision and control of the Senior Superintendent of Police for the district. Cities of 3 lakh to 5 lakh population should have an officer of the rank of Superintendent of Police as the head of its city police force and this head in cities with one lakh to three lakh population could be an Additional or a Deputy Superintendent of Police depending upon the complexities of the problems of that city. At the police station level the problems faced in urban areas are multifarious, and difficult and the people expect a better response from the police at this operational level of the police organisation. This implies that the officer in charge of an urban police station should be of a senior rank, at least that of an Inspector. In police stations, in important commercial areas and in the industrial belts where the police have to face complex situations and frequent breakdowns of law and order it is anticipated that even a Deputy Superintendent of Police could be posted as the officer in charge. (Para 48.14)

49.81 The separation of law and order and detective staff should be at the police station level only and they should all remain under the Station House Officer. Higher officers, i.e., those above the SHO can remain territorially responsible for both law and order and investigation of crimes. It would, however, be advantageous to have a gazetted officer, for close supervision of investigation work regardless of the police station involved. Depending upon the size of the city, the numbers in this supervisory rank can be increased and their ranks upgraded. (Para 48.15)

49.82 Cities should have a local Crime Branch to deal with special crimes while the police stations are left to deal with routine crimes. Broadly speaking, all cities with more than 5 lakh population should have the special squads identified below:

(1) Homicide Squad.
(2) Burglary Squad.
(3) Economic Offences and Forgery Squad.
(4) Robbery/Dacoity Squad.

(5) Kidnapping/Missing Persons Squad.
(6) Automobile Thefts Squad.

These special city C.I.D. squads will function under the control of the Commissioner of Police or the Superintendent of Police, as the case may be. (Para 48.16)

49.83 Urban police forces require a sizeable complement of women police to deal with the problems of women and children. Enforcement of the laws relating to them should involve increasing numbers of women police. The women police officers should be made available down to the police station level and, among other things, they could very profitably be utilised as receptionists in police stations. (Para 48.17)

49.84 Urban police forces, particularly in the larger cities require an effective and well equipped intelligence agency to gather information regarding law and order. It is, therefore, visualised that every city with a population of 5 lakh and above and in the smaller cities there should be a City Special Branch for collection of intelligence relating to law and order. These Special Branches could also look after the special security requirements of airports and other vital installations and perform specialised duties relatable to VIPs. (Para 48.18)

49.85 There should be a provision in the Police Act itself that there should be a Commissioner of Police for all cities with a population of 5 lakh or more. The powers to be exercised by the Commissioner of Police should be those that are spelt out in the Delhi Police Act, 1978. The Code of Criminal Procedure 1973 also requires a suitable modification. Under Section 8 of the Code of Criminal Procedure the term "Metropolitan Area" has been defined as any area in a State comprising a city or town whose population exceeds one million. In Section 20 of the same Code it is provided that some of the powers of an Executive Magistrate could be conferred on a Commissioner of Police in metropolitan areas. The system of conferring powers of an Executive Magistrate on a Commissioner of Police is already in vogue in cities with more than one million population. It has already been recommended that all cities with 5 lakh or more population should be regarded as metropolitan areas. This could only be done if Section 8 of the Code of Criminal Procedure 1974 is suitably amended. It is, therefore, recommended that the term "Metropolitan Area" appearing in Section 8 of the Code should be modified to include "any area in the State comprising a city or town whose population exceeds 5 lakh" as against "a population of one million" as at present. (Para 48.19)

49.86 All large cities generally have an element of the local press in addition to correspondents from the national and State level papers and journals. Incalculable harm is done if there is a communication gap between the press and the police. It not only spreads panic among the people but also tarnishes the image of the police and in the process makes the work of the police all the more difficult. It is, therefore, recommended that in all cities with a population of 5 lakh or more there should be a Public Relations Officer under the Chief of the City Police with the following charter of duties:

(1) To release briefs to the press on news of public interest.
(2) To organise exhibitions and conduct lectures in schools, colleges and other institutions, to educate the public about their rights and responsibilities.
(3) To act as a counsellor to the people when they are in difficulty and guide them correctly in the police procedures and regulations and help them in getting their work done quickly through liaison with the concerned police officers. (Para 48.20)

49.87 In urban areas the police have of necessity to adopt certain specific patterns to ensure their effectiveness. In India there is a system of outposts. It is, however, felt that in urban areas watch and ward outposts will not meet the requirements of immediate registration of offences, and their investigation until such time as, should it be required, specialist squads can take over. In urban areas it would, therefore, be relatively better to have small police stations rather than outposts. Such an arrangement will also provide for better control and supervision of the staff. Every police station need not however, have male and female lock-ups, malkhana, kot and, therefore, sentries. Groups of 2-3 police stations could use these facilities at a larger police station. For easy availability of police to the people and the greater spread of police presence the establishment of more police stations in urban areas and the grouping of these police stations, for purposes of lock-ups, etc., under a larger police station in their middle, is recommended. (Para 48.21)

49.88 Police should undertake the duty of verifying the antecedents of chowkidars whom urban residents collectively or individually appoint, and should, during their night rounds, check if these chowkidars are doing their duty properly. (Para 48.22)

49.89 Patrols on foot and on cycles are more cost effective than those on motor vehicles. Vehicles should generally be kept at various, locations for doing the job of a dispersed flying squad. There should not be an over emphasis on patrol cars as they tend to be impersonal and are very expensive. (Para 48.23)

49.90 We have also seen that urban areas in India are growing very rapidly and new colonies are coming up without adequate provision for police presence through outposts and police stations. As a result these outlying colonies are specially vulnerable to criminals and bad characters. It is, therefore, necessary that police officers should have a say in urbanisation plans of a city by being associated with the development authority or the town planning board so that the police point of view is taken into consideration in drafting the urbanisation plans and the growth of the city. Whenever a new colony or area is to be developed adequate space should be earmarked for the creation of a police station with staff quarters so that in the ultimate development of the city the police is not handicapped by lack of accommodation to ensure its presence. (Para 48.24)

49.91 The requirement of CRPF and BSF should be very limited and request for Army assistance ought to be a very feature indeed. A well organised police system can ensure this. What is required is a police organisation suited to the requirements of the city and working within a suitable framework of laws and rules such as have been recommended. (Para 48.25)

46

NATIONAL POLICE COMMISSION, 1977 – SEVENTH REPORT[1]

Chairman Shri Dharma Vira, retired Governor

Member Shri N.K. Reddy; Shri K.F. Rustamji; Shri N.S. Saksena; Prof. M.S. Gore

Secretary Shri. C.V. Narasimhan

Alterations Shri V. Narasimhan, former Director of Central Bureau of Investigation, functioned as Member Secretary of the Commission from its inception till 19th April, 1980 when he left to take a posting in his parent cadre in Tamil Nadu on replacement of his services from the Central Government to the State Government. After the departure of Shri Narasimhan, Shri M. D. Dikshit, Principal Director of Research, functioned as the Secretary Incharge.

Appointment

Far-reaching changes have taken place in the country after the enactment of the Indian Police Act, 1861 and the setting up of the Second Police Commission of 1902, particularly during the last thirty years of Independence. Though a number of States have appointed Police Commissions after Independence to study the problems of the Police in their respective States, there has been no comprehensive review at the national level of the police system after Independence despite radical changes in the political, social and economic situation in the country. A fresh examination is necessary of the role and performance of the Police—both as a law enforcement agency, and as an institution to protect the rights of the citizens enshrined in the Con-

---

1. Controller of Publications, Delhi, 1982, i + 112 p.

stitution. The Government of India have, therefore, decided to appoint a National Police Commission. The National Commission was appointed under the Government of India, Ministry of Home Affairs Resolution No. VI-24021/36/77-GPAI, dated November 15, 1977.

Terms of Reference

The following will be the terms of reference of the Commission:

(1) Re-define the role, duties, powers and responsibilities of the police with special reference to prevention and control of crime and maintenance of public order.
(2) Examine the development of the principles underlying the present policing system, including the method of magisterial supervision, evaluate the performance of the system, identify the basic weaknesses of inadequacies, and suggest appropriate changes in the system and the basic laws governing the system.
(3) Examine, if any changes are necessary in the existing method of administration, disciplinary control and accountability.
(4) Inquire into the system of investigation and prosecution, the reasons for delay and failure, the use of improper methods, and the extent of their prevalence; and suggest how the system may be modified or changed, and made efficient, scientific and consistent with human dignity; and how the related laws may be suitably amended.
(5) Examine methods of maintaining crime records and statistics and suggest methods for making them uniform and systematic.
(6) Review policing in rural areas evaluate any new arrangements that have been made, and recommend changes that are necessary.
(7) Examine the system of policing required in non-rural and urbanised areas including metropolitan areas, and suggest the pattern that would be the most suitable.
(8) Examine the steps taken for modernising law enforcement, evaluate the work of police communications, the computer network, scientific laboratories and agencies for research and development, and examine whether modernisation can be speeded up; examine to what extent, as a result of the modernisation of Police forces, streamlining of its functions and its restructuring, it would be possible to economise in the manpower in the various areas of its activities.

(9) Examine the nature and extent of the special responsibilities of the Police towards the weaker sections of the community and suggest steps to ensure prompt action on their complaints for the safeguard of their rights and interests.

(10) Recommend measures and institutional arrangements:

(i) to prevent misuse of powers by the police, and to examine whether police behaviour, out-look, responsiveness and impartiality are maintained at the correct level, and if not the steps such as recruitment and training which should be taken to improve them;

(ii) to prevent misuse of the Police by administrative or executive instructions, political or other pressure, or oral order of any type, which are contrary to law;

(iii) for the quick and impartial inquiry of public complaints made against the police about any misuse of police powers;

(iv) for the quick redressal of grievances of police personnel and to look after their morale and welfare; and

(v) for a periodic objective evaluation of police performance in metropolitan area/District/State in a manner which will carry credibility before the public.

(11) Examine the manner and extent to which police can enlist ready and willing co-operation of the public in the discharge of their social defence and law enforcement duties and suggest measures regarding the institutional arrangements to secure such co-operation and measures for the growth of healthy and friendly public-police relationship.

(12) Examine the methods of police training, development, and career-planning of officers and recommend any changes that are required at any time in their service, to modernise the outlook, and to make the leadership of the force effective and morally strong.

(13) Examine the nature of the problems that the police will have to face in the future, and suggest the measures necessary for dealing with them, and for keeping them under continuous study and appraisal.

(14) Consider and make recommendations and suggestions regarding any other matter which the Government may refer to the Commission; and

(15) Any other matter of relevance or importance having an impact

on the subject.

Contents

Organisation and structure of police; State armed police battalions and district armed reserve; Delegation of financial powers to police officers; Traffic regulation; The ministerial staff and administrative work in the police department; Auxiliary to Police—Home Guards; Performance appraisal of police personnel; Disciplinary control; Role of the Centre in planning, evaluation and co-ordination; Policing in the North-East; Summary of Observations and Recommendations; Appendices I to V.

Recommendations

Organisation and Structure of Police

60.1 In restructuring the existing police system, a very high priority should be given to the strengthening of the basic unit of all police work and policing the Police Stations. As Police Station is the most important unit of the police administration, the public expectations from the police can only be fulfilled if the public are satisfied with the integrity, professionalism, fortitude, impartiality, promptness in the services, rendered by the jurisdictional Police Stations. The fulfilment of the organisational roles of the police departments will have its acid test at the level of Police Station and so any reform to strengthen policing either for rural or urban area should start at the organisational, location and working of the Police Station. (Para 50.2)

60.2 In order to earn the acceptance of the people, prevention and detection of crime and handling public order situation, which are onerous duties, should be performed efficiently by the Police Station staff. Efficient performance of duties cannot be achieved merely by addition or creation of specialised units in the organisation as the basic problems will have to be tackled at the level of Police Station. The Police Stations have to be strengthened and made effective and the integrity, professional competence and impartiality of its members have to be improved. It is only then that the public expectations of a high quality of professional work and conduct from police will be fulfilled. Effective civil policing would be in a better position to interact with the public and reduce the need for any larger scale expansion of armed police. (Para 50.8)

60.3 Strengthening of the police ranks at the level of ASIs, SIs, Inspectors, Dy SP will contribute to more efficient public service only if these ranks are freed from political interference and high standard of integrity is ensured. Professional knowledge, etc., needs to be improved by training, periodic refresher courses and job supervision as have been recommended in the Fifth Report. (Para 50.9)

60.4 Police Stations in rural areas are too few and far between and have a very vast and unwieldy jurisdiction. With vast jurisdiction, beats and patrols also become unmanageable and consequently police presence and policing become diffused and diluted. In order to achieve the dual objective of crime prevention and detection and establish community relations, the maximum number of men from the civil police force should be brought as close as possible to the community. If policemen are brought closer to the community they would be able to respond to public needs and expectations and serve the community better. They will be able to provide greater measure of security of life and property to the rural areas which are developing and growing in importance and activity. Better policing will be possible only if the jurisdiction of the large rural Police Stations are delimited and made more compact and manageable. (Paras 50.10 and 50.11)

60.5 Police Station to be effective should be a whole and compact unit, adequate to respond to all needs and assume full responsibility for all the basic police tasks for investigation of crime, maintenance of law and order, traffic control in the areas. The jurisdiction should neither be so large as to defeat the very purpose for which it is created nor so small as to lead to considerable expenditure of resources on more house-keeping functions. The area of 150 sq. km for a rural Police Station may be adequate for the efficient function of a Police Station. Reduction in the size of large rural Police Station is likely to involve expenditure. But this appears necessary as a means for providing a greater measure of security to life and property in rural areas. In urban areas, besides other factors, population density of the community should be one of the main considerations in determining the establishment of Police Station. If the population in any given area exceeds 60,000, it is necessary to bifurcate and carve a new Police Station by delineating the jurisdiction of neighbouring Police Stations. From the crime point of view if a Police Station registers more than 700 crimes annually, another Police Station may be created by rationally adjusting the boundaries of the Police Stations in the neighbourhood. (Paras 50.12 and 50.13)

60.6 Urban areas should have exclusive Police Stations and it is not desirable for a Police Station to cater to both urban and rural areas. (Para 50.14)

60.7 In order to meet the needs of policing there should be a review every 10 years of the jurisdiction of Police Stations. Whenever new Police Stations are sanctioned or the jurisdiction altered and notification under Section 2(S) Cr. P.C. constituting the Police Station should be issued promptly. (Para 50.15)

60.8 Police Stations may be broadly divided into three categories depending upon the number of crimes to be investigated, the area in which law and order have to be maintained and the population which they have to serve. The first category will be a few of the biggest Police Stations in cities investigating over 900 cognizable IPC offences with a Dy. SP/ASP as SHO; the second category will be Police Stations in cities and towns and even in rural areas investigating over 300 IPC offences per year where the SHO should be an Inspector and the third category will consist of smaller Police Stations headed by SI. The main criterion for the formation of the Police Station should be the number of IPC offences investigated, population, area, law and order problems, traffic and other problems, etc. (Para 50.16)

60.9 More compact Police Stations can accomplish better results and ensure closer working relationship and direct control of the SHO. There will be no need also for creation and proliferation of Police Outposts. However, in areas where the terrain is difficult because of mountains, thick forests or where communications are poor due to rain or snow, police Outposts may have to be established as feeder points between the community and the Police Station. The establishment of Police Outposts should be with a view to achieve desired level of policing in any particular areas for reasons of proximity to border or frequent occurrences of disorder or crime of inaccessible topographical features and not to serve on fulfil the desires of influential persons. A Police Outpost should be enabled to register first information report as and when information or complaints about offences are lodged with them direct. (Para 50.17)

60.10 The deployment of police personnel in law and order duties at the expense of investigational work in Police Station arises primarily from inadequacies of manpower resources at the Police Station. There is not always a separate allocation of staff on law and order duties and this makes heavy demands on police manpower resources. It is necessary to assess manpower requirements for law and order duties separately in the light of our experiences in the 1970s and allot staff. Once adequate manpower resources are available at the Police Stations, the need for utilisation of investigation staff for law and order duties may not arise so frequently as is presently taking place. (Para 50.21)

60.11 Placing the two branches, namely, crime investigation and law and order in water-tight compartments has obvious disadvantages. With totally separate lines of command and control for law and order and crime investigation wings, the contact between these two wings tends to be practically eliminated resulting in their isolation from each other. SHO of the Police Station should have an overall control and responsibility for all the police tasks within the Police Station limits and this should be no circumstances be diluted by making the crime investigation wing of the Police Station answerable to hierarchies other than the SHO. The division of duties and functions at the Police Station level should not be carried too far as to make the Police Station appears as a house divided into separate water-tight compartments. The main object of stressing the functional aspects is to ensure that adequate time and attention is given to investigational work which are tending to be neglected due to frequent diversion of staff for law and order duties. (Para 50.22)

60.12 The need for patrolling in all beats is not the same. Some beat require patrolling during certain hours of the day, while certain beats require longer hours and some round-the-clock. (Para 50.24)

In order to establish good relations with the public, render help to public who are in distress, promptly obtain all information of interest, undertake surveillance work over suspects and known criminals, all rural and urban areas, should be divided into convenient beats and specific number of policemen should be put incharge of each beat. The advantages gained by having an effective beat patrolling system would be invaluable. (Para 50.25)

The policemen incharge of beat work have to be of higher quality, and intelligence then those who do this work at present. They should be aware of the social millieu in which they work. (Para 50.26)

Prevention of crime and surveillance work are important aspects of police work and call for considerable planning at the Police Station level. At present this function is neglected and crime prevention programmes are resorted to in a casual and eratic manner without any reference to crime potential and frequency in the region. (Para 50.27)

60.13 The general pattern in most of the States is for as SI of Police to be the SHO of the Police Station regardless of the importance and the quantum of staff manning the Police Station. As the Police Station has to function as a static base for preventive and investigative functions and also as a point of contact between the community, the SHO has to be an officer who can inspire his officers and men and at same time create the right kind of atmosphere under which they can work for the achievements of the organisational goals. A better and higher degree of leadership is required at the Police Station commensurate with the status and importance of the Police Station, the staff posted and the number of crime registered. (Para 50.28)

60.14 In the restructured heirarchy, all Police Stations with a crime figure of 300 IPC offences and above and important Police Stations requiring sizeable manpower should be placed under inspectors. In Police Stations with a crime record of over 900, no officer below the rank of Dy. SP/ASP should be the SHO. Officers with proven ability and integrity should be posted as SHO. (Para 50.29)

60.15 The officer posted as Officer-incharge of the Police Station should be designated as Station House Offer to distinguish him from other subordinate officers, who also can become officer-incharge in the absence of permanent incumbent from the Police Station. The officer next in seniority to the SHO who may be an Inspector or Sub-Inspector, as the case may be, should be designated and posted as second officer of the Police Station. Both the SHO and the second officer, will share responsibilities, allocate duties, monitor manpower requirements and utilisation functions which are at present the most neglected duties in the Police Station. (Para 50.30)

60.16 In order to ensure that the function of the Police Station is not depleted below the level of operational efficiency, adequate reserve for weekly day off, leave, training and emergent duties should be made available. (Para 50.31)

60.17 The buildings housing of the Police Stations are in a state of neglect lacking in the essential minimum needs and amenities for staff as well as the public. The existing dilapidated Police Station buildings should be reconstructed or remodelled along functional lines as per guidelines given in the booklet published by National Building Organisation (1967). The object should to be ensure that Police Stations have good accommodation and are properly equipped for its functions and are decent enough to receive the citizens of a free and progressive country. The staff on duty should be provided with rest rooms and suitable catering facilities should also be made available. A separate reception-*cum*-waiting room for visitors is also necessary. The lock-ups instead of the present dungeons with aweful sanitary conditions should be such in which citizens can be kept without going through extreme hardship and discomfort. Adequate residential accommodation for the staff should be made available near the Police Station building. The Police Station building and its surrounding has to be made neat and clean to suit both the security needs and the aesthetic sense. (Paras 50.32 to 50.34)

60.18 The civil police has to be so restructured that it is able to provide both adequate volume and quality of services to the people. The first basic need is improvement in the qualitative performance without embarking on an undue increase in strength and the same can be brought about within even the existing strength by larger numbers at middle levels of ASI/SI/Inspector offset by smaller numbers at the lower levels of constabulary. There may, however, be Police Stations where additional staff may be needed. (Para 50.35)

60.19 There is urgent need for increasing the numbers of investigating officers. The principle of limitation has been introduced for the first time in the Indian Criminal Law and has been enumerated in Chapter XXXVI of Cr. P.C. 1973. This also underlines the need for speedier investigation. Quickness and efficiency with which individual crimes are investigated by the police with apprehension of offenders and return of lost properties to the victims of crime will determine the police image. The only way to win the trust of the people and refurbish the image of the police is for the Police Station to render expeditious aid to the people who have suffered harm or damage or are in danger. (Para 50.36)

60.20 With correct registration of crime and coming to the aid of the people in trouble, the people will start looking up to the police and the Police Station as a friend in need. Once such a rapport is established, necessary cooperation and support from the people will be forthcoming. The increased registration of cases and their investigation would necessitate considerable increase in the number of investigating officers and middle level officers. Increased numbers at the middle level and an officer orientation of the organisation would enable the police and the Police Station to meet the situation brought about by changing socio-economic scene and shifting values in society in a more competent, effective and above all courteous and honest manner. (Para 50.37)

60.21 The proportionate increase in the ranks of ASIs, SIs and

Inspectors will achieve three important objectives—providing substantially large number of investigating officers for handling individual crimes and defect them to the satisfaction of individual victims of crime; providing motivational incentive in the shape of improved promotional opportunities and avenues within the police system; providing greater number of personnel at the middle level without much additional financial burden. (Para 50.39)

60.22 The people expect from the police a certain capability for response both to act as a deterrent to potential criminals by bringing the culprits to book and to enhance their own skills of investigation. Police will be required to pay the required degree of attention and promptness in the conduct of investigations. Manpower commensurate with the volume of work should, therefore, be available at the Police Stations and each State should set up a Committee aided by Organisation and Method personnel and Operational Research personnel to work out suitable norms. (Para 50.40)

60.23 Operational research must be taken up by every State Police Force to evolve new norms of yardstick based on the new job content of the posts of various ranks. The requirements for investigation law and order, traffic and other police duties differ from State to State. Each State will have to evolve its own yardsticks keeping in view their own needs. (Para 50.42)

60.24 In this context our study of the existing duties and responsibilities of personnel at the various ranks has revealed that every higher rank tends to assume only more and more supervisory roles without much operational responsibility. Supervisory functions must be limited and only incidental to the operative field function of each rank. It is the operative job content which needs to be developed in each rank. Every State should undertake an exercise to re-design the job contents of the existing ranks of Constables, Head Constables, Assistant Sub-Inspectors, Sub-Inspectors, Inspectors and Deputy Superintendents of Police. The restructured police hierarchy will have four levels. (Paras 50.46 and 47)

60.25 Our broad approach in recommending restructuring of the existing 6 basic ranks of Constable, Head Constable, Assistant Sub-Inspector, Sub-Inspector, Inspector, Deputy Superintendent of Police in the Civil Police into 4 levels is designed to ensure that the structure is so organised that not only does it cater to the operational requirements of the civil police for a larger number of investigating officers in levels two and three but also that the structure will make it possible for every employee at a given level normally to get promotion and a higher level after a specified period subject, of course to fitness and suitability. (Para 50.48)

The restructuring of the civil police into 4 levels, providing for a more or less automatic promotion within each level, to every employee who is found to be fit, will lead to the following promotional prospects:

(i) Promotion of constables by horizontal movement to the rank of Head Constable after 8 years of service subject to the rejection of persons with unsatisfactory records;

(ii) Selection to the rank of Assistant Sub-Inspector from Constables and Head Constables who have completed a total period of 6 years of service and above. They will be required to compete in a promotional examination of a high standard. The examination would be so designed that the candidate can give evidence of his academic competence, and knowledge and understanding of police work;

(iii) The promotion of Assistant Sub-Inspectors to the rank of Sub-Inspectors in the second level would be again by horizontal movement after 5th year of service as Assistant Sub-Inspector. We expect all Assistant Sub-Inspectors to get promoted as Sub-Inspector subject to the rejection of those with unsatisfactory record of service and physical unfitness;

(iv) The selection to the rank of Inspector in the third level from Sub-Inspectors in the second level would again be made from those who have completed a minimum of 6 years service and undergone a pre-promotion course of a high standard. The per-promotion course will be designed to improve the knowledge of Sub-Inspectors in law and procedure of police work besides developing their investigational capacity. After this pre-promotion course the aspirants for selection to the rank of Inspectors will have to undergo a competitive examination at which suitable weightage will be given to performance at the written examination, evaluation of the ACRs, personnel interview and physical fitness;

(v) One fourth of the total number of posts of Inspectors should be designated as selection-grade level posts to which every Inspector will get appointed under the criterion of seniority-*cum*-good record; and

(vi) Selection to the rank of Deputy Superintendent of Police will be from the rank of Inspector from among those who have completed 6 years of service as Inspectors. One fourth of the total number of posts of Deputy Superintendents of Police in each grade should be operated in the rank of Additional Superintendent of Police. The appointments to the grade of Additional Superintendents of Police will also be on the basis of seniority-*cum*-fitness. (Para 50.49)

60.26 A bright constable for promotion to the rank of Assistant Sub-Inspector need not necessarily have to pass through the rank of Head Constable. Since the selection to the rank of Assistant Sub-Inspector would be by a competitive examination, it will be possible for a really bright constable to reach the ranks of Assistant Sub-Inspector directly. Similarly a bright and able Sub-Inspector can get selected as Inspectors after serving for a period of 6 years as an Assistant Sub-Inspector/Sub-Inspector since the selection to this rank will be through a competitive examination on the criterion of merit only. In the other ranks within the same level, *viz.,* Constable to Head Constable, Assistant Sub-Inspector to Sub-Inspector, Inspector to Deputy Superintendent of Police we would like the promotion to be on the simple criterion of seniority-*cum*-fitness. (Para 50.50)

60.27 A study was conducted by the Administrative Staff College of India, Hyderabad, at our instance. They have suggested that the personnel from the rank of constables to Deputy Superintendent of Police will have a smooth promotional flow within the system if the total number of persons in different categories are fixed according to the ratio of—constable and Head Constable—45 per cent, Assistant Sub-Inspectors and Sub-Inspectors—32 per cent, Inspectors—16 per cent and Deputy Superintendent of Police and Additional Superintendents of Police—7 per cent. These ratios in the different categories are in the nature of the ideal expected to be attained in the process of restructuring and the same may be kept in view or each State may have a computerised analysis done taking into consideration various input data, namely rankwise strength of police personnel, age of retirement, minimum qualifying service for promotion from one level to another and other relevant variables and determine the relative proportion of posts required at various levels. (Para 50.51)

60.28 The institution of Circle Inspector of Police wherever it exists should be abolished and supervision, coordination and monitoring the performance of Police Station should develop on Deputy Superintendent of Police or ASP as Sub-Divisional Police Officer. He should be the principal supervising officer of investigation of cases, crime control measures, surveillance system and documentation work, etc., in Police Station. He should visit Police Station in order to ensure that all crimes reported at Police Station are registered and all officers conduct their investigation with speed. He should provide the necessary guidance in investigation of difficult cases and will also be required to make a detailed inspection of Police Stations. Keeping in view his duties, Sub-Divisional Police Officer may not be able to supervise the work of more than 3 Police Stations or 1200 IPC cases. Supporting staff like typist and reader Sub-Inspector should be provided. (Paras 50.54 and 50.55)

60.29 In a service like police the integrity of the personnel should not only be kept at a high level but the people's confidence in their integrity should be created and continuously maintained. The statements of the assets of the officials especially of the rank of Inspectors and above may be made available for public scrutiny so as to provide an opportunity to the public to bring to the notice of authorities any false or fraudulent statement made by corrupt officials. The modalities of this exercise have to be spelt out clearly and in careful detail so that honest and straight forward officials are not subjected to harassment and humiliation by unwarranted allegations from mischievous elements. (Paras 50.56 to 50.58)

60.30 The entire exercise of confirmation of police personnel in every grade only generates considerable paper work and takes up a lot of time all-round. Every official should be deemed to be permanent and confirmed in the grade of his appointment automatically on the completion of 3 years of satisfactory service in that grade. If any official is considered unfit for confirmation in that grade, steps to revert or discharge him should be taken well before the expiry of the period of 3 years. This will give the officials a feeling of security and place responsibility on the superior officers to review each case before the expiry of the period of 3 years, if in their view the official concerned is unfit to hold the rank to which he was appointed. (Paras 50.61 and 50.62)

60.31 In view of the vesting of all powers in the District Superintendent of Police for the regulation, control and promotion of order in the district, as recommended in Chapter XXXIX of our 5th Report, the Deputy Inspector General is required to play a more positive role in the functioning of districts under their control. He has to operate as the coordinating authority between the districts and also required to play an important role in the planning and modernising of the force. He must be sensitive judge of public opinion and would be an appellate forum both for the public and for the staff. In order to enable Range Deputy Inspector General to discharge his new functions efficiently he will not be able to supervise the work of more than 5 districts establishments. (Paras 50.63 and 50.64)

60.32 The present charge of the Inspectors General of Police in some of the major States is very unwieldy. With the present day complex and difficult law and order situation, it is obvious that for an Inspector General to function well he should have only a manageable charge. For adequate supervision, larger States should have Territorial Inspectors General who should not have more than 15 to 20 districts or 4 to 5 ranges under his charge. The armed battalion, of the range, should also be placed under the operational charge of the Territorial Inspector General. (Para 50.65)

60.33 In matters concerning police personnel in the organisation, exercising of disciplinary control over them, the financial management of supplies and purchase, and providing the infrastructural facilities for the growth and well-being of the force, the role of the Chief of the Police should be considerably enhanced and strengthened. The internal management of the police force in the States should fall entirely within the purview of the Chief of the Police. To relieve the Chief of State Police in bigger States of much routine work for better supervision, Territorial Inspectors General of Police for districts and Functional Inspectors General of Police for specialised branches like intelligence, armed police should in position so that the Chief of Police can devote himself to the important, but so far neglected, tasks of planning and strengthening the police organisation. To coordinate the functioning of these multifarious Territorial and functional Inspectors General of Police in the States, the Chief of Police of the State may be designated as Director General. The Director General will have for purposes of command and control the benefit of enhanced participative association from his senior colleagues to the maximum extent on a functional and territorial basis. The Inspector General of Police and the Directors General should be persons of high integrity and ability so that the officers and men have great respect for their knowledge and confidence in their ability to improve the force in their respective controls. (Paras 50.66 to 50.69)

60.34 One of the criteria for jurisdiction of posts at various senior levels should be the number of cases registered and investigated. A study conducted at our instance has revealed that if an Investigating Officer puts 10 hours of work daily and is available for duty on 300 days in a year, then 3000 hours of work will be his out-turn in a year and he will be able to investigate different units of work-load of different categories of cases in metropolitan city, urban and rural Police Stations. The study revealed that the officer can investigate 50 to 60 cases in a year. On a broad basis, investigation of cases cannot be the only criterion and the other criteria of compactness of charge, strength of the force, problems, etc., are equally relevant and should be kept in view. (Paras 50.71 and 50.72)

State Armed Police Battalions and District Armed Reserve

60.35 The scale of officering has a great significance in an armed unit particularly when it is put on sensitive law and order duties. It is necessary that the commander of even the smallest unit of as armed battalion, which is put on duty, is an officer with adequate experience and seniority. Without proper leadership, men may over-react to a situation or even feel emboldened to behave improperly and brutally. (Para 51.6)

60.36 We feel that a unit performing a law and order duty, with arms, should not be split into less than a section strength, though it could be utilised in the strength of half-sections if working without arms. In either case, the Commander of a section should be an officer of a rank not less than that of an Assistant Sub-Inspector. It will also be appropriate if each section has two head constables who could lead the half-sections whenever men are deployed a half-sections. (Para 51.7)

60.37 While the platoon can continue to be headed by a sub-inspector, there are distinct advantages in a company being put under the charge of an ASP/Dy. SP. A company is the most common unit which is deployed in the districts. An ASP/Dy. SP as the commander of this would find it easier to liaise with the district authorities, ensure the welfare of his men and provide on-the-spot leadership at an appropriate level. The second-in-command of a company could be an Inspector. A battalion should also have a Deputy Commandant to assist the Commandant in the administration of the unit. (Para 51.8)

60.38 A DIG should be provided for 5-6 battalions, and if there are more than two DIsG, the armed battalions should be headed by an officer of the rank of an IG. Such an officer should be made effective by giving him all the normal financial/disciplinary powers of an Inspector General, leaving only the overall supervision to the IG or DG incharge State Police. (Para 51.9)

60.39 Services of the officers commanding the armed battalion contingents were often requisitioned by the district administration and they were posed as Area Officer or Duty Officers—thus depriving them of the opportunity to be with their men, lead them—guide them and keep then under control. This practice should stop. Officers of a particular unit must invariably accompany their unit and be allowed to remain with their men. Such officers should have to explain if they are found absent from the scene at a crucial moment. (Para 51.10)

60.40 In a number of States, officers with an indifferent record of service or unsavoury reputation are often posed to the armed wing. Treating the armed battalions as the dumping ground of substandard personnel is an approach which must be given up. (Para 51.11)

60.41 In armed police also the direct intake at the intermediary levels of Sub-Inspectors and Dy. S.P. should be phased out gradually. All the recruitment at the initial stage at the level of constable be made in the armed police and after a recruit has served in the armed police for three years, he should be eligible to shift to civil police, depending upon his aptitude and professional competence, to be tested through an examination. Every constable of the armed police, who is desirous of moving to the civil police, should be given two chances to get selected for transfer to civil police no completing of three years but before completion of five years of service. Those who do not succeed should remain in the armed police. It will keep the armed police comparatively young. It will provide an opportunity to everybody in the civil police to be a part of the armed police at one stage. That will remove the hiatus that often develops between the armed and the civil wings. (Para 51.13)

60.42 In case it is not possible to fill all the vacancies of constable with High School pass candidates, candidates of the Scheduled Castes and Scheduled Tribes with even lower educational qualifications may be recruited with a stipulation that they shall pass the High School examination within a specified period, failing which their appointment will not become substantive and they will be liable for discharge from service. In such cases, the department should provide the necessary facilities to enable the recruits to prosecute their studies and come upto the standard. (Para 51.14)

60.43 As the initial entry of every recruit will be in the armed police for the first three years of his service, he should be equipped during the preliminary training for the performance of all the armed duties including duties performed in aid of civil police. This course will have to give a heavier emphasis on the techniques of individual and collective interaction with the public and thorough knowledge of constitutional and legal rights of the citizens. Those, who move to civil police, before they join, should be put through a re-orientation course to prepare them for the new tasks. A long course will not be necessary at this stage as there is considerable overlapping in the job content for the armed and civil police. Considerable stress needs to be laid on courteous and impartial behaviour free from any kind of prejudice and bias. It would be helpful if the conference of IsG reviews the training concept periodically to bring about the required changes in the training content. (Para 51.15)

60.44 Utilisation of such a highly trained force for routine police duties not only is a waste of the intensive training given to such men but it also makes the force ineffective. Such use of armed battalion men should be discontinued forthwith. If any shortage are noticed in the district allocation for handling such routine calls, the same should be examined and removed. (Para 51.17)

60.45 Far too often more force is requisitioned than is absolutely necessary. The District Superintendent of Police tries to play safe and the superior officers also find it expedient to fall in line. Again the force once requisitioned is detained much longer than necessary. While no guidelines can be laid down determining the quantum of force required, as requirements will very according to situation, it must be ensured that the demand is realistic. The superior officers should also feel free to prune the demand. The deployment should be made for a fixed time and unless the same is extended the force should return to Battalion headquarters. (Para 51.18)

60.46 The need for annual refresher training should be fully appreciated. It is to keep men fit and confident for the job they have to do. A company should, as prescribed, be always under training and it should not be taken into account for purposes of deployment. An effort should be made to withdraw men from relatively unimportant duties and conserve force. (Para 51.18)

60.47 A vigorous and faithful enforcement of law, without let or hindrance would reduce occasions when armed support has to be provided. (Para 51.18)

60.48 An intelligent utilisation of home guards will also reduce pressure on the armed battalions. (Para 51.18)

60.49 Shortages in equipments which affect the efficiency of the force need to be investigated periodically and removed. (Para 51.19)

60.50 It would help if a Central enactment prescribing uniformity in the composition, officering pattern, equipment, disciplinary rules, etc., of the State Armed Battalions is passed. The Act should also provide for adequate legal protection to the members of these battalions against any suit or criminal proceedings for any act done by them in pursuance of a warrant or order of a competent authority and against any legal proceedings under the powers conferred by any such Act or rule made thereunder. Such an Act should place the Superintendence and control with the State Government but should also enable the Central Government in an emergent situation to order deployment outside the State. Such a measure will make optimal use of available resources possible. (Para 51.20)

60.51 The district police and its reserve should be the first means to fact a situation. If they act quickly and are able to assemble their resources promptly, many situations which assume distressing dimensions will be controlled and the need for the State armed battalions as also for the Central forces will go down. As the requirements of the district armed reserve have not been reviewed now for quite some time, it is time that the same is done and the reserve is augmented wherever necessary. (Para 51.21)

60.52 There appears to be no need to have a separate closed cadre of the district armed reserve. The sanction of the district armed reserved should be worked out in terms of platoons or companies and they should be provided out of an existing armed battalion for a specified period of time. On completion of this period, this force should be replaced. During their stay in the district, the force should be under the operational and the administrative control of the district S.P. Part of this force in the district could be distributed and placed at sub-divisional headquarters and police stations depending upon the requirements for the manning of the local guards, escorts and bandobust duties, etc. The fixed guards must be of the strength of half a section but they may be allowed to be armed. (Para 51.24)

Delegation of Financial Powers to Police Officers

60.53 Full powers of reappropriation as at present available to the DGs BSF/CRPF within the total sanctioned budget grant should be made available to the Chiefs of State Police. (Para 52.6)

60.54 Chiefs of State Police should have full powers for creation and continuance of temporary posts from the rank of constable to Dy. SP up to a period of two years, provided expenditure is within the budget allotment. (Para 52.10)

60.55 All Chiefs of State Police should be delegated with full powers to make purchase and repair of motor vehicles. These powers should be exercised subject to the laid down financial procedure. (Para 52.11)

60.56 Chiefs of State Police should have powers to condemn motor vehicles and full powers to purchase, repair and condemn wireless equipment in their charge. (Para 52.12)

60.57 The Chiefs of State Police should be delegated with following powers relating to repair and construction of buildings:

Item	Chief of State Police	DIG	SP
	Rs.	Rs.	Rs.
1. For major and minor construction works	5 lakhs	1 lakhs	50,000
2. Repair and maintenance	1 lakh	25,000	10,000

(Para 52.13)

60.58 As regards sanction of telephones (both office and residential), the Chief of the State Police should have the same powers as vested in DG BSF and DG CRPF. In respects of PSs and outposts, Superintendent of Police should be delegated with powers of sanction telephones, both for the office and the residence of SHO. (Para 52.14)

60.59 Full powers in respect of purchase of furniture should be delegated to the Chief of State Police, who would make suitable delegations. (Para 52.14)

60.60 Full powers in respect of purchase and repair of typewriters and other office equipment should be vested in the Chief of State Police. Norms should be laid down for the offices of DIG, SP and SHO and within these norms, they should be given full powers. (Para 52.16)

60.61 The powers of the Chiefs of State Police to purchase locally stationery items should be raised to 20 per cent of the total budget. The Chiefs of the State Police should in their turn delegate powers to the DIGs, SPs and also place suitable amount at the disposal of the SHOs. These powers should also be available for the local printing of miscellaneous materials including purchase of books and periodicals. (Para 52.18)

60.62 The Chiefs of State Police should have full powers up to a maximum of Rs. 5,000 for grant of rewards in each case or occasion. The powers of DIG and SP similarly should be raised to Rs. 2,000 and Rs. 1,000 respectively in each case or one occasion. (Para 52.19)

60.63 Full powers should be delegated to the Chiefs of State Police without involving the Accountant General for sanctioning permanent advance. He should further delegate the powers to the DIsG and SPs. The amount of permanent advance of each office including the PS should be fixed realistically by taking into account the actual needs. (Para 52.23)

60.64 In order to enable the Chiefs of State Police to exercise enhanced financial powers effectively they should be assisted by a Financial Adviser of an appropriate rank. (Para 52.27)

60.65 A contingency grant of about Rs. 1 lakh should be placed at the disposal of Chiefs of Police who may be empowered to spend a sum of Rs. 20,000 at a time for immediate relief in cases of large scale rioting, etc. (Para 52.28)

66.66 The Chiefs of State Police should be given powers similar to the DG BSF and DG CRPF in respect of other items in the schedule of financial powers of DG BSF and DG CRPF. (Para 52.29)

Traffic Regulation

66.67 The control of traffic, enforcement of laws and regulations to facilitate orderly movement of traffic and action to prevent and investigate road accidents are primarily a police responsibility. (Para 53.1)

60.68 The regulations of traffic has two aspects, namely, regulation of traffic inside the municipal limits of a city, and regulations of traffic on the highways. (Para 53.3)

60.69 The basic source of traffic problems in a city is the fact that there is a great concentration of people and vehicles in a small area, this being the limited space by way of roads and urban life demands faster and faster movement. The requirements of safety and of speed do not generally coincide, leading to accidents. (Para 53.4.1)

60.70 No permits for occupation of footpaths should be issued by Local Bodies. Further, mobile vending should not be allowed in shopping and other congested areas. It can be permitted in residential areas. (Para 53.4.2)

60.71 The remedy to the problems of traffic in cities lies in having different lanes for different kinds of traffic, removing encroachments by vendors and cattle and confining pedestrians to pavements by having a 2.5 feet hedge, barricade or wall along all pavements with openings at zebra crossing or at over-bridges and sub-ways. There is need to regard cyclists and pedestrians an important road users and separate tracks with segregations and special lights at intersections should be provided for them. Similarly, crowded market areas should be restricted to pedestrians only during peak hours. Additionally officer hours should be staggered to reduced congestions and in certain crowded arteries, heavy goods carriers should only be allowed during night. (Para 53.4.3)

60.72 Though cities have been growing very rapidly as also the number of vehicles and pedestrians on the streets, there has not been any complementary increase in the number of policemen earmarked for the management of traffic. An adequate increase in the strength of traffic police is recommended. This strength should be determined on the basis of points to be manned, areas for patrolling, enforcement of regulatory measures, education of road users in traffic rules, investigation of accidents and the maintenance of proper records. This manpower should be traced properly by specialists within and outside the police organisation. In addition, it should be obligatory for senior officers-in-charge of traffic regulation to be available on the ground during peak hours to supervise the regulation of traffic. Further, in all large cities the traffic enforcement agency should have a research section to analyse the causes of bottlenecks and serious accidents. While the traffic police should undertake education of road users it would be more worthwhile to include a chapter on traffic sense and traffic rules in any of the text-books of the school curriculum. (Para 53.4.4)

60.73 The management of traffic in urban areas also required that the traffic police by fully equipped with salvage vehicles, radar speedometers, stop watches, walkie talkie sets, close circuit TV cameras, ambulances, photographers, etc. Traffic signals could also be computerised to rapidly adopt themselves to the frequently varying needs of traffic flow by control from a central point. (Para 53.4.5)

60.74 There is at present no standard motor vehicle inspection code which states the minimum standards of safety required for a vehicle to be on road. It is, therefore, recommended that a Standard Motor Vehicle Inspection Code stating the minimum standards of safety required for a vehicle to be on road should be incorporated in the Road Safety Act. All motor vehicles including scooters and motor-cycles should be required to pass a fitness test periodically. This fitness test should include a stringent check of prevent pollution by vehicles. In future it may become necessary to check the fitness of vehicles from the point of view of fuel consumption. Large automobiles or what are called fuel-guzzlers may have to be denied a fitness certificate or discouraged by steep taxation. Institutions could be set up for conducting such tests and they could charge a fee. (Para 53.4.6)

60.75 It should be made compulsory for the manufacturer to provide necessary safety fixtures like safety frames in two wheelers, seat belts and collapsible steering assembly in cars to reduce the severity of accidents. Similarly sharp corners and edges in vehicles should be removed by proper designing. (Para 53.4.6)

60.76 All owners of commercial vehicles before removal of their permits should obtain a certificate from the police that all pending traffic violations have been accounted for. This should be applicable to private care at the time of sale of transfer. (Para 53.4.6)

60.77 The Regional Transport Authority should take due notice of an operator's previous traffic record before issuing a permit to him and where there are more than one applicant, the one with the best record for observance of laws should be selected. (Para 53.4.6)

60.78 Police should be associated with policy decisions regarding issue of permits so that there is no undue pressure on traffic control by a preponderance of vehicles like autorickshaws on the road. (Para 53.4.6)

60.79 The registration of vehicles should included payment for third party insurance. (Para 53.4.6)

60.80 Due to inadequate police records some drivers commit a large number of accidents and continue to keep a driving licence. Some drivers manage to procure more than one driving licence in their name or aliases. The National Crime Records Bureau should also maintain records of registration of vehicles, issue of driving licences and traffic offences committed by individual drivers. When this is achieved and computerised a point count system for giving bad marks to drives on the basis of a scale depending upon the gravity of an offence could be developed. If a driver crosses the prescribed maximum bad marks, his licence should be impounded for a period regardless of where he resides and where he has committed the offences. This would also ensure that before the registration of a vehicle is renewed the owner clears all the finds pending against him.

This would eliminate dangerous drivers and ensure safety. (Para 53.4.7)

60.81 Government should establish a large number of driving schools with adequate instructional staff and to provide applicants with vehicle on rent at the time of the driving test. A person should have a learner's licence for at least two months prior to the issue of a regular licence and for obtaining HTV licence, one has to have a HTV licence for a least two years. Also, Gazetted Police Officers should have the powers to suspend a driving licence if a person has committed an offence which indicates dangerous driving. The character and antecedents of a driver be determined and a minimum educational standard prescribed before a licence is issued. In addition to a stringent driving test, medical examination, physical an physiological test including reaction time, depth perception, vision, hearing and mental faculty should be prescribed for issue of driving licences. There should be an objective type written test to determine the knowledge of road signs and traffic rules. Even renewal of driving licences be done after ascertaining the physical fitness of a driver after periods of 3 or 5 years. (Para 53.4.8)

60.82 Good road engineering is essential for ensuring safe and rapid flow of traffic and also to prevent traffic accidents. The type of road pattern and traffic control devices need necessarily to be decided on the basis of scientific studies and analyses of traffic in a city. On the basis of such studies, which should include consultation with various experts, other measures like segregation of traffic, prohibition, time bound or total, for slow-moving vehicles, heavy commercial vehicles and public transport buses on selected streets, regulations of traffic on one-way streets, should be adopted to ensure smooth flow of traffic. Speed-breakers should be clearly marked with red and white stripes and warning lights. Adequate advance notice should be available to a driver before approaching a speed-breaker or a driver before view to take an integrated approach in the management of traffic in a city it is recommended that every major city should have unified traffic authority under the chairmanships of the Chief of the Police of the city with members drawn from the engineering wing of the local body and the other departments of the Government besides suitable representatives of the public. This body should be suitably set up with sufficient finances and powers for handling the traffic problems in a rational and scientific manner. (Para 53.4.9)

60.83 It is essential to specify under the law that driver of a vehicle should carry with him his driving licence with his photograph and also the registration papers of the vehicle. (Para 53.4.10)

60.84 The adoption of the ticketing system which exists in many other countries is recommended. It should be incorporated in the proposed Road Traffic Act. (Para 53.4.10)

60.85 The regulation of traffic and its control includes all vehicles on the streets including heavy transport vehicles, cars and jeeps, motor-cycles and scooter as also slow moving vehicles like cycles, cycle-rickshaws, hand-carts and animal-pulled carriages. It is felt that a comprehensive legislation under the name "Road Traffic Act" be enacted to cover all matters of traffic regulation including road safety provisions, use of vehicles and equipment licencing of drivers and vehicles, driving instructions, insurance and liability to third parties, punishments and penalties including the ticketing system, general rules of evidence and other miscellaneous matters. (Para 53.4.11)

60.86 There is need for adequate manpower and vehicles equipped with communication aids as highway patrols so that they could not only enforce traffic laws and regulations but also promote safety on roads. As the prevention and detention of highway holds-ups and robberies is also a police responsibility and making roads safe from criminals promotes a sense of security in the community, it is felt that the agency entrusted with the highway patrol and having the necessary infrastructure should also look after the requirements of combating criminals who operate on the roads. These highway patrols should be placed under the concerned District Superintendent of Police and they should operate within the limits of a district. Inter-district co-ordination should be the responsibility of the range DIG. At the State Headquarters level there should be a Traffic Unit for Research into the State's traffic problems as also inter-range co-ordination and co-ordination at the State level with the other agencies like the Engineering Department and the Transport Department while the agency for actual enforcement of traffic laws and promoting safety should be a part of the district police. (Para 53.6)

60.87 The Transport Department before renewing the permits of private carriers of goods and passengers should see that where there are several applicants for a particular route, the permit is issued to the person with the best record for observance of traffic laws and regulations. Weigh-bridges and height barriers should be installed at strategic points to prevent trucks from overloading. It is essential that each barrier be equipped with a truck base so that the highways are not used for parking of trucks. It is seen that other than the local bodies which set up Octroi barriers, several others such as the Forest, Police, Transport, Excise, the Nines and Narcotics Departments also set up barriers for the purposes of conducting checks with the result that vehicles are forced to stop at several places along a highway. It is felt that centralised barriers with the checking staff of all the concerned departments be located at strategic points, as far as possible along the highways, so that all the checkings could be done in one stoppage. If this is done, these centralised and comprehensive barriers could have all the cover facilities like parking bays, meal and rest facilities, service stations, fuel pumps, medical aid and weight-bridges. (Paras 53.7 and 53.8)

60.88 There is a need to have an integrated approach to the management of National Highways where important roads are identified, suitably constructed and adequate enforcement staff is available to control these arteries so that accidents are avoided and smooth flow an safety ensured. It is also recommended that all National Highways should carry road signs in English, Hindi and the regional language. (Para 53.9)

60.89 A Road Safety Cell headed by an Engineer who is an expert in Traffic engineering be created as part of the Traffic Unit in the office of the Chief of State Police so that this cell could work in liaison with the Public Works Department and from time to time review the traffic engineering aspects of the highways, specially where bottlenecks have occurred or the road is otherwise dangerous. Major road accidents require research and analysis to ensure that the defects in road engineering do not lead to such accidents again in the future. For this purpose, it is visualised that the Traffic Unit of the State Police Headquarters having both Engineers and Police Officers would work to ensure greater safety for road users. (Para 53.10)

The Ministerial Staff and Administrative Work in the Police Department

60.90 The ministerial staff, who constitute a small percentage of the total strength of police personnel, should be integrated for all practical purposes with the rest of the policemen in respect of terms and conditions of service, discipline, etc. They should be brought under Police Act. (Paras 54.12 and 54.13)

60.91 In order to enhance the career prospects of the ministerial staff, they should be provided with openings into regular police force. (Para 54.14)

60.92 There should be one combined cadre of all ministerial staff consisting of officials in the clerical and supervisory grades working in various administrative offices. Three levels of non-gazetted ministerial police personnel should be there, namely, Head Constable (M), Assistant Sub-Inspector (M), Sub-Inspector (N) and two levels of gazetted ministerial police personnel, i.e., Inspector (M) and Dy. Superintendent of Police (M). (Para 54.15)

60.93 The Chiefs of State Police Force should take personal interest in making a more effective use of computers, firstly in operational matters and, thereafter, in administrative matters. (Para 54.17)

60.94 Computers could be of immense help in modernising the system of budgeting and financial management, inventory control of the assets in the police, in maintenance of General Provident Fund accounts, pensions, drawal of pay and in selections for training courses and promotions. (Para 54.19)

Auxiliary to Police—Home Guards

60.95 Effective policing has to depend, to a large extent, on self-policing. Self-policing can be by individuals or by groups of individuals who voluntarily organise themselves or who offer voluntarily their services to an organisation constituted with a statutory backing. The Home Guards is one such organisation filling a gap between organised policing and individual self-policing in a society. (Paras 55.1 and 55.2)

60.96 There appears an urgent need to raise functional units of Home Guards in all the States. The creation of such functional units generates the necessary confidence and reassurance in the public at large. (Para 55.18)

60.97 Continuous and excessive call-outs of Home Guards in some States have resulted in induction of a sizeable number of unemployed persons in the organisation. Such excessive deployment of Home Guards on police duties leads to:

(1) recruitment of unemployed persons, as stated above;
(2) destruction of voluntary character of Home Guards;
(3) erosion of the spirit of public service which is the main strain of the organisation;
(4) tendency on the part of the unemployed Home Guards to

identify themselves with the police in the long run; and

(5) creating in them a feeling of comparative deprivation and frustration which will ultimately result in demands of higher wages, discontent, lack of discipline and failure of the organisation. (Paras 55.20 and 55.23)

60.98 The police forces of some States are using Home Guards much too infrequently. In the absence of occasional call-outs, the Home Guards in such States get a feeling that they have been forgotten after their brief exposure to a training course. It appears necessary that while deployment in some States should be reduced and brought to a reasonable size, in others, the police should try to utilise Home Guards on many more occasions. (Para 55.24)

60.99 Where deployment of Home Guards presently is very high, it may be examined if the strength of the Home Guards should be increased. In any case, the 15 per cent cut on the total sanctioned strength of Home Guards needs to be restored to permit more and more persons, with a spirit of public service, to joint the Home Guards. (Para 55.24)

66.100 Home Guards should be changed every three years. That will encourage large sections of public to offer themselves for voluntary service of society in times of need and understand the importance of self-policing. (Para 55.24)

66.101 If this regular use of Home Guards for patrolling proves more cost effective and commands greater public acceptability, this could as well be made a regular feature as this will promote the idea of self-policing. (Para 55.24)

66.102 The Home Guards could be made to play a significant role in protecting the weaker sections of the society. Being men of the locality but having an official support they can do a lot to bring about communal amity and harmony. (Para 55.25)

60.103 At the district level, a nucleus of officers should be regular departmental officers who can be exposed to various training courses and they in turn can pass on the expertise to their subordinate officers and ultimately to Home Guards. (Para 55.26)

60.104 Often the police officers who are posted to the Home Guards organisation are those who have been found inconvenient somewhere else. Such officers for no fault of theirs suffer from the handicap of being considered as rejects and this detracts from their ability to command effectively. It is neither fair to the officers nor to the Home Guards organisation and it must be avoided. Such indiscreet postings dampen public enthusiasm and many excellent men, who would have volunteered otherwise to join Home Guards, desist from doing so. (Para 55.27)

60.105 Deficiencies in training staff, living accommodation and apparatus must be removed wherever they exist. (Para 55.28)

60.106 It should be possible to provide two sets of uniforms to Home Guards so that soiled uniform could be changed and smart turn-out maintained always. Till such time that this is done, everybody must have at least one set. (Para 55.29)

60.107 The daily allowance paid to Home Guards must be realistic and not unreasonably discriminatory. (Para 55.30)

60.108 While the Government servants, when called out on duty as Home Guards, are generally treated as on special casual leave, some of the State Governments have enacted that even the private employer of whom the Home Guards is a regular employee, shall treat the period of his absence on duty as Home Guard to be the period spent in employment with him (the employer). Instances are there where the private employer did not treat this period as on duty and did not pay the salary for such a period. Similar enactments should be passed by other States which should see that the legal provisions are followed and strictly enforced. (Para 55.31)

60.109 In the event of a death or injury to Home Guard in the performance of his duties, liberal financial assistance should be provided to the family/Home Guards. (Para 55.32)

60.110 The services of Home Guards should not be made available to other States in times of need. If there is shortage of officers to command, the contingents going on such deputations, could be provided officers from any available sources like the police, NCC or ex-ARmy officers. Such contingents, when so deployed outside their own State, should be given the powers and extended the legal protection which normally are given to the Home Guards of the borrowing State. A Central legislation can take care of this. (Para 55.33)

66.111 NCC trains lakhs of young boys and girls. This pool of manpower could also be harnessed to large scale law and order situations. Idealism of youth should not be allowed to go waste and particularly in times of war or serious emergency the N.C.C. should move closer to the Home Guards and assist in all duties. (Para 55.34)

60.112 The Home Guards organisation should remain voluntary but their deployment and utilisation should be so planned that training, interest and effectiveness are not lost, their utility in self-policing is maintained continuously, and above all the interest of various cross-sections of the people is kept at the optimum level. (Para 55.35)

Performance Appraisal of Police Personnel

60.113 Performance appraisal forms the basis for making managerial decisions in an organisation. It can be punitive and reductive or it can be developmental and constructive in terms of personnel and organisational efficiency. The use of annual confidential reports for disciplining the employees should give way to treat them as a source of information for administrative purposes and for organisational development through improving the performance of the employee. (Paras 56.2 and 56.3)

60.114 The periodicity of the performance appraisal reporting has to be annual due to administrative expediency, but it should ensure that the assessment of the reporting officer does not reflect the impressions and opinions formed by him during the month or two immediately preceding the report. (Para 56.9)

60.115 The employee should be made aware of the quality of his performance, his shortfall and failures, if any, so that he can correct himself. He should know the criteria against which his performance is appraised. But in areas which are not directly concerned with correction and improvement, the system should continue to remain confidential. (Para 56.9)

60.116 The performance appraisal system should be classified into the following two categories (i) a Continuous Appraisal which is correctional and developmental in its impact, and (ii) the Annual Performance Appraisal, report which is for organisational purposes in the matter of training, placements and promotions. This categorisation of appraisal should apply to all ranks from the Constable upwards. (Para 56.10)

60.117 The critical incidents method be adopted for continuous assessment and correction. Officers of the level of Sub-Inspector and above should be required to maintain a running record throughout the review period for each of his subordinates in the level next below indicating specific instances of good and bad work from week to week or month to month, and a periodical rating of overall performance. (Para 56.12)

60.118 The proximity between the officer reported upon and reporting officer should be maintained at all levels. These appraisals should be within the police force and sufficiently approximate to the level apprised so that the appraisals arise from personal knowledge.

(Para 56.12)

60.119 A monthly or a quarterly counselling session for Constables, Sub-Inspectors and Inspectors should be made compulsory. The police leadership should ensure that the counselling session are carried out systematically. (Para 56.13)

60.120 The objective of the appraisal interview should be aimed at encouragement of person's behaviour of correcting behaviour based on assessed information. It should not be converted into a disciplinary drill. The employee who is doing well needs such appraisal interviews as much as the employee who needs correction. (Para 56.13)

60.121 The superior inspecting officers should record their assessments during their periodical inspections in the Critical Incidents Records. They should also check and correct the shortcomings of subordinates and counsel them suitably during inspections. The impact of such counselling should also be rendered by the immediate superior. (Para 56.14)

60.122 The annual performance appraisal report can continue to remain confidential. This format of the performance appraisal be divided into three parts, the first part dealing with assessment of performance of the employee and the second part should deal with the integrity of the employee, his grading, his fitness for promotion or otherwise and third part should contain the Reviewing Officer's remarks. Whenever any adverse remarks appear in the first part of the report, then the employee should be communicated the whole of the first part. This does not bar the Reviewing Officer from informing the employees the gist of the contents of the third part but this should be left entirely to the discretion of the Reviewing Officer who should taken into account the totality of the circumstances and the necessity for making the employee aware of the contents of the report as a whole so that he can defend himself. (Para 56.15)

60.123 The combination of the graphic rating method and the forced distribution method be adopted. A simple scale of not more than 4 ratings should be applied to a combination of not more than 10 to 12 performance heads and 8 personality traits. The forced distribution ratings could be standardised as Outstanding, Very Good, Average and Below Average. (Para 56.17)

60.124 The formats for the various levels above the Constabulary in the police organisation should be designed as far as possible having regard to the specific nature of duties for each job and based on a detailed job evaluation. It should reflect the essential requirements of performance, personality and managerial indicators. (Paras

56.18 and 56.20)

60.125 Responsibility should be fixed on the senior officers to ensure good behaviour and attitude of helpfulness towards the public on the part of the subordinates. (Para 56.18)

60.126 The reporting, reviewing and countersigning offices for the various ranks in the police are suggested below:

Rank	Reporting officer	Reviewing officer	Countersigning officer
1	2	3	4
Constable/Head Constable	(ASI/SI) SHO	SDPO	—
ASI/SI	SDPO/ASP	SP	—
Inspector	SDPO	SP	DIG
Dy.SP/ASP	SP	DIG	IG
SP	DIG	IGP concerned	Chief of Police
DIG	IGP concerned	Chief of Police	Home Minister

(Para 56.21)

60.127 For ranks above the Constabulary, including the IPS, the individual reported upon should write a short note of the work done during the reporting period not exceeding 300 words. (Para 56.21)

60.128 The performance appraisal for the Constabulary be kept in book from to be known as the Performance Appraisal Register but it should not form part of the Service Book as it is today in most States. Every effort should be made to bring the performance appraisal system for the Constabulary on the same footing as that of higher levels in the police in a phased programme. (Para 56.23)

60.129 The Reporting Officer should communicates the adverse remarks within 15 days of writing the report and certify so in the performance appraisal format. The official reported upon will have a right to make a submission to the Reviewing Officer who may take into account the circumstances of the case and if he so beems fit, interview the employee and expunge the remarks if called for. In case, he decides that the remarks should not be expunged, he should record reason for the same. The official shall have a right to file a revision petition to the Competent Authority whose decision shall be final. If the adverse remarks are frivolous, the reporting authority should be cautioned. If the representation is frivolous, the officer representing should equally be warned. Adverse remarks which show prejudice and *mala fide* on the face of the report should be corrected by higher competent authority without any reference to the employee concerned. Action should be taken against the officers making irresponsible reports to infuse the necessary confidence in the system. (Para 56.25)

60.130 The annual performance appraisal report should contain the integrity column. (Para 56.26)

60.131 The annual property statements submitted by the officials should be scrutinised carefully by the superior officers in cases where the performance appraisal reports or information received otherwise reveal doubtful integrity. It should be open for the superior officers to conduct a full investigation in such cases. (Para 56.27)

60.132 A Cell at the district and the State level be made responsible for follow-up action both on the continuous appraisal as well as the annual performance appraisal. (Para 56.28)

60.133 Every State Police force may have to developed at some stage in future Computerised Performance System. (Para 56.29)

Disciplinary Control

60.134 In view of the vital functions assigned to the police in the democratic system of this country, it is of great importance that high standard of discipline is maintained by all ranks of police-organisation. (Para 57.1)

60.135 Discipline is not merely mechanical enforcement of disciplinary rules and procedure; it is one of the components of good man-management, other components being leadership, grievance-redressal and amelioration of the working conditions of the police and setting up of higher personal example, etc. Supervisory ranks should always make efforts to guide and counsel the police personnel so that they put in their best. However, prompt and effective disciplinary action should be taken when departmental norms are broken severely or some of the personnel tend to be habitual in their misdemeanour. (Paras 57.5 and 57.26)

60.136 In an organisation like police there should be fool-proof grievance redressal machinery for the police personnel on the pattern of staff-council as already recommended in the First Report. But such associations, if not kept under proper control, can become a serious undermining factor for the organisational disciplines. (Para 57.6)

60.137 The new Police Act should contain the following offences relatable to the duties of police personnel to be triable in the Courts of Judicial Magistrates and punishable with imprisonment for one year and fine upto Rs. 500 or both:

(i) Violation of any duty;
(ii) wilful breach or neglect of any provisions of law or any rule or regulation or lawful order which he is bound to observe or obey;
(iii) withdrawing from duty of his office without permission;
(iv) being absent on leave, failing without reasonable cause to report himself for duty on the expiration of such leave;
(v) engaging himself without authority, to any employment other than the police duties;
(vi) being guilty of cowardice;
(vii) being in a state of intoxication with on duty;
(viii) malingering or feigning or voluntarily causing hurt to himself with the intention to render himself unfit for the service;
(ix) disobeying lawful command of superior officers;
(x) being grossly insubordinate to his superior officer or using criminal force to superior officer;
(xi) taking part in procession, gherao, demonstration, shouting slogans or forcing under duress or threats any supervisory authority to concede anything or striking work;
(xii) offering unwarrantable personal violence to any person in custody;
(xiii) entering or searching, without lawful authority of reasonable cause any building or place, etc.;
(xiv) seizing vexatiously and unnecessarily the property of any person;
(xv) detaining, searching or arresting any person vexatiously and unnecessarily;
(xvi) holding out any threat or promise not warranted by laws; and
(xvii) being guilty of any other offence for which no punishment is expressly provided in the Police Act or any other law in force.

(Para 57.8)

60.138 The departmental punishments (i) dismissal (ii) removal and (iii) reduction in rank should be kept in the category of 'major punishments' which may be awarded to the police personnel after drawing up of regular disciplinary proceedings. (Para 57.9)

60.139 (i) Censure; (ii) withholding of increment and (iii)

withholding of promotion should be kept in the category of 'minor punishments' to be awarded to the police personnel through a shorter procedure. According to this procedure the delinquent official should be confronted in writing with the facts of the case and penalty proposed against him. He may be asked to furnish his representation against the same within a specified period; final order may be passed after taking the representation into consideration. (Para 57.10)

60.140 The following penalties should be kept in the category of petty punishments which may be awarded to the members of constabulary in the orderly room:

(i) reprimand;
(ii) confinement to quarter-guard for a period not exceeding 15 days;
(iii) punishment drill, extra guard duty, fatigue or other punitive duty, not exceeding 15 days with out without confinement; and
(iv) fine not exceeding one month's pay in a month. (Para 57.11)

60.141 The following punitive powers should be accorded to various levels of disciplinary authorities:

Disciplinary Authorities	*Extent of Punitive Powers*
(i) Deputy Inspector General of Police	All punishments to police personnel of and below the rank of Inspectors.
(ii) Superintendent of Police	All punishments to police officers of and below the rank of Sub-Inspectors. Minor punishments to Inspectors. Power to suspend all police officers of and below the rank of Inspector.
(iii) Asstt. Superintendent of Police/Deputy superintendent of Police	All punishment except major punishments to police personnel of and below the rank of Sub-Inspector.
(iv) Inspector of Police	Punishment drill, extra guard, fatigue or other punitive duties to constabulary for a period not exceeding three days.

Regular disciplinary procedure against the Police Inspector should be drawn by a police officer in the rank of Superintendent of

Police/Additional Superintendent of Police. In cases where one of major punishments is warranted, the inquiry officer should forward the file to the Deputy Inspector General for passing final orders. Similarly, Assistant Superintendent of Police/Deputy Superintendent of Police should be authorised to conduct the disciplinary proceedings against the police officials of and below the rank of Sub-Inspectors. In those cases where award of one of major punishments is indicated he will forward the findings to the Superintendent of Police. In a similar manner Police Inspectors should be authorised to conduct disciplinary proceedings against the constabulary. (Para 57.12)

60.142 Awarding of major punishments without drawing regular disciplinary proceedings on the grounds of security of the state as per provisions of Article 311(2)(c) of the Constitution should be made use of with great care and caution and it should not be resorted to in a routine manner. (Para 57.13)

60.143 Against any of the major punishments awarded to a police official, there should be provision for only one appeal to the authority just above the punishing authority, followed by one revision if necessary to authority just above the appellate authority. There should be one appeal but no revision against the minor punishments. The existing practice of no appeal against any of the petty punishments awarded to the constabulary in orderly room should continue. (Para 57.14)

60.144 Administrative tribunal should be set up under Article 223(a) of the Constitution to adjudicate and try matters relating to conditions of service of civil servants employed under the State Governments including the Police. This step would be in exclusion of the jurisdiction of all Courts except the Supreme Court in these matters. (Para 57.15)

60.145 Suspension should not normally be ordered without getting the complaint looked into through a preliminary inquiry. Further, suspension should not be resorted to unless facts and circumstances of the case indicated that the likely punishment will be a major one. Suspension should not be ordered for extraneous considerations. Guidelines given in the Central Vigilance Manual regarding suspension should be borne in mind by the disciplinary authority while ordering suspensions. (Paras 57.17 and 57.18)

60.146 The charge must be furnished to the delinquent police officials within a period of 45 days from the date of suspension failing which the incumbent would be entitled to automatic reinstatement.

(Para 57.18)

60.147 The following changes in the departmental procedure be made:

(i) A legal practitioner should not be permitted to appear at the departmental proceedings. However, the inquiry officer may have the discretion to allow a 'friend' of the delinquent to appear where the delinquent officer is not capable of putting up his defence properly. The 'friend' should be a serving police officer of and below the rank of Sub-Inspector, for the time being posed in the same district where the proceedings are being held. The same police official should not be permitted to be a 'friend' in more than one case at a time;

(ii) Appointment of a 'presenting officer' appears unnecessary;

(iii) In order to overcome the difficulties in serving charges and other documents relating to disciplinary proceedings on the delinquent officer, who avoids their service, procedure similar to that prescribed in Sections 62, 64, 65 and 69 Cr. P.C. for service of summons to witnesses may be adopted by the inquiry officer;

(iv) The inquiry officer should have the legal powers similar to those available to civil courts to secure the presence of private witnesses;

(v) Travel and other expenses should be paid to private witnesses who appear before the inquiry officer; and

(vi) Rule should specify the maximum period that the inquiry officer may allow to the delinquent at each stage of inquiry, e.g., replying to the charges, submitting list of defence witnesses, etc. (Para 57.20)

60.148 Whole time, police officers under the control of the District Superintendent of Police should be posted exclusively to conduct disciplinary proceedings in those districts where pendency of such cases is high. (Para 57.21)

60.149 Time limits should be prescribed for completing various stages of disciplinary proceedings. In case such time limits have to be exceeded, specific approval should be sought from the next higher authority. (Para 57.22)

60.150 Exhaustive rules of procedure should be framed governing the disciplinary proceedings for the guidance of the inquiry officers. (Paras 57.19 (vii) and 57.23)

60.151 Police Inspectors should be authorised to conduct disciplinary proceedings in these States where they are not so authorised. (Para 57.24)

60.152 Ministerial and mechanical assistance should be provided to the disciplinary authorities for disciplinary cases. (Para 57.24)

60.153 Various court-rulings and departmental instructions issued on the subject from time to time should be collected at a central place, possibly at the headquarters of Inspector-General of Policy, compiled in the form of a booklet and issued to every unit of police periodically, possibly, every 2 years. (Para 57.24)

60.154 Police officers should be trained in various aspects of disciplinary proceedings before they are allowed to handle these cases. (Para 57.24)

60.155 Adequate supervision and control by supervisory ranks is a must so that this aspect of duty is not neglected by police officers. (Para 57.24)

60.156 For the Armed Police Battalions the pattern obtaining in CRPF with regard to disciplinary and penal provision is recommended except that the criminal offences relatable to the duties of the personnel should be triable by the ordinary courts. With regard to disciplinary proceedings and award of minor punishments, procedure referred to in this Chapter should hold good for the Armed Police Battalions also. (Para 57.25)

Role of the Centre in Planning, Evaluation and Co-ordination

60.157 There is need to streamline the existing system by reallocating a few units from the I.B. and the C.B.I. to the Bureau of Police Research and Development. While the I.B. and the C.B.I. may continue to convene various conferences that they organise at present, the BPR&D should also convene the IsGP conference and the DIsG Crime conference to discuss aspects of policing other than those relating to intelligence and anti-corruption work. The BPR&D should conduct the police sports and duty meets as also all the other conference and meetings which it now conducts. [Paras 58.7 and 58.8(I)].

60.158 In matters of operational research we envisage a dynamic role for the BPR&D. For this purpose, research projects should be taken up on the basis of pro-determined goals and objectives which should be clearly spelt out. Centre should fund the research units of the States through the BPR&D. There is need for bringing Police

Research, Development and Training in the plan sector and instead of the present 0.22 per cent at least 0.5 per cent of the police budget should be earmarked for research and development. [Para 58.8(2)]

The research wing should also have a development wing forming an integrated division of the BPR&D. The Development wing should pay attention to weaponry, fleet management and police vehicles, investigation kit boxes and traffic control equipment. The development wing should produce films for public display and publish journals and periodicals. [Para 58.8(2)]

60.159 For the proper provision of scientific aids to the police and their coordinated growth, functions related to forensic science be placed under the BPR&D under a Chief Forensic Scientist who should also be the Director of Coordination, forensic Science. [Para 58.8(3)]

60.160 For the training of police personnel, the Directorate of Training under the BPR&D should be strengthened to coordinate the training programmes of the various Central Police Organisations without in any manner impinging on their administrative independence. This Directorate should identify courses which are suitable for police officers both within and outside the country in police and non-police organisations and select the trainees so that officers from all parts of the country could benefit from the various courses. [Para 58.8(4)]

60.161 The BPR&D should be developed to render advice to the Central Government on matters relating to the police point of view in legal and organisational spheres as also providing such information as may be required by the Central and State Police Organisations on the profiles of the police organisations existing in the various States. For this purpose a Central Information Unit be developed in the BPR&D. [Para 58.8(5)]

60.162 The Institute of Criminology and Forensic Science be developed into an autonomous institution to take up basic research, train persons from all branches of the Criminal Justice System through multi-disciplinary courses and award degrees by affiliation to one of the Universities in Delhi. The Forensic Science laboratory in the ICFS be developed with the latest equipment and other facilities to undertake original research and to attend to highly intricate cases beyond the capacity of CFSLs and State FSLs. (Para 58.10)

60.163 The Directorate of Coordination, Police Wireless be developed with a view to meeting the future communication requirements of the police. Police Communication is likely to develop into a highly specialised field and for that purpose necessary expertise be developed within the State and Central Police Wireless Organisations so that technical officers of requisite experience are available to man the DCPW at all levels. (Para 58.11)

60.164 A National Crime Records Bureau be formed by integrating the Interpol Division and the Central Finger Print Bureau of the C.B.I. and the Statistical Division of the BPR&D with the Directorate of Coordination, Police Computers. The Centre should also start a Central Crime Records Office and urge the States to take similar steps and collect records on the lines suggested by us in our Second Report. (Para 58.13)

60.165 A Central Police Committee to look after the functions of consultancy and monitoring be created, because an expert agency is required by the Central Government and the State Security Commission to advise them on matters relating to:

(i) Police Organisation and police reforms of a general nature;
(ii) central grants and loans to the State Police Forces for their modernisation and development; and
(iii) budgetary allotments to State Police Forces.

This Committee could also make a general evaluation of the state of policing in the country and provide expertise to the State Security Commission for their own evaluation if they so require. [Para 58.14(1)]

60.166 The Central Police Committee should be of an adequately high standing and independent of the Government and be constituted on the same lines as the State Security Commissions recommended by us. It should have a secretariat for the purposes of its functioning. [Para 58.14(2)]

60.167 An all India Police Institute on the lines of similar professional institutions existing for Engineers, Chartered Accountants and other professionals be created. This institute, when established, should be kept under the proposed Central Police Committee. [Para 58.14(3)]

Policing in the North-East

60.168 The tribal culture has its own social value systems and nothing should be done to upset it. The policy makers in Delhi rightly decided that the solution of the border problem lay in bringing the area into the mainstream of the country's life by properly administering it, and extending to it the benefits of development, but unfortunately they did not quite appreciate the historical perspective and the tribal social structure and temper their efforts to these vital factors. The tribal was not used to too much government and it was a mistake too force our administrative system on them. (Para 59.10)

60.169 The tribal system is still the most suitable system in this area for policing and for satisfying the tribals' social needs. No effort should be maae to interfere with this system on the plea that the modern system of policing as in the rest of the country is necessary. In the interior tribal areas the customary tribal institutions should be allowed and encouraged to continue to administer the area. In the urbanised areas, which are connected by roads or railway a mere formal police structure will require to be established. (Para 59.11)

60.170 In Assam and the plains area of Tripura the modern pattern of policing as prevailing in the rest of the country can be extended. Urbanised areas like Aizawal and Kohima and other areas which have been linked with railway or roads should have the infrastructure of modern policing to cope with the increasing number of crimes and criminals, but it should take seriously into account the tribal laws, customs and institutions. The interior tribal areas should be left to be policed entirely by the traditional tribal institutions. The underlying principle for policing in the North-East should be minimal policing; no interference in the tribal laws, customs and institutions; policing on the basis of the gravity of offence and the sensitivity of the area. (Para 59.12)

60.171 There is no separation between the executive and the judiciary and it is our considered opinion that this arrangement should continue, till socio-economic changes justify any modification. (Para 59.13)

60.172 The tribal councils should continue to deal with the types of criminal offences they are dealing with at present. These tribal councils are discharging a very valuable and important function and any reform made in the law and the police administration should try to strengthen this machinery and not weaken it. The objective is to provide cheap justice to the people with simple procedures on the principles of natural justice without any exploitation by the lawyers. (Para 59.14)

60.173 In the interior places where it may not be necessary to open new police stations, it would suffice if a police party visits these areas periodically. The police in the headquarters should maintain close touch with the village councils. (Para 59.15)

60.174 No criteria can be fixed for the establishment of a new police station. The factors such as population, area, and crime will have to be taken into consideration but the approach will have to be flexible. In areas where mixed population gives rise to disputes between tribals and non-tribals and between different tribes, new police stations/police posts should be opened to inculcate a sense of security. The condition of the buildings of the police stations in this region is uniformly very poor and this needs to be attended to urgently. Proper buildings are also necessary from the security point of view, because of the activities of hostile elements. The system of maintenance of records in the police stations should be simplified, taking into consideration the capacity of an average tribal police officer. A new Police Manual taking into consideration the special requirements of the region should be drafted expeditiously so that the force can start functioning on the right lines. (Para 59.16)

60.175 The main difficulty in dealing with the activities of the insurgents is their identification. While it is true that no insurgency activity can flourish without the support of the people, it must also be appreciated that any action which further alienates the local population will only help the insurgents. Ultimately the problem will have to be tackled by isolating the extremist elements and winning over the local population. The police must be organised on proper lines and it must be allowed to play its legitimate role. In addition, following measures are recommended to deal more effectively with the problem of insurgency:

(i) The police should concentrate more on the border areas and those areas which are known for providing shelter to the extremists;
(ii) The police should be given modern arms and ammunition;
(iii) Identity cards should be issued to all male members of the population over 16 years of age;
(iv) There should be strict control on the sale and stock of explosive material;
(v) There should be very stringent control on the possession of arms and ammunition;
(vi) The police and the security forces operating in the area should have a separate public relations department; and
(vii) Murder of any government official or looting of any public property should be severely and promptly dealt with. (Para

59.17)

60.176 At present the responsibility of Intelligence set up is being shared by many intelligence agencies. It is absolutely essential that the work of all these agencies should be coordinated at some level, say at the level of the Lt. Governor in the Union Territories and at the level of Governor in the States. A Coordination Committee with the representatives of all the agencies as its members should be constituted by the Governor/Lt. Governor. All information should be conveyed directly to the Lt. Governor or the Governor for appropriate action or instructions instead of routing if through their own headquarters as is the practice at present. (Para 59.18)

60.177 It is imperative that only the best officers of the highest calibre are posted to this region. The posts will have to be made much more attractive so that suitable and talented officers with vision and enthusiasm volunteer for them. In some recent cases the government has not cared to look after the officers on return from a successful tenure in the North-East. It is strongly recommended that the following steps should be taken to make these posts attractive:

(i) Generous additional allowances should be sanctioned for all posts in the North-East. This should be at least 50 per cent of the Basic Pay available to the officer in his own cadre;
(ii) On free passage for the officers and their families should be given once a year for travelling to their home state and back;
(iii) If in spite of general allowances/perks senior officers in the same grade show unwillingness to go comparatively junior officers can be sent on rank promotion; and
(iv) A scale of suitable allowances should be fixed for hostel subsidy up to a maximum of 2 children. (Para 59.19)

60.178 It is further recommended that similarly the tribal officers from this region should be encouraged for postings outside the region. The tribal officers should, when posted outside the tribal areas, continue to enjoy the same emoluments and facilities as they are entitled to when posted to the tribal region. (Para 59.20)

60.179 Rules should be framed for recruitment at all levels, and their should be no departure from the norms laid down in the rules. To make it a homogenous force, as far as possible persons from all tribals and sections in the area should be recruited. (Para 59.21)

It should be possible for officers to do much more touring than they have been doing with the available means of communication. There should be closer cooperation between the police administration and the army and the air force, so that full use is made of the available helicopters which frequently go empty. (Para 59.23)

60.18 It would be desirable to increase the training facilities at Barapani and it should be possible for this centre to cater to the needs of all the Union Territories and the States in this region except Assam, which can have its own training institution. Anti-insurgency measures should form an important part of the training syllabus. (Para 59.24)

60.181 The para-military forces, though under the operational control of the local Police Chiefs are not under their disciplinary control, with the result what they have no commitment to the task and are not result oriented. The local police chief must have operational and disciplinary control over these forces. There should be close coordination between them, the local police, the army and the intelligence agencies. (Para 59.25)

60.182 To ensure that local pressures do not adversely affect the efficiency, morale and discipline of these forces, it is recommended that Article 371-A(1)(b) which enables the Governor of Nagaland to have special responsibility for the maintenance of law and order, should be extended to any other state when the problem of insurgency raises its head. (Para 59.26)

60.183 It is recommended that instead of recruiting the armed battalions for each State or Union Territory a North-Eastern Rifles or Armed Police should be constituted for the entire region on the CRPF pattern. Recruitment to these armed battalions should be done from all the 7 States and Union Territories. This should be a composite force for the entire region. The should be rotated under the order of the Governor of the North-East. These battalions when posted in a State should be completely under the operational and disciplinary control of the local Inspector General. (Para 59.27)

60.184 It is recommended that the entire border should be policed by the B.S.F. The army will, of course, have to continue is supportive role. The distance between the existing border outposts is far too long and needs to be reduced to improve their effectiveness. All the forces deployed at the border, should be trained in the anti-insurgency measures. The problem of Chakma infiltrators from Chittagong Hill Tracts in Bangladesh into Mizoram needs to be dealt with immediately before it gets out of hand. (Para 59.29)

60.185 Smuggling is another problem which has already assumed serious proportions in Manipur. There are complaints of connivance by the police and at the political levels. The border police has an important role to play in tackling this evil. (Para 59.30)

60.186 In the absence of social sanction against corrupt methods, which are helping the hostile element, there is no other alternative except to strengthen the anti-corruption machinery. There is need for reorganising and strengthening both the state anti-corruption branches and the zonal office of the Central Bureau of Investigation. Only experienced investigating officers with unimpeachable reputation of integrity should be posed to the Anti-Corruption Branch. Special judges to try these cases expeditiously should be appointed within the State, instead of sending them for trial outside the State, as is the practice in some of the States. The audit machinery should also be strengthened. (Para 59.31)

60.187 The security arrangements of jails need to be tightened. Proper jail buildings should be constructed without any further delay. (Para 59.32)

47

NATIONAL POLICE COMMISSION, 1977 – EIGHTH AND CONCLUDING REPORT[1]

Chairman Shri Dharma Vira, retired Governor

Members Shri N.K. Reddy; Shri K.F. Rustamji; Shri N.S. Saksena; Prof. M.S. Gore

M. Secy. Shri C.V. Narasimhan

Alterations Shri C.V. Narasimhan, former Director of Central Bureau of Investigation, functioned as Member Secretary of the Commission from its inception till 19th April, 1980 when he left to take a posting in his parent cadre in Tamil Nadu on replacement of his services from the Central Government to the State Government. After the departure of Shri Narasimhan, Shri M. D. Dikshit, Principal Director of Research, functioned as the Secretary Incharge.

Appointment

Far-reaching changes have taken place in the country after the enactment of the Indian Police Act, 1861 and the setting up of the Second Police Commission of 1902, particularly during the last thirty years of Independence. Though a number of States have appointed Police Commissions after Independence to study the problems of the Police in their respective States, there has been no comprehensive review at the national level of the police system after Independence despite radical changes in the political, social and economic situation in the country. A fresh examination is necessary of the role and performance of the Police – both as a law enforcement agency, and as an institution to protect the rights of the citizens enshrined in the Con-

1. Controller of Publications, Delhi, 1983, i + 116 p.

stitution. The Government of India have, therefore, decided to appoint a National Police Commission. The National Police Commission was appointed under the Government of India, Ministry of Home Affairs Resolution No. VI-24021/36/77-GPA.I, dated November 15, 1977.

Terms of Reference

The following will be the terms of reference of the Commission:

(1) Re-define the role, duties, powers and responsibilities of the police with special reference to prevention and control of crime and maintenance of public order.
(2) Examine the development of the principles underlying the present policing system, including the method of magisterial supervision, evaluate the performance of the system, identify the basic weaknesses of inadequacies, and suggest appropriate changes in the system and the basic laws governing the system.
(3) Examine, if any changes are necessary in the existing method of administration, disciplinary control and accountability.
(4) Inquire into the system of investigation and prosecution, the reasons for delay and failure; the use of improper methods, and the extent of their prevalence; and suggest how the system may be modified or changed and made efficient; scientific and consistent with human dignity; and how the related laws may be suitably amended.
(5) Examine methods of maintaining crime records and statistics and suggest methods for making them uniform and systematic.
(6) Review policing in rural areas, evaluate any new arrangements that have been made, and recommend changes that are necessary.
(7) Examine the system of policing required in non-rural and urbanised areas including metropolitan areas, and suggest the pattern that would be the most suitable.
(8) Examine the steps taken for modernising law enforcement, evaluate the work of police communications, the computer net work, scientific laboratories and agencies for research and development, and examine whether modernisation can be speeded up; examine to what extent, as a result of the modern-

isation of Police forces, streamlining of its functions and its re-structuring, it would be possible to economise in the man-power in the various areas of its activities.

(9) Examine the nature and extent of the special responsibilities of the Police towards the weaker sections of the community and suggest steps to ensure prompt action on their complaints for the safeguard of their rights and interests.

(10) Recommend measures and institutional arrangements:

(i) to prevent misuse of powers by the police, and to examine whether police behaviour, out-look, responsiveness and impartiality are maintained at the correct level, and if not the steps such as recruitment and training which should be taken to improve them;

(ii) to prevent misuse of the Police by administrative or executive instructions, political or other pressure, or oral orders of any type, which are contrary to law;

(iii) for the quick and impartial inquiry of public complaints made against the police about any misuse of police powers;

(iv) for the quick redressal of grievances of police personnel and to look after their morale and welfare; and

(v) for a periodic objective evaluation of police performance in a metropolitan area/District/State in a manner which will carry credibility before the public.

(11) Examine the manner and extent to which police can enlist ready and willing co-operation of the public in the discharge of their social defence and law enforcement duties and suggest measures regarding the institutional arrangements to secure such co-operation and measures for the growth of healthy and friendly public-police relationship.

(12) Examine the methods of police training, development, and career-planning of officers and recommend any changes that are required at any time in their service, to modernise the outlook, and to make the leadership of the force effective and morally strong.

(13) Examine the nature of the problems that the police will have to face in the future, and suggest the measures necessary for dealing with them, and for keeping them under continuous study and appraisal.

(14) Consider and make recommendations and suggestions regarding any other matter which the Government may refer to the Commission; and

(15) Any other matter of relevance or importance having an impact on the subject.

Contents

Accountability of Police Performance; Looking Ahead; Police Act; Epilogue; Summary of Observations and Recommendations; Appendices I to VII.

Recommendations

Accountability of Police Performance

65.1 Accountability is liability to account for proper performance of assigned task. In a democratic society, the police is accountable for its performance to the people. Then, all activities of the police are governed by various provisions of law and each action of the police is to conform to the law of the land. So the police has an accountability to law. Finally, the police functionaries are accountable for their performance to the organisation (Paras 61.4, 61.5 and 61.6)

65.2 The departmental instructions regarding stay in the rural areas for 90 days in a year must be strictly complied with by all officers of the level of SDPO and SP. Such stays would help them to come in close contact with the common people, know their problems in detail, and seek their cooperation in various police-activities. (Para 61.9)

65.3 An important aspect of inspections carried out by supervisory officers is to assess the qualitative performance of policing, its impact in that area on citizens and feeling of security prevailing in the community. The Inspecting Officer should not take inspections as a routine drill but they should introduce inter-action with the people which will enable them to elicit the maximum information regarding the views of the people in regard to the functioning of the officials in the area. (Para 61.10)

65.4 Among the various sources which would aid the State Security Commission to have an objective evaluation, one would be the Annual Administration Report submitted by the Chief of Police every year. Besides, the State Security Commission should have under it an independent Cell to evaluate police performance. This Cell should function outside the State police organisation and may have experts from various fields according to the need. The State Security Commission would also be receiving the assessment report regarding the state of policing from the Central Police Committee recommended by us in the Seventh Report. These three reports emanating from different channels will provide a reliable base to enable the State Security Commission to assess the police performance in an objective manner. Based on these reports, the State Security Commission should prepare a final report on the performance of the State police to be placed before the State Legislature. (Para 61.12)

65.5 Although a totally direct accountability of the police to the people is beset with various difficulties, it is not impossible to introduce a near-direct accountability of the police to the people. This would involve among other things creation of awareness in the police functionaries at various levels regarding accountability to the people. The police functionaries individually as well as in groups should be sensitised to the idea of accountability to the people. (Paras 61.14 and 61.15)

65.6 During the inspections, inspecting officers should seek out people in order to get the necessary feed-back to assess the functioning of operational level policing. During such inspections, the inspecting officers should call meetings of cross-section of people and discuss their problems. At the district level, they should hold meetings not only with the cross-section of people but also with the representatives of the people in the Municipality and Zila Parishad and with the MLAs and MPs of the constituency. (Para 16.16)

During such inspections, the inspecting officers should devote special care to scrutinise and review the overall pattern of complaints that are received. If a particular nature of complaint is repeated or frequent complaints are noticed from a particular areas, the inspecting officer should investigate the causes. Selective inspections should be carried out so that the complaints as well as the results thereof could be ascertained in detail. (Para 61.17)

65.7 The responsibility should be squarely fixed on the officers of the level of SP and above to carefully watch the reputation of SHOs and take appropriate measures wherever warranted. Any failure on their part in this regard should be seriously viewed. In those circumstances where the supervisory officer may either fail to assess the reputation of the SHO or fail to take appropriate action in a particular instance, the people have a right to petition to the State Security Commission. In the event of such complaints, the State Security Commission should gauge the reputation of the SHO concerned and take such action as may be required. (Para 61.18)

65.8 When the Range DIG or SP of the District feels that the particular station house or other operational level is not providing necessary satisfaction to the people, he should go into the causes in depth and try to remove the same. If the attitude of a particular SHO or his method of functioning is not in the interest of the people of the locality, the higher officer should not hesitate to shift the officer from that particular area and to take corrective or disciplinary action against him to mend his attitude and behaviour. (Para 61.20)

65.9 Section 132 and Section 197 of the Cr.P.C. 1973 provides protection to various categories of public servants against any prosecution brought against them relating to performance of official duties. The protection available to the police officers under these sections should be withdrawn so that the private complainant is free to press his complaint against police official for a judicial pronouncement without there being a provision to obtain prior permission of the competent authority for such prosecution. However, the police officer against whom a complaint is brought in a court of law should be defended at the cost of the Government. Officers of and above the rank of Superintendent of Police should be authorised to order defence of their subordinates. An order from the State Government should be necessary in these cases when a complaint is filed against the police officer of the rank of IGP or DGP and also in case the complaint against the police officer is of rape, or murder. Such defence at the Government's cost should extend upto the appellate stage. In thoses cases where the court comes to the finding that the case is unfounded, it should by law be empowered to take the explanation of the complainant, and if the explanation is unsatisfactory, to inflict suitable punishment on the complainant. Suitable amendment should be made in this respect in the law. High Courts may impress upon subordinate courts that such complaints against police officials should be disposed of on priority basis. The High Court may further draw the attention of the lower courts to the provisions of 202 Cr.P.C. and advise them generally to ask for a report from the District Superintendent of Police on the complaint filed before them. It would be the responsibility of the District SP to either make an inquiry himself or have it made by a sufficiently senior officer and submit a factual report to the court before the latter decides to proceed further with the case. On mere filing of a complaint, unless there is a prima facie case and justification for the same, transfer of the concerned official should not be ordered. (Paras 61.26 to 61.36)

65.10 The following yard-sticks should be adopted by the State Police Organisations for evaluating group-performance of the police at various levels:

(1) *Prevention of Crime*

(i) Sense of security prevailing in the community;
(ii) People's willing cooperation and participation secured by the Police in preventing crime.

(2) *Investigation of Crime*

(i) Correct registration of crime;
(ii) Prompt visit to the scene of occurrence;
(iii) Speedy investigation; and
(iv) Honesty and impartiality in investigation.

(3) *Law and Order*

(i) Extent to which law and order is maintained taking into account the forces which promote lawlessness; and
(ii) The manner in which law and order is maintained. Two factors have to be judged – (a) People's cooperation, (b) Use of force.

(4) *Traffic Management*

(i) Smooth flow of traffic in urban areas and control of fatal and seriousness accidents by prosecution of persistent offenders.

(5) *Service*

(i) General spirit of service, especially to weaker sections, physically handicapped women and children;

(ii) Quality of service rendered in a distress situations like cyclone-havoc, flood-damage, famine, etc.; and

(iii) Specific instances of service-oriented functions performed by the Police which drew special appreciation and gratitude from the public.

(6) *Reputation of Integrity and Courtesy*

(i) General reputation.

(ii) Police collusion with criminals organisation illicit distillation, gambling, economic crimes, prostitution, etc.

(iii) Reputation for courteous behaviour.

(iv) Prompt and satisfactory enquiry into complaints against policemen. (Para 61.42)

65.11 Functionaries in the department at each level should be held accountable only with respect to the functions and duties assigned to him and accountability should not extend to duties over which he has no direct control. Therefore, police functionaries from SHO to that of Chief of Police cannot be held accountable for each isolated incident in a particular region in their respective jurisdiction, however serious it may be, unless it is proved that the particular incident occurred because of act of omission or commission on the part of the police functionary or such incidents have been widespread and the official has failed to react adequately. (Para 61.43)

The sanction of fixing unreasonable or impossible targets which cannot be achieved except through illegal or irregular means should be effectively discouraged. (Para 61.44)

Looking Ahead

65.12 The object of looking ahead is to determine what the police organisation has to do *now and from now on* to adequately discharge its responsibilities. (Para 62.1)

65.13 So far law and order problem has been an urban phenomenon, but the last couple of years have shown that the awakening in the rural areas is leading to bitter and brutal caste and class conflicts. In addition unrest emerging from organised demand in the rural areas also for more money for what they produce is another emerging factor of importance. Hitherto this phenomenon was confined to the urban workers only. When this ferment is viewed against the background that about 80 per cent people live in the rural areas it is evident that the most serious threats to law and order will in future arise in the rural areas. (Para 62.20)

65.14 So far organised crime has grown almost unchecked. The police will have to develop special expertise to tackle it. Another such crime is terrorism the spectrum of which embraces the rural terrorism of dacoits and Naxalites, kidnapping in urban areas and hijacking of aircrafts. (Para 62.23)

65.15 The factors that cause crime are increasing in strength and intensity. Some of these factors are population, internal migration, urbanisation and development of slums combined with increasing unemployment and iniquitous distribution of wealth. Our cities and towns are in a chaotic state and the services, particularly the civic amenities, have been unable to keep pace with the constantly increasing urban population. Thus problems of water supply, power, sanitation, housing transport are becoming more and more acute. With the deterioration in the quality of life in our towns and cities, the problems of police are bound to become more acute. (Paras 62.25 to 62.28)

65.16 The agricultural sector is already saturated with as much manpower as it can absorb. Rapid growth of the industrial sector which alone can absorb more and more of the working population has yet to come about. Already unemployment is very sizeable and if it continues to increase the emerging phenomenon of educated unemployed or under-employed youth taking to a life of crime may become about the most intractable police problem of the future. (Para 62.30)

65.17 The problems of police in 2000 AD are not likely to be uniform all over the country. Even as several centuries can be seen to exist on our roads–bullock-carts, horse-drawn carriages, cycles, cycles-rickshaw, mopeds, motor-cycles, motor-rickshaws, the latest Mercedes and, occasionally, a jet screaming overhead – the various parts of the country are facing various kinds of police problems in varying degrees. The problems faced by the police in Bombay today may be faced by Delhi in another five years, and by Bangalore, Hyderabad, Lucknow in another fifteen years. The problems faced by cities like Lucknow, Allahabad, Tiruchirapally today may be faced by numerous smaller cities by 2000 AD. Accordingly, no single model can be applicable to the whole country although certain essential features would have to be common all over the country because of improved means of transport and communication available to criminals. (Para 62.32)

65.18 Of the answers to the police problems that are developing the most important is self-policing. Self-policing means (1) taking adequate preventive measures to protect life and property; (2) resisting an attempt on life and/or property, should it take place in spite of preventive measures undertaken by exercising the right of private defence, and (3) active involvement in the processes of the criminal justice system. The present practice of police, however, is a hindrance to self-policing in the sense that the right of private defence cannot be exercised by a person without running the risk of prosecution by police and conviction by a court of law. (Paras 62.33 and 62.34)

65.19 The various sub-systems of the criminal justice system have to be harmonised structurally so that they may work together for the common objective of protecting society from such acts of individuals or groups of individuals as can damage it. At present the sub-systems are at cross-purpose and a frequently visible posture is confrontation. (Paras 62.35 and 62.39)

65.20 As the entire work of the Commission has been about the response of the police, in the preceding chapters of various reports it has already suggested how the Police is to be prepared for the problems and challenges it is facing and will have to face. (Para 62.40)

65.21 While the constant endeavour has been to prepare the police for the new challenges and tasks, factors having a bearing on crime and disorder are complex and any inflexible planning for the future is neither advisable nor possible. Accordingly it is suggested that the Bureau of Police Research and Development and the State Research units must make a periodical analysis of the police problems and the police performance. Such an analysis should take into consideration the projections which had been made in the past and see to what extent they proved to be accurate. If they went away, what were the reasons for it? Having done so, they would be in a position to say, with an amount of accuracy, about the future. The Central Police Committee and the State Security Commissions that have been recommended in earlier Reports will naturally have a significant role to play in this. (Para 62.42)

Police Act

65.22 For the incorporation of our new recommendations, it is necessary to replace the existing outmoded Police Act of 1861. A draft new Act has been given as an Appendix. (Paras 63.1 and 63.2)

65.23 We recommend that the Central Government may enact the necessary legislation for the constitution of the Central Police Committee, define its role and functions, and such other details in terms of our recommendations delineated in detail in paragraph 58.14 of our Seventh Report. (Para 63.3)

RAILWAY ACCIDENT INVESTIGATION REPORT ON DERAILMENT OF NO. 2 DOWN AHMEDABAD-DELHI MAIL AT KM 18/6.2 BETWEEN AJARKA AND BAWAL STATIONS ON THE BANDIKUI-REWARI SINGLE LINE METRE GAUGE SECTION OF WESTERN RAILWAY AT ABOUT 05.18 HOURS ON NOVEMBER 23, 1977 – REPORT[1]

November 23, 1977 – March 31, 1978

One Man Commission Shri P.M.N. Murthy, Additional Commissioner of Railway Safety

Appointment

The Commission was constituted under Ministry of Tourism and Civil Aviation (Commission of Railway Safety) in accordance with Rule 4 of the Statutory Investigation into Railway Accidents Rules, 1973 vide Notification No. RS. 13-T(8)/71 dated April 19, 1973 on November 23, 1977.

Terms of Reference

To enquire into the Derailment of No. 2 Down Ahmedabad-Delhi Mail at km 18/6.2 between Ajarka and Bawal Stations on the Bandikui-Rewari Single Line Metre Gauge Section of Western Railway at about 05.18 hours on November 23, 1977.

Contents

Summary; Inspection and Inquiry; Relief Measures; The Train; Local

---

1. Delhi, Controller of Publications, 1980, 20 p.

Features; Summary of Evidence; Observation and Tests; Discussion; Conclusions; Remarks and Recommendations; Annexure; Railway Board's Comment on Various Paragraphs of the Report.

Conclusions

Cause

On full consideration of the factual, material and circumstantial evidence, I have reached the conclusion that the Derailment of No. 2 Down Ahmedabad-Delhi Mail at km 18/6.2 between Ajarka and Bawal stations on the Bandikui-Rewari single line metre gauge section of Western Railway at about 05.18 hours on 23-11-1977 was the result of unauthorised interference with the track, by persons unknown.

A full length rail (11.9 metres) on the left of the track about 13.50 metres ahead of km. 18/4, was disjointed by unfastening the fishplates at both ends and the rail displaced from its former intact position to the left away from the alignment, after disengaging it from the steel sleepers.

Responsibility

Detection of such discontinuity in the track in time being impossible, no responsibility lay on the Driving Crew in connection with this accident.

Relief Measures

(a) Apropos Section II of the Report, the relief measures were generally satisfactory.

(b) The Railway Administration may in a suitable manner convey their appreciation to:

(i) S/Shri M.L. Kaushik and Sultan Singh, Sarpanchs of the neighbouring villages Tihara and Shahpur respectively, who looked after the stranded passengers by providing them tea and eatables; and

(ii) The Medical-Officer-in-Charge, Primary Health Centre, Bawal, Medical Officers of the Civil Hospital, Rewari and the

Chief Medical and Health Officer, Alwar who promptly responded to the Railway's call, rushed to the site and rendered necessary medical assistance.

Recommendations

54. It would appear from the evidence of the Northern Railway's Assistant Engineer at Rewari and the Divisional Engineer at Bikaner [paras 24 and 25] that there was some apprehension of tampering with track on that region (following a case on the Moradabad Division) and the Deputy Commissioners concerned (including Mahendragarh—the district in which this accident occurred), as well as the Police Authorities had been addressed on 9-11-77 to advise the sensitive locations warranting patrolling. In fact, pending such advice, the Divisional Engineer, Bikaner, had on his own introduced patrolling on certain stretches on the Rewari Subdivision with effect from 11-11-1977. The Western Railway Administration had, apparently no information in this regard. The need for greater coordination and expeditious consultantion in such matters not only with the State Authorities, but also between contiguous Railway Administration is indicated.

55. The pace of welding of rails on the trunk routes and main lines may be accelerated, priority being given to routes in 'sensitive' areas and those on which high speed trains operate, e.g., the Pink City route on which this mishap took place.

56. Neither the Assistant Engineer, Rewari nor the Additional Permanent Way Inspector, Ajarka (who was the first Civil Engineering, Railway Official to reach the site) were aware of the instructions in force [vide Appendix J of the Western Railway's Accident Manual] that:

(i) Gangmen proceeding to the site of accident in the first instance should not carry any tools with them; and

(ii) It is to be ensured that tool boxes of Gangmen sent to the site of accident are not opened until they have been checked by the Police.

Also no joint inventory of the materials taken over by the Police was made, nor were they under joint custody as enjoined in Para 204 of the Accident Manual.

Copies of the Accident Manual may be supplied to all Supervisory staff (of the concerned Departments) and their adequate knowledge of its provisions assured through periodic checks by Inspecting Officials.

57. (a) The Postal Van which was the 3rd coach and the 2 Air-conditioned-cum-First Class coaches—the 5th and 6th—which were all wooden bodied, were severally damaged in the accident. The advisability of placing only steel bodied coaches on Mail and Express trains may be examined and the change-over effected on priority.

(b) Adverting to Para 50, the Commission of Railway Safety had expressed its reservations on the view held that the behaviour of rivetted designs of steel coaches maybe taken as equivalent to all welded integral coaches, vide letter No. RS. 25-T(26)/77 dated 23rd/24th September 1977 addressed to the Secretary, Railway Board. This issue may be urgently reviewed in the light of the happenings in this accident in which the roof and sides over almost half the length of the 4th coach (36640 GSCNW) which was steel bodied, were smashed.

58. The speed chart of the locomotive indicated that the Driver had touched speeds of over 80 km/h at 8 locations between Bandikui and the accident spot. Cases of overspeeding must be viewed with concern and necessary corrective action taken to curb this tendency. It may also be examined if the existing system of checks is adequate for the purpose.

59. The speed indicator-cum-recorder fitted on loco No. YDM4 6402 had no arrangements for illumination, making it difficult to read it during night hours. The need for improving the standard of maintenance of speedometers is emphasized.

60. The procedure in vogue in the Loco Shed at Bandikui for the issue and fitment of charts on speed-recorders should be bettered and made more systematic [paras 23 and 41]. Instructions should also be issued that Mechanics deputed to replace the charts should check and set the clocks to correct timing.

61. Adverting to my recommendation made in the Report on the Derailment of No. 4 Down Assam Mail between Samuktala Road and Salsalabari stations on the N.F. Railway on 28th September 1967, reproduced in Annexure I, the question of providing an additional speed-indicator-cum recorder or repositioning the exiting one on YDM4 locos for easy reference by Drivers in both positions of driving, may be decided and implemented expeditiously.

Railway Board's Comments on Various Paragraphs of the Report

Para 54: The recommendations made by the Commissioner of Railway Safety has been noted by the Railway Administration who have brought this to the notice of State authorities also. In fact it is always the endeavour of the railways to introduce security patrolling of track on vulnerable sections as and when the need for such patrolling is felt in consultation with the civil authorities and also maintain a close liaison with the Civil/Police authorities in this regard.

Para 55: It is the policy of the Railways to lay short welded rail panels and long continuous welded rails on trunk and main lines on a programmed basis at the time of carrying out track renewals. Considerable progress has been made in this respect. A proper watch is being kept on the laying of welded rails. As for the section, where the subject accident took place, laying of long welded rails is not permitted on technical considerations as the track consists of 60 lb rails.

Para 56: The Railway Administration have reiterated the instructions contained in the Accident Manual for the guidance of the staff, and have also directed the supervisory officials to test the staff in their knowledge of the extant instructions.

In this connection, it is also mentioned that instructions already exist that in cases of sabotage, a factual note should be prepared about the conditions obtaining at the site of accident and that this note should be signed jointly by the Police and Railway authorities. Instructions about preservation of clues *vis-a-vis* signing of the joint inventory of fittings and notes/sketches by the Police at the site of accident have also been issued to the Railways vide Board's circular letter No. 78/W6/PRA/9 dated 25-10-1979.

Para 57(a): Instructions are being issued that as far as possible, coaches which carry maximum number of passengers like, GS, Sleepers, first class coaches, etc., should be steel bodied in case of Mail/Express trains. Since there are a large number of wooden bodied Postal Vans, Dining Cars, Air-conditioned coaches, both on B.G. and M.G. and MG SLRs, they would be progressively replaced by steel bodied coaches on Mail/Express trains, subject to the limitation of manufacturing capacities and availability of funds.

Para 57(b): The issue is under examination.

Para 58: The speed charts are checked regularly by the supervisory officials, and corrective action is taken against the drivers whenever over-speeding is noticed. The existing system of checks is considered adequate. The subject was again discussed in Chief Mechanical Engineer's Conference and Railways have been asked to reiterate instructions contained in Railway Board's letter No. 59/467/46(M)/ (M&P) dated 26-6-67.

Para 59: The cab light arrangements for providing illumination for speed recorders are normally considered adequate. Instructions have, however, been issued to the Railways vide Board's letter No. 77-M(M&P)/7/2/W dated 7-11-78 to devise ways for self-illuminating the instruments and arranging for its installation.

Para 60: The subject was discussed in detail in the Chief Mechanical Engineers' Conference held at Madras on 12th and 13th December, 1979 and it was decided as under:

(i) Drivers shall henceforth be responsible for changing the Speed recorder charts. This is to provide against multiple recording and to ensure that charts are changed every trip, as well as to ensure regular collection of charts and their inspection at the base sheds;

(ii) It will also be the drivers' responsibility to see that the correct chart is properly fitted in the Speed-recording instruments on their locomotives and that it is recording correctly.

Necessary instructions have been issued to the Railways vide letter No. 77M(M&P)/467/7 dated 19-1-80.

Para 61: Instructions already exist that two speedometers should be fitted on YDM IV locos, and the same are being followed. However, in the cases of locomotive No. YDM IV-4602 which hauled the ill-fated train, second speedometer could not be fitted by DLW due to non-availability of the same from the only indigenous supplier, viz., M/s. International Instruments Pvt. (Ltd), Bangalore whose supplies are irregular.

49

WORKING GROUP ON TECHNICAL EDUCATION, 1977 – REPORT[1]

Chairman Shri P. Sabanayagam

Members Shri Samar Guha; Dr. B. Ramachandra Rao; Dr. A.L. Mudaliar; Prof G.R. Damodaran; Shri Ravi L. Kirloskar; Shri Nanu B. Amin; Dr. C.J. Dadachanji; Shri Harish Mahindra; Shri M.S. Padmanabhan; Shri Satyendra Tripathi; Dr. A Ramachandran; Dr. Ajit Mozoomdar; Shri V. Krishnamurthy; Prof. M.G.K. Menon; Shri B.B. Lal; Dr. S. Varadajan, Shri N.B. Prasad; Shri A.C. Banerjee; Shri C.S.V. Rao; Shri S.K. Bose; Rear Admiral Krishna Dev; Prof. A.K. De; Dr. S. Paul; Dr. Y.K. Alag; Prof. Malathi Bolar; Dr. Y.V.N. Rao; Prof. T. Subbarao; Dr. S.N. Saraf; Prof. D. Banerjee; Shri P.K. Umashankar; Shri H.S. Shahani; Shri C.S. Sridharan; Shri B.N. Guha Biswas

Secretaries Shri K.R. Sivaramakrishnan; Shri M.S. Srinivasan

Appointment

The Government of India in the Ministry of Education and Social Welfare set-up a Working Group on Technical Education in November 1977.

Terms of Reference

To review the present status of the Nation's needs during the coming decade and to suggest reorientation and improvements to the existing programmes.

---

1. New Delhi, Ministry of Education and Social Welfare, 1978, XXIV, 134 p.

Contents

(a) Report of the Working Group, (b) *Appendices* – (i) Position Paper for the Working Group; (ii) Minutes of the Ist Meeting of the Working Group for Technical Education held at New Delhi on 19-11-77; (iii) Report of the Sub-Group on Technical Manpower; (iv) Report of the Sub-Group on Research and Development; (v) Report of the Sub-Group on Diversification and Redesigning of the existing programmes; (vi) Report of the Sub-Group on quality improvement; (vii) Report of the Sub-Group on Industry Institutional Collaboration; (viii) Recommendations of the All India Council for Technical Education on the Reports of the Working Group.

Recommendations of the Working Group

3. *Manpower Needs*

3.1 A tentative overall quantitative assessment of engineering and technical manpower requirements for the next decade indicates that the present annual admission capacity of 3,000 for post-graduate courses, 25,000 for first degree courses and 50,000 for diploma courses is adequate. Same is true also of facilities in management education vis-a-vis manpower requirements. It should be possible for the existing institutions to increase the supply of manpower by improving the efficiency and effectiveness of the system through optimum utilisation of available resources and improvement in the instructional process. Changes in demand in different specialities (disciplines) should be made by appropriate shifts in disciplines within the existing total sanctioned intake capacity.

An objective review for reorientation of the existing course facilities should be made to provide for diversification to meet the emerging specialised manpower needs.

Within the approved annual intake capacity each institution should increase the supply of technical manpower by improving the efficiency and effectiveness of educational processes. Shifts in the intake capacities between disciplines may be effected to cater to the emerging manpower needs.

3.2 All new courses should be based on established and well defined manpower needs.

3.3 A reliable information system is a perquisite to planning, specially in the field of technical education and training. In the absence of up-to-date and meaningful manpower information, it will neither be possible to anticipate areas of growth in the field of science and technology nor plan for technical manpower development. Such a system is at present not available; the necessary data are not even collected, much less updated, systematised and stored suitably for retrieval as and when necessary. From the available data it is not possible to undertake studies relating to productivity of the educational programmes or absorption patterns of the educated in the employment market. A number of personnel with the background of science education is also deployed in Industry. It is necessary for any Survey of Technical Manpower to take cognizance of this factor. It is, therefore, necessary to establish a national manpower information system. In order to make such a system operational, it is necessary to establish effective coordination of efforts among the data generating and collecting agencies through a well-knit countrywide organisation. The Regional Engineering Colleges and other selected technical institutions could assist as nodal points in the operations of the information system and thereby benefit from the system. Manpower information can also be used usefully for purpose of placement through agencies such as the Boards of Apprenticeship Training.

A reliable information system is a pre-requisite to Planning, specially in the field of technical education and training. A national manpower information system should be established with a lead centre in the Institute of Applied Manpower Research for the storage, updating, retrieval and analysis of manpower information to assist technical education planning. The Institute of Applied Manpower Research should be suitably strengthened for this purpose with provision of requisite facilities.

4. *Measures for Improvement*

4.1 *Courses/Programmes to Meet Industrial and Community Needs*

4.1.1 There should always be opportunity for self development. A person starting his career as a craftsman should also have the opportunity to develop himself as a technician or engineer, if he has the right aptitude and abilities. The present pattern of courses is based on rigid entry and exit points and does not encourage horizontal or vertical mobility.

The adoption of a credit system with the prescription of maximum and minimum number of credits that can be taken in a semester/academic year will bring in an amount of flexibility in the system. This will enable multi-point entry options to persons depending on their initial preparations/professional background, thus providing opportunity for continuing/further education at their pace and abilities. This provision can also lead to diversification, interdisciplinary programmes and modular courses.

Credit system with provision for multi-point entry in part-time and full-time programmes, be introduced.

4.1.2 The impact of research and development activities so far undertaken has been felt in the various sectors of development including rural and community services. Although 'problem-oriented' and 'application oriented' programmes have been undertaken, there is a need for a greater emphasis on such research programmes which will tackle industrial and rural development problems in keeping with the national needs.

Industrial and rural development problems be identified, and greater emphasis on research programmes to tackle such problems keeping in view the national needs, be given. Technical education institutions having the potential and capability to undertake problem-oriented and application-oriented programmes should be selected and properly supported to facilitate substantial contribution to rural and community development.

4.1.3 Involvement in consultancy work, and testing/service activities on selection basis will promote interaction between the institution and the industry, which will be mutually beneficial. It will build up expertise and confidence of the staff and students and the image of the institution. To undertake and promote such activities, a Consultancy Centre should be established in each institution. A separate development fund should be created from out of the earnings through consultancy, which could be used for further development of the Consultancy Centre.

Institutions should be encouraged to set up Consultancy Centres to promote consultancy activities.

4.1.4 Managerial skills are crucial for engineers and technicians, who are very often required to perform the managerial functions in industry.

Relevant management education be integrated with professional courses at degree and diploma levels.

4.1.5 The pattern of courses in management at all Management Institutions is heavily oriented towards large scale industries. Considering the great need for managerial manpower for small and medium-sized industries, it is suggested that at least a part of the present intake of recognised management institutions be diverted to this sector. Sectoral needs of transport, power, health, education and agriculture should also be taken care of through specialised management programmes offered by these institutions.

Courses in management education be restructured to provide for managerial manpower for small and medium-sized industry as also for sectoral needs such as transport, power, health, education and agriculture.

4.1.6 Some Polytechnics have shown initiate to interact with the environment by organising programmes and activities to meet the community needs. Such institutions could act as focal points to promote transfer of technology to the rural sector. Development projects beneficial to the community could be undertaken towards this end.

Selected Polytechnics act as focal points to promote transfer of technology to the rural community. Such Polytechnics be designated as 'Community Colleges' and adequate support provided.

4.1.7 Professional role of a technician varies from industry to industry. The education of a technician in the institutions necessarily, therefore, is broad-based. However, when once the technician takes up employment, he is called upon to occupy a variety of job positions. It is necessary to give him the skills required for this purpose to cope up competently in this role with his responsibilities. To meet diverse requirements and challenges in his profession, a technician will have to be provided facilities for his continuous education and for acquiring new competencies. Advanced technician courses would be useful in this context. Quite a few of the Polytechnics in the country have the potential to conduct such courses and to contribute to the development of diverse manpower needs.

Selected Polytechnics should be given central assistance to conduct advanced technician programmes.

4.1.8 The technical education to be relevant, has to keep pace with the changing practices in science and technology. The role of curriculum development in this context, is a crucial one, and can hardly be over-emphasised. A continuous review of curricula should, therefore, be a permanent feature in the technical education system. Considerable curriculum development work has been done at the various centres established for this activity, particularly at the diploma level. Such efforts are to be co-ordinated and strengthened. Dissemination of information and ideas from these centres to all concerned agencies should take place freely.

Support be provided to strengthen the work of curriculum development and research related to problems of technical education.

4.2 *Staff—Students, Development, Appraisal*

4.2.1 The minimum qualifications for recruitment to teaching posts laid down by the UGC/AICTE is considered generally adequate. The only lacuna identified is the inadequate emphasis on industrial experience. Faculty recruitment should be based on precise job descriptions.

In addition to minimum academic qualifications laid down by AICTE, one year's industrial experience for Lecturers and two year's for Senior staff is considered essential. All recruitment

should be strictly on merit, by open competition and on All India basis, subject to reservation because of constitutional requirements.

4.2.2 **To ensure sustained high quality performance appointments to Senior teaching posts (i.e., Professors and Heads of Institutions) should be on contract basis for five years, renewable after assessment.**

4.2.3 Due to lack of promotional opportunities at senior levels, bright young faculty with proven ability have to stay in the same category for long periods of time. Such a situation is detrimental to the motivational climate of institutions.

Personal promotion schemes should be established to enable promotion to deserving young faculty stagnating at a particular level. Such promotion be restricted to 20 per cent of the sanctioned strength.

4.2.4 At present teacher appraisal is done primarily for administrative purposes. Confidential reports hardly represent profiles and the strength and weakness of the teachers. The appraisal by the students is also considered desirable and should be taken as an important factor in assessing teacher's competence.

An appropriate staff appraisal scheme based on a methodology acceptable to the faculty be introduced. This would also enable identification of the needs of staff development.

4.2.5 Most of the existing faculty members at the collegiate level already possess Master's Degree, which is the minimum qualification prescribed. It is desirable that faculty in engineering colleges upgrade their qualifications for effective discharge of their responsibilities. It is, therefore, recommended that more opportunities be provided under the faculty development programme for Ph.D.

Master's Degree training under the Quality Improvement Programme be phased out and in its place, additional provision be made for doctoral programmes. Considering the number of teachers involved, it is suggested that provision be increased to enable 250 teachers every year to enroll for doctoral programmes.

4.2.6 For a teacher to be effective, in addition to subject matter competence, he should have expertise in educational technology his pedagogical skills must be well-developed. This is important both for Collegiate and Polytechnic teachers.

Provision be made to organise short-term courses for Polytechnic and collegiate teachers in educational technology.

4.2.7 For Polytechnic teachers, a Bachelor's degree has been prescribed as the minimum qualification for initial recruitment. A very large proportion of the Polytechnic teachers are only Diploma holders. It is essential that opportunities are provided to these teachers also to acquire Bachelor's degree.

Selected Engineering Colleges should organise under Quality Improvement Programme three-year courses to enable Polytechnic teachers with Diploma qualification to get Bachelor's degree.

4.2.8 Higher attainment for Polytechnic teachers should be in tune with the requirements of Polytechnic education. Master's Degree courses are not appropriate to fulfil these requirements. For Polytechnic teachers, the courses should be primarily industry-oriented or in the fields of technical education and its management.

Polytechnic teachers should be sponsored under the Quality Improvement Programme for Industry-Oriented Post-Graduate Diploma Courses Organised for the Purpose.

4.2.9 The expertise and capability of executives, managers and technical personnel from industry, research institutions and professional bodies would be of benefit for the educational programmes in institutions. Improvement of quality of instruction is possible through the faculty acquainting themselves with the variety of live problems in the industry. This would also enable identification of industrial problems and open up avenues for consultancy in problem-areas.

In order to ensure purposeful and meaningful interaction and collaboration between industry and institutions, "Adjunct Professorship" in the institution for willing and capable personnel from the industry, be instituted. Similarly 'Residency' for institutional

faculty be provided in the industry. Additional budgetary provision of staff to the tune of 20 per cent be made to finance these schemes.

4.3 *Students*

4.3.1 Selection of students with proper aptitudes and abilities plays an important role in the development of the right type of technical manpower. Reliance on the percentage of marks obtained by the students at the qualifying examinations does not seem to be fair, in view of the fact that there is wide variance in the standards of different examining bodies. Further, in view of the different grading systems being followed now, admission procedures need a change.

Admission to both degree and diploma courses be on the basis of carefully designed entrance tests. These tests could be conducted state-wise, common to all institutions.

4.3.2 In spite of the best methods of selection, the student body always has a percentage of weak students, who need special attention. This problem is particularly acute in the case of students admitted under reserved quotas.

In order to reduce drop outs and other forms of wastage, it is necessary that special efforts in the form of remedial courses be carried out to help weaker students.

4.3.3 Opportunities for continuing education should be available to those who are already in the profession to enable them to professionally advance according to their abilities and convenience through part-time full-time courses based on the credit system and multipoint entry.

Flexible programmes of continuing education through part-time/full-time courses be introduced at all levels for serving personnel.

4.3.4 Participation of students in the academic bodies would generally result in greater commitment of the student community.

Representation be given to students in academic bodies of the institutions.

4.4 *Instructional Support Services*

4.4.1 The non-teaching technical supporting staff has a direct bearing on the technical education process. Apart from assisting in laboratory experimentation and workshop practice, they are primarily responsible for the maintenance of laboratory equipment, instruments, etc. Training needs of this category of personnel deserve immediate attention to ensure optimum and effective utilisation of resources for instruction.

Schemes for training of technical supporting staff be started under "Quality Improvement Programme".

4.4.2 With the vast amount of published literature and the newer methods of information retrieval, the role of library in the teaching-learning process has become important. To get maximum benefit from this resource, it is essential that the efficiency of the library services should be improved.

To ensure better and more effective library services, qualified and trained library staff be provided.

4.4.3 Developments in the field of educational technology have made available a variety of audio-visual aids and reprographic facilities, which could make the instructional process more effective.

Adequate support be given to institutions to organise audio-visual and reprographic services.

4.4.4 The role of resource centres in the instructional process is very significant. Such centres can help individuals the instructional process and make it more student-oriented. Remedial instruction to weaker students become easier through a variety of instructional alternatives, which the students could choose according to their level and background. Learning resource centres also offer facilities to the teacher to design his instructional strategies around and material and equipment available and to prepare his own instructional material and aids.

On an experimental basis, Learning Resource Centres be established in a few selected institutions.

4.4.5 There is a definite shift in the approach towards the aims of laboratory instruction. Conventional laboratory experiments of the 'verification of theory' type are found to be ineffective and these are making way to 'learning by doing' type laboratory assignments. Some of the laboratory equipment acquired by institutions in the early 60's have become obsolete, in view of curricular changes. To keep up with this trend in laboratory instruction and to meet the requirement of curricular changes, the laboratories should be gradually modernised with relevant and useful equipment and components.

The replacement of laboratory equipment, which have become obsolete due to technological and curricular changes, be examined. Laboratories be modernised gradually with relevant, and versatile equipment, with more instructional potential.

5. *Management of the System*

5.1 The tasks of planning and organizing the education system, to cater to the technical manpower needs from craftsmen to technologists, can be effectively performed through an integrated approach. To ensure such an approach for balanced development of the system, all the tasks mentioned above should become the responsibility of a single agency.

The tasks of planning and organising technical education from the level of craftsman to that to technologists be brought under a single national agency, both at the centre and the states to ensure balanced development through an integrated approach.

5.2 Effective co-ordination of post-graduate and research efforts is essential for ensuring optimum utilisation of resources, balanced development in tune with national needs and dissemination and exchange of innovative ideas. Such a co-ordinated approach will also prevent duplication of efforts. At present, planning, organisation and funding of post-graduate activities are under the auspices of different agencies. It is essential to avoid diffusion of efforts. It is recommended that effective support to all centres based on potential and proven capabilities be extended. This equally applies to management education at the Indian Institutes of Management and University Departments.

It is essential to optimise the utilisation of available resources and provide impetus to all the centres engaged in post-graduate programmes and research. The planning, organisation and funding of post-graduate and research programmes conducted at Universities, Indian Institutes of Technology, Indian Institutes of Management and affiliated College be undertaken by a single agency at national level.

5.3 At present short-term courses are being planned and organised by a variety of agencies like the Indian Society for Technical Education and other Quality Improvement Programme Centres. Co-ordination of the efforts of the various agencies will optimise the impact of these courses in terms of quality improvement of faculty and instructional processes.

A national agency be set up to co-ordinate the organisation of short-term courses.

5.4 The available potential of the industry to provide facilities for training of students during or at the end of educational programmes should be effectively utilized.

The Regional Boards of Apprenticeship Training to adequately staffed and strengthened with a view to ensure purposeful planning and supervision of apprentice training programmes.

5.5 The AICTE recommended that the State Boards of Technical Education be made statutory. This is a very important step towards reorganisation and reform of Polytechnic education. The Boards of Technical Education should be what the University is for degree education, with the difference that there will be only one Board for each State.

The State being the implementing agency for most educational programmes the State Directorates have a variety of academic, professional and managerial roles to play. This requires reorganisation of the State Directories.

The State Board of Technical Education be reorganised and vested with statutory powers to be more effective in their functions.

The Directorates should have organs dealing with manpower assessment, planning, co-ordination, controlling, monitoring and evaluation of educational programmes. Re-organisation of directorates to enable them to perform these professional functions effectively be undertaken as a matter of urgency.

5.6 It is necessary that institutions are in a position to react to the needs of the region in which they are situated. They should also be alive and alert to the changing requirements and organise programmes accordingly. This is possible only if the Principals and the Faculty members have the freedom to design courses and undertake projects and implement them. To enable such a situation to develop and grow, institutions need autonomy not only academically, but also administratively and financially. Such autonomy will release tremendous energies now available and remaining dormant in technical institutions.

Administrative autonomy and powers of financial control be given, by bringing all technical institutions including Government institutions, under suitably constituted governing councils and academic autonomy be given on a selective basis.

5.7 **The concept of 'Adoption of Polytechnics' by industry already recommended by the All India Council of Technical Education be pursued.**

5.8 The efforts towards improvement in instructional processes for the education and training of the right type of technical manpower will bear fruit only when the organisational climate in the institutions in conducive to development and growth. This, in turn, calls for effective management based on scientific management principles with regard to resources utilisation, human relations, organisational development, etc.

Short-term courses under Quality Improvement Programme, in

Educational Management be organised for training Heads of Institutions and Heads of Departments.

5.9 Technical Education in the country has reached such a stage of development that the growing innovative efforts in the institutions will have to be supported, encouraged and optimised. Increased professionalism on the part of the 'managers' of technical education in the areas of administration, planning, decision-making and organisational development has become vital. A Staff College for technical education could provide a solution to this problem by offering facilities for training in educational management, assisting Government agencies to plan and bring about policy changes in technical education and to monitor and evaluate the effect of these policy changes. This would also enable the technical institutions and other concerned agencies in the promotion and diffusion of new ideas.

Setting up a Staff College for Administrators of Technical Education be examined by an Expert Committee.

5.10 An objective assessment of the existing programmes should be undertaken and further support should be considered only on the basis of proven performance. Even for starting of new courses in the existing institutions, identification of new centres, support for research activities and project work, etc. it is desirable that an evaluation of the institutions, both from the point of view of their professional competence and future capability for advanced work, is done.

Continuous evaluation of institutions for maintenance of standards, as also total performance in respect of programmes, is essential. This will also enable identification of institutions with professional competence and capability to launch new programmes and projects and consolidate the existing programmes.

A National Evaluation and Accredition Agency be set up.

5.11 The All India Council of Technical Education has played a very important role, in the first two decades after independence in maintaining uniformity of standards in the technical education system in the country. Recent trends, however indicate that many important recommendations of the Council having a direct bearing on the improvement of quality of technical education have either been neglected or overlooked. Quality of technical education is vital to the maintenance of standards. If the All India Council of Technical Education is to be effective in ensuring balanced development of technical education in terms of quantity and quality, the Council should be vested with statutory powers like the Indian Medical Council.

The All India Council for Technical Education be vested with statutory powers for ensuring effective implementation of policies and programmes and maintenance of standards.

6. *Financing of Technical Education*

6.1 Linkage of engineering education with general education stands in the way of making adequate Plan provisions in tune with the objectives of engineering education. As with other sectors of professional adduction – like health and agriculture – technical education should be organised, managed and administered separately from general education, since it is essentially an investment for national development.

The plan allocations for technical education be commensurate with the developmental outlay of the other user departments, since technical education is developmental investment.

6.2 It is always not possible to get adequate financial support from Government agencies alone. In order to meet the increasing cost of technical education and provide proper inputs, it is increasingly necessary that Governmental efforts should be supplemented by all user agencies including public and private industry. In order to encourage industry to support technical education, it is recommended that as in the case of industry contributions for scientific research, contribution for technical education be deducted for purposes of Income Tax by amending Section35(1)(ii).

To provide the necessary incentive to industry, expenditure by industry on technical education including management education be deductable for purposes of Income Tax assessment.

6.3 Because of financial constraints at the State level, even the

Plan funds agreed to during the Plan discussions for purposes of technical education, are not always available, since allocations are not ear-marked for technical education. This has seriously affected the implementation of the approved schemes of technical education. To enable the system of earmarking of funds being spent on technical education, it is recommended that the pre-fourth Plan funding arrangement of making available directly to the institutions the Central Government's matching share of expenditure on approved schemes, be restored.

The system of making available the Central Government's share for approved schemes directly to the institutions, should be restored.

Recommendations of the All India Technical Council

The Council noted that the Ministry of Education had appointed a Working Group to review the present status of technical education including management education at all levels, to identify areas for development in the context of the nation's need during the coming decade, and to suggest re-orientation and improvement to the existing programmes.

The Council further noted that the Ministry of Education would prepare the Sixth Plan proposals on the basis of the recommendations of the Council on the report of the Working Group.

The Council thereafter examined various recommendations made by the Working Group and resolved as under:

1. Within the approved annual intake capacity each institution should increase the supply of technical manpower by improving the efficiency and effectiveness of educational processes. Shifts in the intake capacities between disciplines may be effected to cater to the emerging manpower needs.

2. All new courses should be based on well established and well defined manpower needs.

3. A reliable information system is a pre-requisite to planning, especially in the field of technical education and training. A national manpower information system should be established with a lead centre in the Institute of Applied Manpower Research for the storage, updating, retrieval and analysis of manpower information to assist technical education planning. The Institute of Applied Man-

power Research should be suitably strengthened for this purpose with provision of requisite facilities.

4. Credit system with provision for multi-point entry in part-time and full-time programmes should be introduced.

5. Industrial and rural development problems be identified and a greater emphasis on research programmes to tackle such problems be given in keeping with the national needs. Technical education institutions having the potential and capability to undertake problem-oriented and application-oriented programmes be selected and properly supported to facilitate substantial contribution to rural and community development.

6. Institutions be encouraged to set up Consultancy Centres to promote consultancy activities.

7. Relevant Management Education be integrated with professional courses at degree and diploma levels.

8. Courses in management education be restructured to provide for managerial manpower for small and medium sized industry as also for sectoral needs such as transport, power, health, education and agriculture, cooperation and cooperative banks.

9. Selected Polytechnics act as focal points to promote transfer of technology of the rural community. Such Polytechnics should be designated as 'Community Polytechnics' and adequate support provided.

10. Selected Polytechnics should be given central assistance to conduct advanced technician programmes.

11. Support be provided to strengthen the work of Curriculum Development and Research related to problems of technical education.

12. In addition to minimum academic qualifications laid down by AICTE, one year's industrial experience for lecturers and two years for senior staff is considered desirable. All recruitment should be strictly on merit, by open competition and on all India basis, subject to reservation because of constitutional requirements.

13. To ensure high quality performance, appropriate measures be taken for providing the necessary facilities. In this context the feasibility of making appointments to senior teaching posts (i.e., Professors and Heads of Institutions) on contract basis for five years, renewable after assessment be considered.

14. Personal promotion schemes should be established to enable promotion of deserving young faculty stagnating at a par-

ticular level. Such promotion be restricted to 20 per cent of the sanctioned strength.

15. An appropriate staff appraisal scheme based on a methodology acceptable to the faculty should be introduced. This would also enable identification of the needs of staff development.

16. Facilities for Masters' degree training under the Quality Improvement Programme be progressively reduced. Considering the number of teachers involved, provision for Doctoral Programme under QIP be increased to enable 250 teachers every year to enrol for Doctoral Programmes.

17. Provision be made to organise short-term courses for Polytechnic and Collegiate teachers in educational technology.

18. Selected Engineering Colleges should organise under Quality Improvement Programme three-year courses to enable Polytechnic teachers with diploma qualification to get Bachelor's degree.

19. Polytechnic teachers should be sponsored under the Quality Improvement Programme for industry oriented post-graduate diploma/degree courses organised for the purpose.

20. In order to ensure purposeful and meaningful interaction and collaboration between industry and institutions, "Fellowship" in the institution for willing and capable personnel from the industry be instituted. Similarly 'Residency' for institutional faculty be provided in the industry on the lines of QIP. Additional budgetary provision on staff to the tune of 20 per cent should be made to finance these schemes.

21. Admission to both degree and diploma courses be on the basis of carefully designed entrance tests. These tests should be conducted State-wise common to all institutions.

22. In order to reduce drop outs and other forms of wastage, it is necessary that special efforts in the form of remedial courses be carried out in the initial stages to help weaker students.

23. Flexible programmes of continuing education through part-time/full-time courses be introduced at all levels for serving personnel.

24. Representation be given to students in bodies concerned with farming the curricula.

25. Schemes for training of technical supporting staff be started under "Quality Improvement Programme".

26. To ensure better and more effective library services,

qualified and trained library staff be provided.

27. Adequate support be given to institutions to organise Audio-Visual and Reprographic services.

28. On an experimental basis, Learning Resource Centres be established in a few selected institutions.

29. The replacement of laboratory equipment which have become obsolete due to technological and curricular changes be examined. Laboratories be modernised with relevant, and versatile equipment with more instructional potential.

30. The tasks of planning and organising Technical Education from the level of craftsmen to that of technologists be brought under a single National Agency both at the Centre and States to ensure balanced development through an integrated approach.

31. It is essential to optimise the utilisation of available resources and provide impetus to all the Centres engaged in Post-graduate Programmes and Research. The Planning, organisation and prescription of norms for post-graduate and research programmes conducted at Universities, Indian Institutes of Technology. Indian Institutes of Management and affiliated Colleges should be coordinated by the Board of Post-graduate Engineering Education and Research of the AICTE.

32. The organisation of short-term courses under QIP be coordinated.

33. The Regional Boards of Apprenticeship Training be adequately staffed and strengthened with a view to ensure purposeful planning and supervision of Apprenticeship Training Programmes.

34. The Directorates should have organs dealing with Manpower Assessment, planning, coordination, controlling, monitoring and evaluation of technical educational programmes. Reorganisation of Directorates to enable them to perform these professional functions effective be undertaken as a matter of urgency.

35. Administrative autonomy and powers of financial control be given to all technical institutions including Government institutions by bringing them under suitably constituted governing councils. Academic autonomy be given to institutions on a selective basis.

36. The concept of 'Adoption of Polytechnics' by industry already recommended by the All India Council for Technical Education be pursued.

37. Short-term courses under Quality Improvement Programme in educational management be organised for training Heads of in-

stitutions and Heads of Departments.

38. Setting up a Staff College for Technical Educators be examined by an Expert Committee.

39. Maintenance of uniform standards in technical institutions in the country is the constitutional responsibility of the Central Government. It is therefore, necessary to coordinate and strengthen existing evaluation agencies.

40. To ensure effective implementation of polices and programmes of the Council, measures other than making it statutory, may be considered for the present.

41. The Plan allocations for Technical Education should be commensurate with the developmental outlay of the other user departments, since technical education is development investment.

42. To provide the necessary incentive to industry expenditure by industry on technical education including Management Education be deductible for purposes of Income Tax Assessment.

43. The system of making available the Central Government's share for approved schemes directly to the institutions should be restored.

50

WORKING GROUP ON ENERGY POLICY, 1977 – REPORT[1]

Chairman Shri N.B. Prasad

Members Prof. M. Datt Chaudhury; Shri S.N. Roy; Dr. M.G. Krishna (replaced by Shri S.C. Sinha); Dr. I.B. Gulati; Prof. A.K.N. Reddy; Shri R.K. Bhargava (replaced Shri C.R. Vaidyanathan); Dr. M.R. Srinivasan (replaced Shri J.C. Shah); Shri S. Chattopadhyay; Shri B.K. Agarwal (replaced Shri M.G. Nair); Shri S.K. Bose (replaced Shri S. Chattopadhyay); Smt Otima Bordia; Dr. K.C. Majumdar (replaced Dr. Y.K. Alagh); Shri T.R. Satish Chandra; Shri Nitin Desai; Dr. R.K. Pachauri; Dr. J. Gururaja

Secretary Shri T.L. Sankar

Appointment

The Working Group on Energy Policy was constituted by an order of the Planning Commission on December 6, 1977, with a view to "carry out a comprehensive review of the present energy situation in the light of recent development both within the country and outside, to develop a perspective for the next five to fifteen years and to recommend appropriate policy measures for optimal utilisation of available energy resources including non-conventional sources of energy.

Terms of Reference

(a) to estimate the perspective energy demand in the different sectors of the economy and regions of the country by 1982-83 and a decade thereafter;

---

1. Delhi, Controller of Publications, 1980, 121 p.

(b) to survey the present and perspective supplies of energy;

(c) to recommend measures for optimum use of available energy resources; and

(d) to outline the National energy policy for the next five years, fifteen years and the longer term conservation policy.

Contents

Chairman's letter forwarding the Report; The Approach; Tends in Energy Consumption; Forecast of Demand for Energy; Energy resources in India; Energy in the Household Sector; Energy in the Industries Sector; Energy in the Transport Sector; Policy for the Power Sector; Oil Policy; Coal Policy; Rural Energy Policy; Costs and Prices in the Energy Sectors; Research and Development in the Energy sector; An Overview; Annexures I and II.

Recommendations

15.1 The Working Group commenced its work in early 1978. The events in the international energy system during the past year and half (while studies and discussions were being carried on by the Group) have had a strong impact on the approach and the recommendations made by the Group in this Report. In the first half of 1978, it was widely recognised that the energy supplies, especially the oil supplies, would gradually run short of demand and that the previous trend of steadily increasing oil demand and matched supplies would yield place to new situation of declining total oil production in the world, irrespective of demand. It was expected that the transition from the past trends to the new situation would be managed in an orderly fashion through a combination of market forces and positive intervention by the Governments through public policies to regulate the consumption of oil products. But the events in the last few months—the disruption of oil supplies from Iran and the steep increase in oil prices twice within one year—have forcefully brought home the realisation that any energy policy formulation will have to start with the assumption that there can be no guarantee of steady oil supplies to any importing country in future.

15.2 The experiences within the country and out side have shown that there are severe limitations to the pace at which supply could be increased from conventional energy sources like coal, nuclear power and hydro-electric resources. The growing realisation of the dwindling supply of conventional energy resources and the resulting rise in the real price of energy are expected to bring about some economies in the use of fuels in general and of oil in particular. The estimates of Reference Level Forecast drawn up by the Group reflect the Group's view that even if no deliberate measures are adopted to restrain and regulate energy consumption, the rates of growth of demand for energy in the coming years would be somewhat moderate as compared to those observed in the past.

15.3 The demand for coal and oil arises not only for direct use as sources of energy but also for conversion into electricity and for non-energy uses. Taking all the requirements into account, the Group has estimate that by the year 2000 AD the coal requirements would increase to 530 million tonnes, oil to 92 million tonnes and electricity generation to 550 TWb under the RLF.[2] It is to be noted that the consumption of coal for power generation by the year 2000 AD as per this forecast would be around 220 million tonnes and the non-energy uses of oil and oil used for power generation would amount to 18.5 million tonnes. The overall rate of growth of requirement of coal increases as per this projection at the rate of 7.7 per cent year and of oil 5.6 per cent per year and electricity at 8 per cent year from 1978-79.

15.4 The Working Group felt that it would not be desirable and might not even be feasible to step up the supply of energy to these levels and that ways and means should be explored to bring about an overall reduction in the energy demand, of which the reduction in the demand for oil products should be the highest. The exercises to seek reduction in the energy demand, however, should assume that the growth of the economy in terms of GNP should not be reduced from the levels adopted for the Reference Level Forecast. The result of these exercises are set out as the Optimal Level Forecast in the Report (see Chapter III).

15.5 The Group has examined a large number of propositions and has recommended a number of measures to optimise the level and the pattern of use of energy. The major thrust of the policy prescriptions are towards:

---

2. These figures have been rounded off to the nearest conventional digits from Table 3.4. The requirement of coal and oil include quantities used for power generation and non-energy uses.

- — the curbing of consumption of oil to the minimum possible level;
- — conserving the use of energy by increasing the efficiency of its utilisation;
- — reducing the overall energy demand by lowering the intensity of energy consumption in the economy, particularly in the industries sector;
- — an increased reliance on renewable energy resources; and
- — a reappraisal of our economic development strategies, especially those elements of the strategy which have a direct link to energy consumption like technology choice, location policies, urban growth, mechanisation in agriculture, etc., with reference to the new awareness of the energy supply and demand in future.

15.6 Theoretically, options for substitution of oil by any other fuel should be examined case by case on techno-economic considerations. But under the current anticipation of rapidly increasing oil prices and possible discontinuities in the supply from time to time, the Group felt that it would be more pragmatic to examine all possible ways by which the consumption of oil could be restricted only to uses where it cannot be substituted.

15.7 In deriving the Optimal Level Forecast, the Group has suggested certain targets for the improvement in the efficiency of energy use which could be achieved at different points of time upto the end of the century. As the improvement in efficiency will require the replacement of capital stock which is currently in use by equipment which would be more efficient in the utilisation of energy, the targets for efficiency improvement have been assumed to be very small in the next five years but higher in each succeeding sub-period.

15.8 The Group feels that the targets for energy conservation suggested for different sectors in the report are moderate and could be improved upon if adequate institutional arrangements are made for each sector. It is necessary to examine the technological processes and the achievable levels of efficiency for each industry or equipment, and to prescribed the standards of efficiency to be achieved by energy users or equipment manufacturers. The systematic monitoring and the acceptance of all these norms may result in much higher levels of conservation than what has been assumed in the report. It is relevant to note that in countries where the efficiency of energy utilisation was higher compared to our country, it has been possible in the last few years to achieve substantial savings in energy consumption without affecting the rate and pattern of growth of the economy. The consumption of energy in industry in the United States is reported to have declined at the rate of 1.2 per cent per year on the average between 1973 and 1978, though a GNP increase of 2.3 per cent was registered during this period, and that the reduction was accomplished by conservation, recycling and burning of waste products. Given the relatively lower levels of efficiency of energy utilisation in many of our industries, it should be possible to achieve large savings in energy consumption by adopting appropriate conservation measures.

15.9 The pattern of growth especially in the industries sector which has been evolved in the last three decades on the assumption of continuously available and relatively cheap energy supplies, requires to be restructured now. The Group felt that within the overall industrial production there is too large a share of some of the very high electricity consuming industries like aluminium, ferro silicon, etc., and this results in the overall energy intensity of the industries sector being very high. In the transition towards the optimal level of energy consumption, measures to restructure the industrial strategy with low energy intensity industries deserve serious consideration.

15.10 The Group has also emphasised the scope for greater reliance on renewable energy resources. Among the renewable resources, hydro-power is the most important one as the technology for its greater utilisation is readily available. The share of hydro-power generation in the total electricity/energy supply has to increase in the coming decades. In consultation with Central Electricity Authority which is currently making a reappraisal of the hydro-electric resources, the Group has suggested a level of utilisation of hydro-electricity which is much larger than what has been contemplated in the past and which has become possible due to the upward revision of the estimation of hydro-electric resources. The Group has also indicated that there is scope for setting up micro-hydel power stations in the hilly areas and that the possibilities of developing low head hydel resources along canals should be pursued.

15.11 The Group has suggested that the use of agricultural waste and fuel wood should be encouraged in future. While the increasing agricultural production would give rise to increased agricultural waste, the increase in the level of its utilisation would depend on the development of appliances and technologies which would make it convenient to use this kind of fuel. The fuel-wood resources could be increased by taking up forest plantations at the village level which would enable there use as a household fuel without any change in technology and without increasing the costs of transportation and transformation. In general the Group has placed great reliance on renewable resources to supply the increasing needs of rural areas.

15.12 Though the Group has given anxious consideration to the utilisation of new energy sources like solar energy, wind power, tidal power, etc., it was felt that in the absence of reliable data regarding the investment requirements as most them are yet to the commercially tested and the cost benefits of these technologies are still uncertain, it would be hazardous to assume any supplies from such sources up to the year 2000 AD. The Group has, however, recommended R&D efforts on new energy resources as they might have to play a big role in the years beyond 2000 AD.

15.13 The strategy of economic growth adopted in our country has no doubt taken into consideration the endowment of resources and the major constraints to growth. The overall direction of growth, however, has been influenced by the internationally available technologies and the energy perspective of the world market in which abundant and inexpensive supply of oil and other relatively inexpensive forms of energy were the major elements. This has resulted in the ratio of energy consumption to GDP being high in our country. While it is generally maintained that there is a direct correlation between GDP and energy consumption, we do not have a full understanding as to why the intensity of energy consumption varies widely as between countries which are almost at the same level of economic well-being. A number of countries in the centrally planned economies seem to have high GDP even with low energy inputs. In our country a substantial portion of the energy supply is obtained in the form of non-commercial energy, animal power and human labour. One would expect that as a consequence of this, the consumption of commercial energy per unit of GDP in India would be low, but the facts indicate the opposite position. To some extent, this is due to the problem of computing GDP on a comparable basis for different countries at different levels of economic development. It is also due to varying levels of efficiency in energy utilisation. Even though more studies are required to understand the causes for the seemingly high energy intensity of the Indian economy, the Group is convinced that it is not only possible but necessary to reorient our strategies of economic growth in such a manner that the input of energy required to produce a given level of goods and services is reduced gradually over time. This would require a detailed study of the specific operations which should be mechanised in agriculture and industries, the type of technology that should be chosen to produce a given set of goods, location of different production activities in the country so as to reduce the requirements of transport of the inputs and outputs of production activities, the extent of urbanisation and various other factors. In other words, the economic growth strategies would have to be realigned so as to be consistent with the current expectations of increasing scarcity and price of all energy products in general and of oil in particular. The Group has made some broad recommendations in this regard but these are not based on any detailed consideration of factors other than energy which might also have a decisive influence on these issues.

15.14 The Group has felt that the decentralised energy systems also would have a place in future especially if production activities are likely to be decentralised. The extent to which this could be achieved is not predictable at this stage.

15.15 The Optimal Level Forecast has been drawn up based on the above assumptions. The implementation of measures proposed in the Report would bring down the requirements of energy to 427 million tonnes of coal, 69 million tonnes of oil and 457 Twh of electricity. The OLF reduces the demand for oil by 25 per cent as compared to RLF. Consultations with experts connected with coal, oil and electricity production suggest that the stepping up of the production to these levels in the next 20 years might not be very difficult in the case of coal and electricity. In the case of oil, however, there are serious misgivings about the possibility of obtaining the oil supplies to the level of 69 MTs by the year 2000.

15.16 The Group has assumed that in view of the limited resources of oil identified so far and the some-what sluggish rate at which additions to oil reserves are being made, the production of indigenous crude in the year 2000 would be about 24 million tonnes. This would mean that over 45 million tonnes of crude would have to be imported then. Though this would represent a very small fraction of the overall oil trade in the world, it would be unrealistic to assume that we could get increasing supplies of oil when the world production is likely to decline in absolute terms. On the basis of the current knowledge of resources and market conditions the general anticipation is that world oil production might peak some time during the eighties. Some time between 1980 and 1990 the maximum level of production would be reached and then the level of world production might decline. At that stage, all importing countries would compete to obtain a fair share in the available supplies. Whether the problem is resolved by market-forces or by physical quota allocations, it would be unreasonable to expect that India would be able to obtain steadily increasing quantities of oil during the nineties.

15.17 It therefore, appears imperative to prepare ourselves for the contingency of not being able to import all needed to the levels implied in this Report. The options to be considered in response to such a situation are either to increase further the production of crude from indigenous wells or to develop some liquid fuel which could substitute oil and which could be produced from renewable sources like agricultural products, either primary or waste products. Unless very large new oil discoveries are made, which are not anticipated in this Report, the increase of oil production would only shorten the life of our known resources. Theoretically, liquid fuels could be obtained from coal also. However, as the coal production for the other needs themselves add up to a substantial quantity by the year 2000, this proposition can be pursued only to a limited extent. Another option is the production of liquid fuels from renewable agricultural resources and to bio mass.

15.18 The production of liquid fuels to a level of twenty million tonnes might not be possible by merely utilising available agricultural waste, as the quantities of waste required to produce about 20 million tonnes of liquid fuel cannot be obtained by collecting agricultural waste. The production of large quantities of liquid fuels from bio mass would therefore require cultivation of an appropriate agricultural product like sugarcane or cassava on lands which are allocated exclusively for energy plantations. The Group was not able to examine in detail the viability and feasibility of diverting lands in use now for cereal production for energy plantations, as the decision has to be based on a study of all factors that determine optimal land utilisation. India with its large population and a meagre land-man ratio, might have serious limitations of the extent to which this option could solve the problem of liquid fuel shortages. The Group would, however, like to recommend that this option should be pursued to the extent possible.

15.19 The sombre fact that emerges from this study is that international action is inevitable to ensure the supply of even the minimal levels of oil consumption required essentially to support our economic growth. The fact that India would be requiring in per-capita terms very meagre quantities of oil and that shortfalls in obtaining even this quantity might affect the growth of the economy, the Group hopes, would be recognised in any system of oil supply to be devised in future in the international energy system to ensure equitable distribution of a scarce resource essential for the well being of the world. In the absence of such a support, the basic objectives of economic development of improving the economic level and quality of life of our people would be difficult to achieve.

15.20 While on the one hand the international community should become sensitive to the needs of India securing a certain minimum level of oil supply to achieve her economic and social goals and should evolve a system that could allocate the minimum needs at reasonable prices, on the other hand, all efforts should be made within the country to secure a low energy growth and to optimise the fuel utilisation pattern. These domestic efforts cannot be successful, if the action of energy issues are not pursued in a sustained and comprehensive manner under a central direction. The Working Group is of the view that energy policy-making could no longer be an exercise to be undertaken at periodic intervals, but should be a continuous one. Various policy measures suggested in this Report are only the broad outlines of policy for which the details would have to be worked out, implementing agencies identified and efforts for increasing production of energy supported with investment decisions. The efforts made in one sub-sector of the energy economy would have to be consistent with efforts made in other sub-sectors. The Group feels that such a coordination cannot be obtained under the present institutional arrangements. There should be a nodal agency which should take the responsibility for evolving the future energy policy options on a continuous basis, operationalising the policies into specific programmes, identifying agencies which must implement the programmes etc.

15.21 The Group discussed a number of alternative administrative structures which could achieve these ends. It felt that the best arrangements could be to have in the Energy Ministry the energy supply departments, viz., Coal, Petroleum, Electricity and Nuclear Power. In addition, there could be Wing within the Ministry to deal with energy policy formulation and coordination. The task of evolving suitable policies towards non-commercial energy resources and new energy resources could be specifically entrusted to this Wing. Though such an arrangement would involve the creation of a very large Ministry, which by itself might give rise to certain problems, the Group felt that on balance, this would be the most practical, effective and least expensive of the various alternative arrangements.

15.22 If, for any reason, it is found not feasibility to re-organise the Departments of the Government dealing with different forms of energy under a single Ministry of Energy, the alternative arrangements could be creation of an Energy Commission. Such a Commission should work directly under the Prime Minister and should report on issues of energy policy and its implementation so that the Prime Minister could coordinate effectively the activities of the relevant departments.

15.23 The broad conclusion that emerges from the studies of the Group is that Indian can no longer afford to take a fragmented and short-term view of energy policy issues. The growth rates that have been assumed for the economy are believed by experts as the minimum required to achieve the economic and social objectives of improving the quality of life of the people and alleviating poverty. If the present strategies of growth are continued without change to attain the projected levels of growth, the quantities and the pattern of energy requirements would reach levels which cannot be met. It is, therefore, necessary that measures towards optimisation of energy use are initiated from now on and implemented efficiently, so that supply of adequate energy would not set a constraint to growth of the economy. The Group would like to urge that all sections of the economy have to realise that the 'energy crunch' is not likely to be a transitional problem but a continuing one of increasing acuteness in the foreseeable future. Comparison of the levels of the energy consumption in India with those of developing countries with comparable population like USA, USSR and China, would not be very rational as the *per capita* energy resources available in India are far below what is available in these countries. In this context, the Group feels that while all attempts are made to conserve our resources of conventional fossil fuels by more efficient production and utilisation measures, the need to rely increasingly on renewable resources of the traditional types like firewood, agricultural and animal waste and on new energy resources like solar energy and energy plantations, cannot be over emphasized. If the importance of energy to support our plans of economic and social development is not fully recognised and action is not initiated in the right directions as indicated in this Report from now on and pursued vigorously, the Group feels that energy will become the major constraint to the growth of the economy. The Working Group herewith submits this unanimous report on the Energy Policy for the future.

51

COMMITTEE ON PANCHAYATI RAJ INSTITUTIONS, 1977 – REPORT[1]

Chairman	Shri Asoka Mehta
Member	Shri Karpoori Thakur; Shri Parkash Singh Badal; Shri M.G. Ramachandran; Shri B. Sivaraman; Shri Mangal Deo; Shri Kunwar Mahmood Ali Khan; Shri Annasaheb P. Shinde; Shri E.M.S. Namboodiripad; Shri S.K. Dey; Shri Siddharaj Dhadda; Prof. Iqbal Narain; Shri Vallabhabhai Patel
Secretary	S.K. Rau

Appointment

The Government accords the highest priority to rural development, so as to increase agricultural production, create employment, eradicate poverty and bring about an all round improvement in the rural economy. The Government considers that the maximum degree of decentralisation, both in planning and in implementation, is necessary for the attainment of these objectives. It has accordingly been decided, in consultation with the State Governments and Union territories, to set up a Committee to inquire into the working of Panchayati Raj Institutions, and to suggest measures to strengthen them, so as to enable to decentralised system of planning and development to be effective.

The cabinet secretariat in their Resolution No. 14/1/2/77-CF dated December 12, 1977, appointed the Committee on Panchayati Raj Institutions.

---

1. New Delhi, Government of India, Ministry of Agriculture and Irrigation Department of Rural Development, 1978, 301 p.

Terms of Reference

(1) To review the existing situation regarding democratic decentralisation in the States and the Union Territories, and the working of the Panchayati Raj Institutions from the district to the village levels, so as to identify shortcomings and defects. In particular, to examine the working of these institutions in respect of—

(a) Mobilisation of resources,
(b) Planning and implementation of schemes for rural development in an objective and optimal manner, and in looking after the interests of the weaker sections of society.

(2) To examine the methods of constituting the Panchayati Raj Institutions, including the system of elections, and to assess their effect on the performance of the Panchayati Raj system.

(3) To suggest the role of Panchayati Raj Institutions, and the objectives which could be attained through them, for integrated rural development in the future.

(4) To suggest measures for reorganising the Panchayati Raj system, and removing the short-comings and defects, with a view to enable these institutions to fulfil their future role.

(5) To recommend the form and content of the relationship that should exist between the Panchayati Raj Institutions, the official administrative machinery, and the cooperative and voluntary institutions involved in rural development.

(6) To make such other recommendations, including those on financial matters, as may be necessary to ensure adequate availability of funds for the discharge of the responsibilities that may be entrusted to the Panchayati Raj Institutions.

Contents

Introductory; Panchayati Raj : Review and Evaluation; Dynamics of Development; Panchayati Raj—An Imperative; Structures, Composition and Elections; Functions; Planning; Weaker Sections; Administration; Financial Resources; Human Resources Development; Relationship with other Institutions; Approaches and Recommendations; Annexures 1 to 12 and statements 1 to 8.

Recommendations

1. We are departing from the conventional mode of presenting our views, suggestions and recommendations in the form of an itemized summary because our main endeavour throughout has been to lay down a new approach towards the Panchayati Raj Institutions—not in the usual point-by-point way but rather in concentrical circles, as they interact and depend on one another. The formulation of structures, functions and the utilisation of financial, administrative and human resources of Panchayati Raj Institutions should, in our opinion, be determined on the emerging functional necessity of management of rural development. In our Report, we have attached importance to the direction rather than specifics on certain items usually done and hitherto highlighted in various cognate Reports. The institutional, structural and functional specifics of Panchayati Raj would, in our opinion, vary over time as well as space; we can do no more than indicate the spectrum of possibilities while the various State Governments would have to work out the actual details keeping in view their changing requirements. Whatever be the variations, they have to be round the crucial theme of linking institutions of democratic decentralisation with socially motivated economic development.

2. In the approach, it is not necessary to dwell too long on the past, except to locate the trend and draw guidance for the future. The dis-association of the growing and complex programme of development with Panchayati Raj Institutions which were considered inadequate, the inability of the bureaucracy to be attuned to execute the programme through elected bodies, the lack of political will to foster these institutions, several internal deficiencies in the functioning of Panchayati Raj Institutions and, above all, the lack of clarity about the concept itself have weakened the entire system.

3. Part of the disappointment arises from the syndrome that they have not been assigned significant functions and tried continuously and with zest. The developmental programmes were not channelled through them. Some of the comments like the emergence of oligarchic tendencies are inherent in the social milieu, and some others are common to other tiers of the polity also. Panchayati Raj Institutions should not be singled out for these comments. It has many achievements to its credit in introducing a process of democratic seed-drilling in the Indian soil, in breaking the gulf be-

tween the bureaucratic elite and the people and in generating a new leadership not merely relatively young in age but pro-social change in outlook.

4. Panchayati Raj, like democracy at the national and State levels, is both an end and a means. As an end, it is an inevitable extension of democracy; as a means, it would continue to be responsible for discharging obligations entrusted to it by the national and State Government in spheres not yet transferred to its exclusive jurisdiction. Altogether, both as an end and a means, Panchayati Raj should contribute to the philosophy as well as practice of a rich, rewarding life in rural India.

5. The establishment of democratic bodies below the State level is an imperative from the political and socio-developmental perspectives. Democratic institutions with periodic elections at all levels will provide a forum for the assertion of their strength in large number by the weaker sections. With the people and political parties having adequate opportunities to exercise power at various levels, national energy in political recrimination will yield to constructive competition and mutual co-operation in development activities among political parties.

6. Our recommendation to transfer substantial quantum of powers from the State Government to the local bodies, is bound to have concern with the existing scheme of distribution of powers between the Union and the States, which would require a detailed but separate consideration. In order to achieve requisite status as well as continued functioning, the Committee agree that some provision in the Constitution deserves a careful consideration of the Government of India.

7. On account of growth of the span, spatial scatter and the complexities of the development activities, as also significant changes in the strategies, the context of institution-building in rural India has undergone a change since the submission of the Report of Balvantray Mehta Study Team in 1957.

Among the striking changes in rural India, considered in Chapter II, the most important have been (a) imparting of dynamism to agriculture which was previously stagnant, (b) the enlargement of the concept of agriculture to cover allied occupations like dairy, piggery, fishery, social forestry, etc., which are of special relevance for the economy of the weaker sections, (c) assured availability, on an increasing scale, of new agricultural technology including scientific utilisation of major and minor irrigation, (d) emerging shifts in national policies towards cottage, village and rural industries at localised production points, (e) increasing possibilities for absorption of institutional credit for effective implementation of productive projects, (f) growing importance of marketing, involving a series of extra-local transactions, (g) the emergence of growth centres and need for tackling the rural-urban continuum, (h) increasing emphasis on group action and conjoint activities, (i) growing concentration on special efforts to organise and assist the weaker farmers in particular and poorer sections of society in general and finally, (j) coupled with the development urges, the evolving need for provision of the welfare and municipal utilities requiring, in the rural areas, different types of technical servicing functions.

8. The institutional, structural and functional contours of Panchayati Raj have to be in conformity not only with the accelerating pace of development but also with its strategies and policies. New structures of development administration or local level development management will have to take into account the functional necessities of the on-going development thrust. Panchayati Raj Institutions in the coming decades should, therefore, be equipped to undertake democratic development management under conditions of rapid changes, continuous growth and sustained innovations in all spheres of rural life.

9. State Governments should realise the social costs of administering expanding development programmes from a distance or through only governmental machinery. When they delegate the responsibilities for implementation to lower levels, they can concentrate on refinement of strategies and higher-level policy-making in the management of challenges of development administration in areas such as rural land structural deficiencies, agricultural modernisation, rural industrialisation, credit universalisation and planning for fuller utilisation of natural resources.

Structures, Composition and Election

10. The institutional design for Panchayati Raj should take into account the functional necessity of propelling the on-going developmental thrusts, build upon the intricacies at the appropriate levels and transmit the impulse to the people through location-specific involvement.

11. The emerging scenario of the dynamics of development necessitates that the technical expertise of a high order be made available at levels below the State to sustain the momentum of rural development, which, in many cases, has been already administratively decentralised at the district level. The inescapable compulsion, therefore, is that the district should be the first point of decentralisation, under popular supervision, below the State level. (IV.6)

12. Below the district level, the balance between technological requirements and possibilities for meaningful participation by the people in development management can, in our view, be best achieved, by grouping a number of villages to constitute Mandal Panchayats. These would not only ensure an economic viability; this will enable the people's representatives to exercise democratic supervision over the large number of micro-projects which are to be implemented at the local levels in the coming years. Most of these projects are not entirely village-based but would require a span of technology beyond the capacity of a Village Panchayat. The attention to the family-based programme, often covering as many as four hundred families, needs larger unit to tackle them than at present. Such a Mandal Panchayat would cover a population of 15,000 to 20,000 and would also facilitate the forging of necessary linkages with schemes for development of local points and growth centres and would ensure efficient management of the growing rural-urban linkages. (IV.2 to IV.8)

13. While our preference is for two tiers—a district-level Zilla Parishad and a Mandal Panchayat—we are conscious of the fact that two other tiers are already in existence and it may take time for the suggested institutional design to take shape and become fully operational. The block-level Panchayat Samitis, where they exist now, would be converted into non-statutory executive committees of Zilla Parishads and when the Mandal Panchayats become active, most of their functions would be taken up by the Mandal Panchayats. As a transitional structure, the Block can, therefore, continue as per the convenience of the States keeping in view their requirements and the stage of development. At the village level, the people would be involved in Mandal Panchayats through Village Committees which would look after the municipal functions and related welfare activities. Till the Mandal Panchayats are constituted, a federation of existing Village Panchayats may be desirable. (IV.6, IV.6.1 and IV.6.2)

14. Regarding the composition of the various tiers of Panchayati Raj, we would like to suggest only a broad pattern. We would, however, like to make it clear that whatever be the structural arrangements, the directly elected element must preponderate over the others at all levels. In the elections, the Scheduled Castes and Scheduled Tribes should get representation on the basis of their population. The Chairman of Zilla Parishad will be elected indirectly. The President of the Mandal Panchayat may, however, be elected directly or indirectly as the States may decide. The term of all the elected tiers should be 4 years, and, as far as possible, election to all these bodies should be held simultaneously. (IV.11.3 and VII.8.3)

15. Our proposals regarding the structures would have to be necessarily modified in case of areas with predominant tribal population or in hilly or desert areas. Thus, in tribal areas Mandal Panchayats may be formed for smaller population as necessary. Again, in tehsils/blocks where strong traditional tribal organisations are functioning, they may be allowed to look after their social functions. Similarly, structures established by the Constitution under Schedule VI need not be disturbed. (IV.7.1, IV.7.2, IV.8.1 and IV.8.2)

16. The Zilla Parishad should consist of six types of members, viz., members elected from suitably demarcated electoral divisions, President of the Panchayat Samitis on an *ex-officio* basis, nominees of bigger municipalities, nominee of district level cooperative federation, two women who have secured the highest number of votes in the Zilla Parishad elections (in the event of no women coming forward for election, to women may be co-opted) and two co-opted members—one with special interest in rural development and the other drawn from University/College teachers. The Chairman of the Zilla Parishad would be elected from amongst the directly elected and *ex-officio* members by all the members.

17. (a) The Zilla Parishad would function through a number of Committees, the more important ones being constituted for Agriculture, Education, Small Industries, Finance and Public Works. The composition of all the Committees would be on the basis of proportional representation so as to ensure representation to all sections and shades of opinion. A Committee of the Chairman of these Committees will function as the Standing Committee of the Zilla Parishad. There will be a Committee

on Social Justice in Zilla Parishad as well as at other levels also.

(b) All members of the Zilla Parishad and M.L.As., M.L.Cs. and M.Ps. from the concerned district shall constitute the Planning Committee at the district level for plan formulation and periodic review.

(c) A suitable Committee for dealing with the problems of Education staff like transfers to be comprised of members of Zilla Parishad, a representative of the State Government and the District Education Officer with a view to bring in evenness and method in transfers and postings. (IV.10, IV.15, VII.10.1, VII.10.2, VI.11 and V.5.3)

18. Panchayat Samitis, till they continue to exist, should consist of the following categories of members: (1) Presidents of the Mandal Panchayats, where they have been constituted, on *ex-officio* basis, (2) Zilla Parishad members elected from electoral divisions in the Mandal Panchayat areas, (3) nominees of smaller municipalities and block-level cooperative federations, (4) one co-opted member, having special interest in rural development. The President of the Panchayat Samiti would be elected from amongst the *ex-officio* and directly elected members of the Zilla Parishad from the Samiti area by all the members. In approximately 1000 Talukas/Blocks (where either the Scheduled Castes constitute 20 per cent of total population or the Scheduled Tribes are majority of population) the Chairmanship of Panchayat Samitis can be reserved for them. (IV.9, VII.8.4)

19. The Mandal Panchayat would consist of the following categories of members:

(a) fifteen members directly elected on village' *cum*-population basis;

(b) representatives of Farmers' Service Societies; and

(c) two women securing the highest votes in Mandal Panchayat elections (if none contested, two women may be co-opted).

The President of the Mandal Panchayat would be elected by the directly elected members from amongst themselves. The President may, however, be elected directly as the States may decide. Seats may be reserved for Scheduled Castes/Scheduled Tribes on a population basis in the Mandal Panchayat. A Committee with all women members of the Panchayat represented on it would also ensure that decisions are made by women themselves on priorities and choices in welfare and development programmes specifically for women and children. (IV.9, VII.9.2 and X.10.2)

20. The Village Committees would consist of the following categories of members: (1) members elected to Mandal Panchayat from the respective electoral unit, (2) members elected to the Zilla Parishad from the respective electoral units, (3) representatives of small and marginal farmers. The Village Committee will be presided over by the Member of Mandal Panchayat elected from the village concerned. (IV.9)

21. The Gram Sabha has an important role in activating the democratic process at the grass-roots and deserves genuine encouragement. The proposed Village Committees would have the special obligation to organise two Gram Sabha meetings every year to explain to the people what programmes the Mandal Panchayats are executing in their area and to channelise the people's feedback to the Mandal Panchayat. (IV.5)

22. The Nyaya Panchayats like the Gram Panchayats were adopted as institutions for dispensation of justice at the local rural level.

The working of Nyaya Panchayat has shown mixed results, in most cases they remained inactive. The administration of justice on a decentralised basis has its merits but the functioning of the existing Nyaya Panchayats have not been able to elicit popular satisfaction.

The Committee are of the view that Nyaya Panchayats should be kept as separate bodies and should not be mixed with the people elected for development panchayats. The members of development panchayats wield executive powers and there are chances that justice may suffer if the two functions are combined.

The Committee are in favour of a combination of a qualified judge to preside over a bench of separately elected Nyaya Panches. The elected Nyaya Panches will not be entitled to seek re-election; they should serve in an area other than that from which they have been elected. (IV.18, IV.18.1, IV.18.2 and IV.18.3)

23. Panchayati Raj elections should be conducted by the Chief Election Officer of the State in consultation with the Chief Election Commissioner. (IV.16.1)

24. The State Government should not supersede the Panchayati

Raj Institutions on partisan grounds and if supersession becomes necessary, these should be replaced by an elected body within six months. The State Governments should not postpone elections of Panchayati Raj Institutions. (IV.16)

25. Participation of political parties in Panchayati Raj elections would ensure clearer orientation towards development programme and facilitate healthier linkages with higher level political process. Direct elections coupled with programme-based contests, would offer great scope to weaker sections for availing of the opportunities offered by the political system. (IV.14)

Functions

26. The functions developed upon Panchayati Raj Institutions being highly location-specific, exhaustive list of functions, in an all-India perspective, will not have much operational relevance. Local priorities in all development programmes vary from region to region and it is, therefore, necessary that the States and the Union Territories should have adequate scope for evolving their own list of functional priorities.

27. Our basic approach with regard to decentralisation is, that of spectrum of functions and tiers; development being a dynamic process, functions cannot remain static. Periodic adjustments would, therefore, have to be made in the functions devolved upon Panchayati Raj Institutions to suit the changing requirements. But this does not mean that decentralisation can be viewed as a political charity or administrative concession. The functional agenda of Panchayati Raj Institutions would be inescapably determined by the unfolding logic of "dynamics of development"; in the interests of effective implementation State Governments would have no choice but to decentralise adequate powers and functions and provide proportionate financial resources at the relevant local levels.

28. Keeping in view the foregoing approach, all the development functions relating to a district which are now being discharged by the State Government would have to be placed under the Zilla Parishads. Some of the functions which can be so decentralised include: agriculture and allied sectors, health, education, communications, rural industries, marketing, welfare of backward classes, family welfare, etc. Even under these heads certain parts may have to be with the State Government. Thus, functions such as agricultural research, college

and university education, medium irrigation projects and other similar items involving complications or cutting across district boundaries may not be transferred to Zilla Parishads. (V.4)

29. Under the new scheme envisaged by us, the decentralisation would commence with the district as the first point and further movement below will take place depending upon the situation in each State. Broadly, the Zilla Parishad will handle all the decentralised State programmes and plan for them at the district. The Mandal Panchayat will handle the implementation work. (V.3.2)

30. Mention is needed of cooperation (which should remain outside the purview of Panchayati Raj Institutions) and education (which must be entrusted to Panchayati Raj Institutions). In our view, cooperation should not be under the Zilla Parishad as it would be placing one set of elected bodies under another. The Panchayati Raj Institutions can limit themselves to motivating and organising the co-operative movement at this stage. As regards education, we feel that it can be transferred to Zilla Parishad with the proviso that a committee should be specifically constituted to look after transfers and postings. Supervision by local bodies will, in our view, not only improve the attendance of teachers but it is anticipated that the ratio of drop-outs will decrease. The programmes on adult education will also be accelerated. (V.5.1, V.5.2 and V.5.3)

31. The entrustment of development functions to Panchayati Raj Institutions would remain incomplete unless all the Panchayati Raj Institutions are vested with the authority to take their own decisions and plan according to their own requirements. Planning would, therefore, be an important function to be discharged by the Zilla Parishads. (V.6.1)

32. The functions of the Mandal Panchayats would have to be viewed from a new angle. They would be responsible for implementation of the schemes and projects assigned by the Zilla Parishad. These would be many. They would have to play a promotional role in activating community action, build up organization and project formulation. They would continue to perform the functions conventionally assigned to them under various statutes. They would have increasing role to play in the sphere of municipal and welfare functions. (V.7)

33. Elaboration of an omnibus list of Mandal Panchayat functions has no relevance unless there is genuine decentralisation accompanied by corresponding resources. The foregoing classification

of the Mandal Panchayat functions would, indeed, facilitate the process of decentralisation by helping the task of identification of areas in which further decentralisation can take place. What is, therefore, needed at the Mandal Panchayat is purposive work allocation and transfer of money component alongwith the functions assigned to them for implementation. This would not only introduce clarity into the expenditure pattern, as also help the State-level Heads of Departments in specifying the operational procedures for execution of various plan projects. In general, Mandal Panchayats have to administer coordinate, and provide institutional supervision to on-going field level projects. (V.7, V.7.3, V.7.4, V.7.5 and V.7.51.)

34. The Panchayati Raj Institutions in general and the Mandal Panchayat in particular can play an important role in the sphere of municipal and welfare functions by supplementing the State Plan outlays in this regard. Many of these requirements might be so local that even such comprehensive programmes as the R.M.N.P., may not be able to cover them; but the Mandal Panchayats are more intimately concerned about such items. (V.9)

35. In view of the fast moving developments and transitions, the regulatory functions may continue to be vested in the Collector but such regulatory functions which are germane to implementation of various development programmes should be assigned to the appropriate tier of Panchayati Raj. Further, the Revenue Department should be reoriented to encourage and facilitate the working of Panchayati Raj Institutions. (V.10, V.10.1 and V.10.2)

36. The devolution of regulatory functions upon the Panchayati Raj Institutions may be reviewed in due course of time when the Zilla Parishads have been properly established and are in a position to make and implement their own plans with the quantum of resources available or placed at their disposal. (V. 10.5)

37. The Mandal Panchayats would have to be suitably integrated with growth centres. They would have to take the necessary decisions concerning marketing, input supplies, credit and servicing and welfare requirements in association with other organisations in this regard. (V.11)

38. In due course of time the Mandal Panchayat will have to be the base-level organisation for project implementation and as such they would not only take over the functions of the Block but higher level technical expertise will be made available at lower levels. Some of the block-level functions would have to be moved upwards as only

the district-level body would be competent to discharge them. (V.12.1 and V.12.2)

Planning

39. With the district as the strategic level for economic planning, the Zilla Parishad should be made responsible for planning at the district level. The appreciation of the total resources, the credit availability and the necessary strategy formulation covering several blocks would be feasible at the district level. An elected Zilla Parishad would also provide the much needed correctives to the techno-economic plans. The production and employment programmes prepared at the Block level will fit into the totality of the plan. (VI.1, VI.6.1 and VI.8)

40. A professionally qualified team should be stationed at the district level for preparation of district plans. The composition of this group would be on the lines suggested by the Expert Group on Block level Planning. While formulating the plans, the expertise of the district level staff should take into account a cross section of all shades of public opinion relevant to the district. (VI.9.1, VI.9.2)

41. The State Government would have to provide continuous assistance in the process of district planning. It would have to ensure that the national objectives relating to weaker sections are pursued by the Panchayati Raj Institutions. They will also have to provide the financial and physical parameters as well as technical expertise to the technical group. It should also ensure equitable allocation of resources and fixation of long-range priorities. (V.10)

42. The district plan prepared by the technical group would be placed before the "committee of the whole" of the Zilla Parishad where the MPs, MLAs and MLCs are also members. (VI.11)

43. The State Government should provide necessary machinery for examining the district plans to enable formulation of the State Plans. It should also hold a dialogue with the Zilla Parishads in this regard. (VI.12)

44. The District Planning should take care of urban-rural continuum. The District Plan should also analyse data on growth points and growth centres in order to provide for necessary economic flows. (VI.13.1, VI.13.2)

45. Intensive exploitation of new opportunities of resources earmarked for the Weaker Sections should be a part of the plan process

itself. The District Social Justice Committees will be of considerable help in this regard. (VI.13.3)

46. The on-going exercise of District Planning should also take into account the formulation of sound projects and short-terms action plans covering areas of specific endowments, poverty belts and specific target groups. (VI.13.4)

47. In order to avoid the problem of non-implementation and non-absorption of the many "delivery systems" which are already functioning, the several implementation components of all the local-level projects should be analysed in advance and greater attention should be paid towards synchronization and orchestration of the activities of the project-level functionaries of the different disciplines. Coherent activity analysis, standardized micro-project plans including flow-charts of goods, services and functionaries will also have to be prepared so that the Mandal Panchayat can play an effective role in administrative coordination and institutional supervision. (VI.14.1, VI.14.2)

48. At present, some districts are too large to facilitate drawing up of composite plans. Keeping in view, among others, the guidelines of compactness, effectivity, manageability and the number of representatives in the Zilla Parishad, smaller districts would be desirable. (VI.15)

49. To begin with, the Mandal Panchayats may be limited to implementation and promotional roles, but they would have a key role in supplying the necessary information about the various schemes and suggest the potential areas of development as well as their requirements to the Zilla Parishad. They would have to play this role on a continuing basis and not merely by holding a meeting to consider the draft plan or sending their comments on it to the Zilla Parishad. The planning unit at the district level should take note of the views articulated by the Mandal Panchayats from time to time. (VI.17)

50. The total credit inflow for agricultural development is expected to rise significantly in the years to come. The Panchayati Raj Institutions should, therefore, pay greater attention to the institutional finance rather than concentrating on budgetary sources as in the past. This would be possible only if the Panchayati Raj Institutions pay due attention to ensuring greater responsiveness in project implementation by ascertaining the views of the beneficiaries since these require considerable people's participation like the Revised

Minimum Needs Programme. (VI.18, VI.19)

51. The Panchayati Raj Institutions should not only be regarded as a forum for obtaining the views of people's representatives but, in due course, they should become capable of planning for themselves within the resources available to them. (VI.20)

Weaker Sections

52. The Scheduled Castes and the Scheduled Tribes constitute the bulk of the rural poor and their welfare has been enjoined by the Directive Principles of State Policy. Besides, a number of development programmes have been launched for this purpose. The inability as well as the structural inadequacies of the Panchayati Raj Institutions to benefit the weaker sections of society have made us very anxious to provide structural as well as programmatic remedies to ensure that they derive, in adequate measure, the benefits of the planned development of the country. Their confidence in the developmental role of Panchayati Raj Institutions and participation in the functioning should be assured through several measures.

53. Among the institutional devices for ensuring adequate representation commensurate with their numbers we would like to recommend the following: (i) In order to provide a fair deal to Scheduled Castes and Scheduled Tribes their representation in all Panchayati Raj Institutions should be on the basis of their population, (ii) 666 talukas/blocks where the Scheduled Castes constitute more than 20 per cent of the population and in 329 talukas/blocks where Scheduled Tribes constitute a majority of population, the principle of reservation should be extended to elective offices, (iii) the reservation system can be supplemented by formation of Social Justice Committees where the Chairman should be only from Scheduled Castes/Scheduled Tribes, (iv) with a view to provide political support to the objective of protection of the interests of the weaker sections, a Committee of the Legislature with, as far as possible, majority representation of MLAs/MLCs belonging to Scheduled Castes/Scheduled Tribes should be set up to review the working of the programmes meant for these communities. This Committee would also be responsible for social Audit of funds earmarked for Scheduled Castes/ Scheduled Tribes. (VII.9.2, VII.9.3, VII.10.1 and VII.10.2)

54. In order to ensure that the weaker sections of society derive maximum benefits from the various plans we would like to suggest

that there should be an independent authority to carry out 'Social Audit' of the funds and programmes earmarked for the Scheduled Castes and Scheduled Tribes and ensure that projects designed for them are implemented in a way that the desired impact is not diluted. To begin with, a separate wing may be created in the existing audit set up and the Collector may be made responsible for supplying to the Government all the data required for Social Audit. (VII.11.1)

55. Development programmes leading to diversification of occupational pattern have a great degree of relevance for the Scheduled Castes and Scheduled Tribes; the Panchayati Raj Institutions should be involved in opening up these occupational vistas in rural areas in such fields as dairying, poultry farming, piggery, fisheries, scrub jungle forestry, etc. (VII.131 and VII.14.2)

56. Panchayati Raj Institutions as people's institutions can provide the field-level support to Finance/Development Corporations for Scheduled Castes/Scheduled Tribes, (which are in operation in some States and should be established where not yet in existence) providing financial and technical assistance for various programmes beamed at Scheduled Castes and Scheduled Tribes. (VII.15)

57. It should be the special responsibility of the State Government to ensure, through purposeful administrative measures (both protective as well as developmental), that the scale-neutrality of the new technology is maintained, credit flow is made accessible to the poorer sections of society for credit-worthy programmes and development of their skills is continuously fostered. A number of physical resources are still available under the control of Panchayats and Panchayat Samitis which are not being fully realized for the benefit of the poorer sections of the community. In some cases certain influential people in the village have encroached upon such resources. The State Governments should undertake necessary eviction proceedings and launch a vigorous drive to restore these to the Panchayati Raj Institutions; it is also necessary that the relevant regulatory functions should be placed under the Panchayati Raj Institutions as part of their developmental functions. (VII.16.1 and VII.16.2)

58. Among the various development programmes which can be implemented for the benefit of Weaker Sections on the hitherto unused or neglected communal resources we would like to make a special mention of social and farm forestry and brackish water pisci-

culture. Composite culture of brackish water fish and prawns has an immense economic potential which must be harnessed for the benefit of the Weaker Sections. The scientific utilisation of unused areas under reserve forests and protected forests as well as the areas lying between villages and reserve forests where various easement rights prevail can be used to settle landless labour as well as provide effective support to animal husbandry. A time-bound programme to link up the development of such land and water resources with the poorer families should be made an important part of States' responsibility to be implemented through Panchayati Raj Institutions and continuously monitored by the Social Audit Agencies, the Social Justice Committee and the Committee of Legislature. (VII.16.3, VII.16.4, VII.16.5 and VII.16.6)

Administration

59. Our basic approach to remoulding of the administrative organisation of Panchayati Raj Institutions is that administration must drape well with the body politic and fit its contours. With the decentralization of the functions of the State Government, all the concerned district-level officials would, therefore, have to be placed under the Zilla Parishads and lower tiers. A separate development administration functioning on a decentralized basis would, thus, develop along with a composite Zilla Parishad Secretariat. (VIII.1, VIII.2.1 and VIII.2.2)

60. The Constitution of elective organisation to supervise and direct development programmes would certainly upset the existing administrative routines but the various problems of personnel management and personal adjustments should not be allowed to stand in the way of this change over; the administrative apparatus would have to adapt itself to this fundamental change. (VIII.3.1, VIII.3.2)

61. The Maharashtra and Gujarat experience provides many pointers to tackle the problems relating to promotions, protection of pay and other emoluments and maintaining uniformity in service conditions. Generally speaking, all staff of Gazetted rank in Class I and Class II should continue to remain on the cadres of the State Government while the Class III and Class IV should be fully handed over to the Panchayati Raj Institutions. There should be adequate provision for inter-changeability between the State level officers and

Class I and Class II working under the Zilla Parishads. The recruitment of the Zilla Parishad staff may be done by independent State—and district-level boards. (VIII.3.3)

62. All developmental staff with the Zilla Parishad should be placed under an officer to be designated as the Chief Executive Officer of Zilla Parishad. The Chief Executive Officer will achieve horizontal coordination *vis-a-vis* the other district heads who will be Secretaries of the respective subject committees of the Zilla Parishad with Chief Executive Officer being an invitee to the Committees' sittings. (VIII.4, VIII.5.1)

63. Zilla Parishad will be responsible for policy formulation supported by any specific decisions taken by its committees, but the main responsibility for the entire implementation work should be that of the Chief Executive Officer. The development executive should be of a sufficiently high rank; a person who has successfully "done" a district for a period of not less than 3 years should, therefore, be appointed as Chief Executive Officer. (VIII.5.2, VIII.5.3)

64. Some transitional, mainly personnel, problems involved in division and transfer of the entire district staff into State and District cadres are inevitable. (VIII.6)

65. Even after the decentralization of district-level functions to Panchayati Raj Institutions, the State Government would continue to maintain some district-level staff for the execution of its schemes but the extent of dualism of staff would be restricted to State functions which would be determined at the time of decentralizing the powers to the Zilla Parishad. (VIII.7)

66. The Collector would continue to exercise the regulatory, revenue and other functions assigned by the State Government. He would also organize and help the conduct of 'Social Audit'. The role of the Collector may have to be reviewed later when some of the regulatory functions of the State are sought to be transferred to the Zilla Parishad. (VIII.9)

67. Mandal Panchayat would be handling the developmental as also municipal and welfare functions. It would, therefore, be possible for them to have a full-time Panchayat Executive Officer, instead of part-time assistant. His salary and emoluments should be appropriate to attract sufficiently qualified personnel. There is considerable staff of different development departments at the field level: in due course, this staff (e.g., such officials as the Agricultural Extension Officer, the Veterinary Stockmen, the Fisheries Extension

Assistant, Commercial Crop Extension Workers, Small Industries Promotion staff and the health sub-centre staff, etc.) should move to the Mandal Panchayat level. (VIII.10.1)

68. As far as technical inputs are concerned, the line-hierarchy will not be broken. The staff in the Zilla Parishad will be under the control of their superiors for technical matters giving scope for technical line control but they would be under the Chief Executive Officer for purposes of administrative control. The Confidential Character Rolls of the District level technical staff written by the Chief Executive Officer will, therefore, be countersigned by the concerned Head of Department. The Confidential Character Rolls of the Chief Executive Officer, written by the Chairman, could be countersigned by the Commissioner of the Division. (VIII.11)

69. On account of increase in the volume of development work and their growing complexity, it would be necessary to constantly study the developmental requirements and mould the structures and functions of the State-level departments looking after the Panchayati Raj Institutions. There should be a Minister for Panchayati Raj whose main tasks would be as follows:

(a) Enactment of Panchayati Raj legislation;
(b) Elections to Panchayati Raj Institutions;
(c) Training of elected officer bearers and executive officers and administration of all Training Centres meant for the Panchayati Raj system as a whole;
(d) Promotion of Audit of Panchayati Raj Accounts;
(e) Review of Panchayati Raj activities for report to the State Legislature; and
(f) Promotion of camp training of elected members of Panchayati Raj.

For the routine administrative work, a strengthened Directorate of Panchayati Raj and a Secretariat Department under a Development Commissioner would be necessary but all the development departments would have to play a role in the successful working of Panchayati Raj Institutions. (VIII.13.2, VIII.13.3 and VIII.13.4)

70. As a part of the evolution of a new administrative culture, the Heads of Departments from the State Headquarters can call on Chairman, Zilla Parishad on their visits to the district to acquaint him with the essential features of the visit. The Chairman, Zilla Parishad

should also establish rapport with the various State level Directors for achieving smoother and streamlined delivery systems. (VIII.12)

71. The Panchayati Raj statutes should be so framed as to facilitate the transfer of full powers. The responsibility of the Council of Ministers at the State level is particularly significant in this regard as two Committees of Legislature will be looking after the entire performance of Panchayati Raj Institutions. (VIII.13.5)

72. The State Government should also arrange for periodical independent evaluation of the working of Panchayati Raj Institutions by independent agencies including educational institutions with the Universities playing an important part. (VIII.13.6)

73. The Government of India also have the special obligation to strengthen the process of democratic development management at the rural level. They have to ensure that development programmes falling in the district sector do not, in any way, by-pass the Panchayati Raj Institutions. The suggestions made by us such as increasing the training facilities will require the Centre to play a positive role. (VIII.14)

Financial Resources

74. The current situation in the flow of funds to Panchayati Raj Institutions from diverse channels has been analysed and the possibilities have been pointed out for either strengthening or emulating the procedures from other States, for augmenting the resources. While this process may have to continue for sometime, it requires to be emphasised that any proposals for financial devolution of financial decentralization should not emanate from a traditional approach but from our basic commitment to the logical imperatives of the dynamics of development which clearly postulate the entrustment of a great deal of developmental functions at the district level, with the Mandal Panchayat playing a key implementation role. (IX.12.1)

75. Apart from the budgetary devolution from the State Government, the Panchayati Raj Institutions also should mobilise enough resources of their own. No democratic institution can continue to maintain its operational vitality by depending upon external resources. The thesis "no taxation, only representation" should be discouraged. For this purpose, all Panchayati Raj Institutions should have compulsory powers of taxation. A select list of taxation powers should be given to the Panchayati Raj Institutions and out of them

some should be made compulsory. It is not possible to have a standard list for all States. But certain taxes like house tax, profession tax, entertainment tax, special taxes on 'land and buildings' should be levied compulsorily by the Panchayati Raj Institutions at appropriate level. (IX.12.2, IX.5.4)

76. The taxation powers given to the Panchayati Raj Institutions should be limited and specific and must not operate inequitously. Certain occupations and professions in whom the weaker sections predominate should be exempted, through statutory provisions, in order to ensure social justice. (IX.5.4)

77. Incentives can be offered for optional taxes realised. These may take the shape of award of prizes or provision of matching grants. (IX.10.4)

78. In addition to taxes, the Panchayati Raj Institutions should levy fees/taxes for services like lighting, sanitation, water supply, etc. The maxima and minima of these fees should be laid down to avoid arbitariness or lack of uniformity. (IX.12.3)

79. At this stage, land revenue, cess on land revenue, cess on water rate, surcharge on stamp duty, entertainment tax and show tax, etc., should also be assigned to the Panchayati Raj Institutions with higher percentage to Mandal Panchayats. To provide local initiative, the Panchayati Raj Institutions must be statutorily empowered to request the State Government to increase the cesses. In this context, the Committee recommend the complete transfer of land revenue to Panchayati Raj Institutions in a phased manner over a period of five years taking into account the buoyancy of other taxes. (IX.12.4, IX.8.2 and IX.8.3)

80. In the emerging rural development programme, the transfer of public properties such as porambokes, grazing lands, unreserved forests, orchards, public lands, cattle ponds, fishery tanks, ferries, quarries, etc., would have great significance and these should be statutorily vested in the Mandal Panchayat in cases where it is not already done. This is not a mechanical transfer but for the purposes of maximising the yield out of these resources; this activity will increase as a part of their functions. In the emerging context of escalation in their potentialities and fiscal worth, markets, hats, shandies, fairs, etc., will be a significant source of revenue. Hence, custody of such fairs, hats and other markets should be vested with the Panchayati Raj Institutions. (IX.12.5)

81. With a sizeable population-base and a territorial jurisdiction

covering a number of "markets" the Mandal Panchayat would be able to tap a more diversified resource-base with greater intensity and elasticity. It is these revenue yielding sources that should be built up both with budgetary support of Government and institutional finances. Such sources will be mostly with Mandal Panchayats but can be transferred to Zilla Parishad, depending upon the size of the source. A scheme of support by State Government from budgetary sources carrying small or no interest supplemented by institutional finance would go a long way in helping the Panchayati Raj Institutions to proceed with their aims of establishing remunerative enterprises. (IX.11.3)

82. Apart from the taxation powers of their own and transfers effected through several possibilities indicated earlier, a permanent annual grant of not less than Rs. 2.50 per capita should be available to the Mandal Panchayats. It should be the objective; the quantum of several transfers should be, at least, to this target. (IX.12.6)

83. As the power to impose taxes should not be divorced from the responsibility for their collection, the officials of the Panchayati Raj Institutions should themselves collect the taxes. (IX.6.1)

84. Combination of Patwari and Secretary as per the suggestion of the Santhanam Team is not desirable. At the time of consolidation of holdings, the provision for reserving areas for common purposes should be strictly enforced and these should be entrusted to the Mandal Panchayats. It would be possible for the Mandal Panchayat to economise on too many part-time or full-time low paid Secretaries and get the services of a better paid Secretary who would look after the collection of taxes and also be responsible for the other functions entrusted to the Mandal Panchayats. (IX.6.2, IX.6.3)

85. The burden of collection of land revenue should be left optional to the concerned Panchayats, but the Mandal Panchayats collecting land revenue should get a commission commensurate with the results so as to provide a built-in incentive. When the Mandal Panchayat comes into full-fledged existence the policy may, however, be reviewed again. (IX.6.4)

86. When all functions relating to Plan implementation at District level are transferred to the Zilla Parishad, this will also involve transfer of the finance along with the projects. The allocation of the projects/plan funds has to be done on a formula worked out to achieve equity among the Districts and weightage to backward areas. Further, the non-plan expenditure incurred at the District of lower

levels should also be under the administration of the respective tiers, since it would be conducive for composite development work and build up the capabilities of Panchayati Raj Institutions. (IX.9.4)

87. Administrative expenditure on the salaries, allowances, etc., of the staff transferred as on the date of transfer, be given as a grant to the Zilla Parishads or to the other concerned tiers. (IX.10.3)

88. The appointment of a State Finance Commission does not appear to meet the situation. The major need is more to achieve an equitable distribution of plan allocations. (IX.10.9)

89. The establishment of a new financing body, like a Panchayati Raj Finance Corporation, dependent partly on public borrowing, is not likely to add to the total availability of the credit. What is required in this context is a greater rural orientation to all the financial institutions to facilitate greater flow of credit to rural areas. (IX.11.6)

90. The pattern of budgeting, followed by the Panchayati Raj Institutions, should be simple. (IX.13.2)

91. The State Governments also will have to evolve a budgetary procedure which will indicate the transfers of different types of the Panchayati Raj Institutions. (IX.13.4)

92. Each State Government may, taking into account the local circumstances, prepare comprehensive guidelines for the use of their officers and Panchayati Raj Institutions for preparation as well as for approval of budgets. (IX.13.5)

93. An important element to be emphasised both in the preparation of the budget as also in its format is the emphasis need to be placed on sufficient allocation and earmarking of the funds for the projects for the Weaker Sections. The quantum provided and the appropriate utilization for the target-group would be within the jurisdiction of the Social Audit. (IX.14.6)

94. Approval of budget by a higher authority seems to be a desirable practice, as it provides a linkage and also enables the higher level tiers of Panchayati Raj to know what is happening at the lower tiers and also to make suggestions for better utilization of such funds. (IX.13.7)

95. A sufficiently high ranking finance officer should be placed at the district level as the entire plan and non-plan funds would be under his supervision. (IX.13.8)

96. Every State should endeavour to present consolidated finance accounts of Panchayati Raj Institutions to the Legislature. (IX.14.1)

97. State Governments should immediately review the delay in audit which is partly caused by inadequate staff and partly by lackadaisical procedures. (IX.14.2)

98. Quick clearance of the outstanding audit objections pertaining to Panchayati Raj Institutions has special importance in view of the proximity and involvement of people's representatives with the expenditure at these grass-root levels. (IX-14.3)

99. A concurrent audit by the Examiner of Local Funds Accounts should be made operative instead of post audit. (IX.14.4)

100. Procedures for submission of utilisation certificates by the Panchayati Raj Institutions for the grants given by Government must be made simpler. (IX.14.5)

101. The State Governments should consider the establishment of a Committee of the Legislature to be specifically concerned in the financial and physical performance of Panchayati Raj bodies. Alongwith the consolidated finance accounts, the State Government should also lay on the Table of the Legislature, an Administrative Report on Panchayati Raj Institutions. (IX.15, IX.16)

Human Resources Development

102. The human factor is not only a component of growth but also shapes the texture of the society. In many ways, therefore, the human resource is more vital than the financial. Development of human resources should be, therefore, a primary feature of Panchayati Raj Institutions. (X.1)

103. There should be three types of training: (i) for officials; (ii) for elected representatives; and (iii) combined courses for both officials and elected representatives together. The programme content would vary as suited for each participating group. (X.3, X.4 and X.5)

104. The training programmes, covering officials as well as non-officials, would be of a staggering dimension. This would require not only the activation of the existing institutions but also considerable augmentation of their numbers and resources. Suitable remedial measures should also be taken to resuscitate and revitalize the State-level training institutions. (X.6, X.7 and X.7.1)

105. The National Institute of Rural Development should be the apex all-India institution for training of trainers, field studies, developing consultancy capabilities, research work and improvement in the level of training in the States. Its faculty should be

strengthened and upgraded for this purpose. The Government of India has an important role to play in this regard. (X.7.3, X.7.4 and VIII.14)

106. There should be an evaluation for each of the training programmes so that it will be possible to make necessary modulations from time to time. (X.7.5)

107. Importance should be attached to the programmes for adult education to develop the latent civic consciousness in all the people and thus strengthen the faith in the working of the Panchayati Raj Institutions. The Panchayati Raj Institutions should have a major role in organising such programmes. (X.8)

108. As a large segment contributing for the successful operation of a democratic system, special attention is to be paid to the role of women in Panchayati Raj Institutions. Their role could be strengthened in two ways: by allowing them to participate in the election processes more actively and also by giving them opportunities for decision-making. (X.9 and X.10.1)

109. To secure their participation in elections, for the two seats reserved for women in the Zilla Parishad and Mandal Panchayat, any women who gets the highest number of votes in the election, even if she does not win, should be taken in as a coopted member. (X.10.2)

110. There should be a Committee of Women to operate and look after specific programmes which largely concern women and children. This would ensure that they do not become victims of the process of change and that decisions are made by women themselves on priorities and choices involved in their programmes. Such a Committee should have the powers of the Mandal Panchayat with reference to the programmes specifically assigned to them. (X.10.3)

111. In designing the Rural Industrialisation programmes there should be special efforts to concentrate on programmes to provide gainful employment to rural women. This will also strengthen their management capabilities. (X.10.4)

112. The formation of Mahila Mandals should be encouraged. (X.11)

113. The present and the future success of the democratic process through Panchayati Raj Institutions lies with the rural youth. (X.12)

114. Rural youth is not yet fully covered by the Yuvak Mandals; this weakness had to be attended to. Young farmers clubs can be formed to activate the interest of the rural youth both in Panchayati

Raj Institutions and rural development. (X.13)

115. The Yuvak Mandals should be given the status of an associate body in Panchayati Raj Institutions through suitable legislative measures. (X.13)

116. Panchayati Raj Institutions have a motivational task in organizing Nehru Yuvak Kendras. (X.14)

117. It would be advantageous to organise National Service Scheme camps through the Panchayats. (X.15)

118. The role of voluntary agencies in mobilizing people's support for Panchayati Raj will be crucial. They should be strengthened and encouraged to supplement the efforts of the Panchayati Raj Institutions. The motivational and promotional role of the Panchayati Raj Institutions should be clearly spelt to build up and facilitate the work of voluntary agencies and women's organisations. (X.11, X.17)

119. Voluntary agencies with requisite expertise, proven standing and well-equipped organization can assist Panchayati Raj Institutions in the planning process. They can be involved in formulation of projects and schemes and to create strong public opinion in support of measures aimed at social change. (X.18)

Relationship with other Institutions

120. The Panchayati Raj Institutions are expected to take up the overall view of the economic and social well-being of the people, while the cooperatives have to meet the economic requirements. The relationship between the Panchayati Raj Institutions and cooperatives has thus to be coordinate rather than of a subordinate character. (X1.2, X1.3)

121. The pattern of functional relationship between the Panchayati Raj Institutions and the cooperatives will broadly be of five types:

(i) Functions which could more appropriately and effectively be discharged by Cooperative Institutions;
(ii) Functions requiring concurrent and conjoint action of Panchayati Raj and Cooperative Institutions;
(iii) Cooperatives functioning as agents of Panchayati Raj Institutions;
(iv) Functions in respect of which Cooperatives require facilities from the Panchayati Raj Institutions; and

(v) Where Cooperatives participate in functions which are essentially the responsibility of Panchayati Raj Institutions. (XI.3.1, XI.3.2)

122. Panchayati Raj Institutions should undertake the promotional and coordination work like motivation and organisation of cooperatives. The regulatory functions in respect of cooperatives should be done by the cooperatives themselves. (XI.4)

123. Representation from the cooperatives on the Panchayati Raj Institutions will be helpful in providing an institutional dialogue between the Panchayati Raj Institutions and the Cooperatives. A reciprocity of representation of Panchayati Raj Institutions on the cooperatives does not appear to be necessary. (XI.5)

124. Urban-rural relationship is to be viewed in the context of needs of a developing economy and the attendant processes of affording higher level of services and facilities. Integration of rural-urban areas in a balanced reciprocity of economic and social growth can be achieved by linking up the rural areas with urban focal points. (XI.6)

125. With the existing small panchayats, in due course, giving place to larger Mandal Panchayats, the relationship between the Mandal Panchayats and small municipalities would become more purposive and meaningful; with some amount of equality, they can even enter into formal relationship for supplies and services. (XI.8.1)

126. The merger of small municipalities with Mandal Panchayats would be desirable. The local points and growth centres will facilitate this process. (XI.8.2)

127. For purposes of composite planning, the District Plan should encompass the developmental aspects of urban areas and the civic aspects of rural areas. (XI.8.3)

128. The representation of the municipalities in Zilla Parishad and other appropriate areas will strengthen the process of urban bodies integrating their work with that of the Mandal Panchayats. (XI.8.4)

129. Smaller Municipalities should be treated at par with Mandal Panchayats for providing benefits flowing through various Special Agencies such as SFDA, MFAL, etc., to the people living in these towns. (XI.8.5)

130. Panchayati Raj Institutions can assist the Centre and State-sector corporations and boards established particularly for commer-

cial activities with promotional and marketing components. In this context, the role of Panchayati Raj Institutions would consist of creating the local organization and locating the area-wise specialities. (XI.9)

131. Zilla Parishad will be responsible for assessing the over-all credit requirements and arranging for its inflow by localizing the needs and locating the areas. The lower tiers should follow this up. (XI.10)

132. Mandal Panchayats should assist in the establishment of Regional Rural Banks by providing necessary infrastructure and also help the banks in verification procedures or in the analysis of the viability of loan proposals. (XI.11)

52

WORKING GROUP ON EDUCATIONAL TECHNOLOGY, 1977 – REPORT[1]

Chairman Shri P. Sabanayagam, Secy., Government of India, Ministry of Education and Social Welfare

Members Shri Mushir Ahmed (Represented by Shri K.K. Garg); Shri Ajit Bhattachajea (did not attend the meetings); Shri Anil Bordia; Shrimati Nirmala Buch; Shri E.V. Chitnis (represented by Shri B.S. Bhatia); Dr. Ishwar Dass; Shrimati A. Dayanand; Shri M.V. Desai; Shri L.S. Gaur; Dr. O.P. Gautam (represented by Shri S.K. Mukherji); Shri A.S. Gill (did not attend the meetings); Shri Girdhari Lal; Shri Giri Lal Jain (did not attend the meeting); Shri T. Jankiraman; Dr. S.K. Mitra; Mrs. V. Mulay; Dr. D. Shankar Narayan; Smt. Padma Ramachandran; Shri C.G. Rangabashyam; Shri Ramesh Chander; Dr. S.N. Saraf (represented by Shri T.N. Dhar); Shri H.S. Shahani (did not attend the meetings); Shri A.P. Shinde; Shri Krishan Sondhi; Shri Anil Srivastava; Shri D.M. Sukhthankar; Shri S.H. Vatsyayana

M. Secy. Miss S. Rahman

Appointment

The Union Ministry of Education and the State Departments of Education are deeply concerned with the need to improve the quality of education, to widen access to education and to reduce the existing disparities between the different regions of the country as well as different sections of the population. The task has to be carried out expeditiously, effectively and within the limitations of available

---

1. New Delhi, Ministry of Education and Social Welfare, 1978, 145 p.

resources. The Educational Technology Programme aims at contributing to the achievement of these objectives by deploying the modern communication technology, notably the mass media in the educational process. The recent Satellite Instructional Television experiment has established the potential of satellite broadcast television by showing that it is possible to reach effectively and at low cost, very large number of school children, adults, teachers and extension workers in remote areas where communication and educational facilities were inadequate. The expansion of the television network in India and the availability of INSAT by 1981 promise a bright future for educational development provided the educational planners and administrators can create an appropriate infrastructure for exploiting the new technologies to the fullest possible extent. Needless to say the Educational Technology Programme has assumed much greater importance in the wake of the high priorities accorded to universalization of elementary education on the one hand and adult education on the other.

So the Ministry of Education set up a Working Group on educational technology in order to identify the role of educational technology in education, to determine the priority areas, to workout detailed schemes and to indicate their financial implications in December 1977.

Terms of Reference

(i) development of a concept of educational technology in relation to Indian conditions;

(ii) formulation of a set of broad guidelines for the development of educational technology programmes;

(iii) strengthening the three implementing agencies, i.e., Centre for Educational Technology, Educational Technology Cells and Educational Technology Unit in the light of experience gained;

(iv) provisions for guidance and coordination at the Central level between educational and media organisations;

(v) identification of the roles and functions of governmental and non-governmental organisation concerned with the development of the programme;

(vi) provision of continued financial support from the Central Government on a greatly enhanced basis, in continuation of earlier assistance to all the states and throughout the Sixth Plan Period.

Contents

Foreword; Introduction; Report of the Working Group; Appendices from I to VIII, Enclosures from I to IV.

Recommendations

Report of the Working Group

1. *Review and Problems*

Review

Early beginnings: The Educational Technology Programme is essentially aimed at improving the quality of education and widening access to education through the utilization of the media of mass communication and all instructional technology. Government's interest in improving the quality of education by the use of technological aids and devices goes back to 1947 when the audio-visual scheme was included in the educational development plan. It had the limited objective of promoting the use of educational films and sound broadcasting in addition to the other projected and non-projected aids.

Over the years almost all States set up audio-visual units. These units maintain film libraries for loan to schools and educational institutions which have projectors. Films are also screened by mobile vans in local schools which do not have projectors. In a few States the units have developed some expertise in the maintenance and repair of equipment and training teachers in the production and use of simple audio-visual materials. In the area of educational broadcasting, the audio-visual units have promoted the purchase of receiving sets by schools but made little effort towards ensuring the utilization of the educational programmes broadcast by the All India Radio.

On the whole the programmes has not taken root and in most States today it has come to a virtual halt. The failures of the audio-visual programme were dud to several reasons. In the first place, it was not conceived as an integral part of the educational system and was thus not provided adequate material and manpower support. Most State units have small budgets and an audio-visual education officer, an odd-job-man, and projectionist-cum-clerk.

Secondly, a programme mainly based on the use of educational films, required support of an indigenous film production movement with roots in all States of arrangements for large scale adaptation and dubbing of selected films produced elsewhere. This support is still not available. Other audio-visual materials, such as filmstrips and educational charts, were also not freely available. Nor did the schools have adequate production facilities to enable even interested and trained teachers to produce the simple aids needed by them. Furthermore, it has taken a long time for teacher training colleges to realise the importance of audio-visual education and to integrate it in their training programme. Thus the production and availability of software, training of teachers in audio-visual methods and provision of hardware in schools were all far from adequate. In these circumstances the use of audio-visual aids remained an optional or peripheral exercise with only the interested and competent teachers making use of the limited provisions.

Although this programme did aim at supplementing the resources at the disposal of the teachers, its coverage remained limited mostly to better off institutions in the urban areas and its benefits could not be extended to the institutions in the rural and economically backward areas. This resulted in widening the disparities between different institutions and groups covered by the formal system. The audio-visual programme also failed to make any substantial contribution to educational programmes outside the formal system.

Broadcasting was a medium that could reach large number everywhere and at low cost, but educationists were unable to realise or to take full advantage of its potential for educational purposes in the formal system. Radio sets were not provided in adequate numbers and teachers found it difficult to integrate a centrally produced and broadcast programme with the varying requirements of classroom schedules in different institutions. The educational support in the planning and production of programmes was inadequate in most States.

Educational Technology Project: A second beginning was made in 1971-72 with the development of the Educational Technology Project as a new scheme for the Fourth Five Year Plan. This Project was intended to stimulate the use of television as well as other instructional media, notably radio and film, to improve the quality of education. However, the scheme was formulated with a distinctly different emphasis, the objective being to *create an infrastructure* necessary for the utilization of television facilities for education which were to become available under the Satellite Instructional Television Experiment and also under gradually expanding terrestrial television in the country. The infrastructure would involve collaboration on a systematic basis between media agencies and educational institutions in the planning, production and use of media programmes, preparation of support materials, provision and maintenance of hardware, training of user teachers and a variety of other personnel, undertaking research and investigation in the implications arising out of the induction of these media in the educational system.

The scheme was conceived as a broadbased and collaborative effort among the Ministry of Education, the Ministry of Information and Broadcasting and the Indian Space Research Organisation. It underlined the importance of inter-agency coordination, systematic planning, scientific research and proper utilization. Operationally, the project sought to extend the benefits of technology to large groups, particularly those in rural areas. Its stated objective was to improve the quality of education at all levels, to reduce stagnation and wastage and eventually to restructure the methods of education.

The scheme was centrally sponsored and envisaged the setting up of three agencies: (a) an Educational Technology Unit in the Ministry of Education for policy formulation, coordination and financing the ET programme; (b) a Centre for Educational Technology in the NCERT for research, training and prototype production in support of ET programmes; and (c) Educational Technology Cells in the State Department for Education for promoting the use of Educational Technology for the expansion and improvement of education in the State.

Assistance was initially provided for three years. However, as the scheme was slow in taking off and as the States wanted assurance of assistance for five years, the Ministry of Finance agreed to extend assistance beyond the Fourth Five Year Plan. Under present arrangements five years of assistance (or till the end of 1978-79 whichever is earlier) is available. ET Cells have been set up in 17 States.

During the Fourth Five Year Plan a token amount of Rs. 21.32 lakhs was allocated. During the Fifth Plan, the overall provision amounted to Rs. 26906 lakhs. The expenditure incurred up to September 1978 was Rs. 133,20,945. The Statewise and yearwise expenditure on the ET Cells is indicated in Table 1. A detailed review of the development of the Educational Technology Project is given in Appendix VIII.

Programme Operation in SITE States: Although the programme was initiated in 1971-72, it took off only with the launching of the Satellite Instructional Television Experiment in 1975-76. Under SITE, instructional television programmes were transmitted directly from the satellite to reception sets in rural areas. The experiment covered 2,330 villages in widely separated clusters in six States (Andhra Pradesh, Bihar, Madhya Pradesh, Karnataka, Orissa and Rajasthan). The television programmes were transmitted in the morning to primary school and in the evening to general population. The television sets were placed mostly in primary schools, community halls or *Panchayat ghars.*

The Educational Technology Cells provided support for the proper use of educational television programmes in the primary schools. They also assisted in the organisation of the evening television programmes broadcast for other sectors of the population. The ET Cells were made responsible for, among other things, appointment of custodians, reimbursement of salaries, payment of electricity bills, keeping and rendering accounts. This work, although not properly falling in the domain of the functions of the ET Cells, underlined the importance of creating State level agencies for ensuring the proper use of mass media. In this process, the ET Cells gained some insight into the complexity of organizational and management structures necessary for large scale planning for the use of media.

As part of their functions, the ET Cells arranged the training of uses teachers in the handling of television sets and use of television programmes. They prepared, translated, printed and distributed the support materials, supervised and evaluated the experiment in the participating schools. They also assisted in the planning of programmes and training of script writes. Some ET Cells undertook in depth studies of the impact of educational television programmes. These studies have been instrumental in bringing about a better understanding of the implications of the television process in education. As a result, the ET Cells are beginning to plan the post-SITE television programmes with greater understanding and clarity. Also they are engaged in promoting the use of radio in primary schools not covered by television. They also employ radio and TV for training primary schools teachers to avoid dislocation, to cut down avoidable training costs and to maintain continuous contact with the teachers during and after the training.

TABLE 1: Grant-in-aid to State Government for ET Cells

Name of State	(Fourth Plan) 1972-73	1973-74	(Fifth Plan) 1974-75	1975-76	1976-77	1977-78	1978-79	Total (in Rs.)
1	2	3	4	5	6	7	8	9
1. Maharashtra	50,000	1,70,048	1,28,000	1,44,193	1,75,730.35		—	6,14,971.35
2. Rajasthan	—	75,762	31,943	3,12,752.50	1,85,800	1,01,717	—	7,07,974.50
3. Andhra Pradesh	—	—	1,22,608	3,07,250	1,90,643	81,120	1,84,480	8,86,101.00
4. Bihar	—	—	66,680	2,76,874.38	1,55,025.38	22,743	26,520	5,47,842.76
5. Karnataka	—	—	63,179	2,74,683	3,05,756.76	1,13,119	—	7,56,737.76
6. Madhya Pradesh	—	—	83,261	2,78,613	1,78,527	49,593	1,34,925	7,24,919.00
7. Orissa	—	—	1,10,784	3,41,900	1,67,282	96,990	1,60,212	8,77,168.00
8. Gujarat	—	—	—	88,500	—	74,500	—	1,63,000.00
9. Punjab	—	—	—	1,49,700	—	79,456.87	69,500	2,98,656.87
10. Tamil Nadu	—	—	—	—	1,70,872	1,17,750	50,000	3,38,622.00
11. Uttar Pradesh	—	—	—	—	50,000	40,881	—	90,881.00
12. Himachal Pradesh	—	—	—	—	—	1,00,000	—	1,00,000.00
13. Jammu & Kashmir	—	—	—	—	—	1,40,000	—	1,40,000.00
14. Nagaland	—	—	—	—	—	72,150	—	72,150.00
15. Manipur	—	—	—	—	—	1,06,588	95,680	2,02,268.00
16. Meghalaya	—	—	—	—	—	9,200	—	9,200.00
17. Sikkim	—	—	—	—	—	—	1,00,000	1,00,000.00

The ET Cells also participated in large scale teacher training programmes organized by the CET through a multi-media approach. These programmes trained about 47,000 teaches in two phase and involved a large organizational effort in planning the package and using it.

Programmes Operation in non-SITE States: The ET Cells in Maharashtra and Tamil Nadu have built up an infrastructure for educational television broadcasts by the Television Stations in Bombay and Tamil Nadu respectively. The ET Cell in Tamil Nadu has done pioneering and substantial work in providing, through a special drive, radio sets to almost all primary, middle and secondary schools. It has also taken several measures to integrate the broadcasts with the school system. The ET Cell in Punjab is planning ia thematic approach to schools broadcasting. The ET Cell in Gujarat has launched a training programme involving 10,000 primary school teachers aimed at improving English teaching. The programme consists of a carefully planned series of radio broadcasts and printed materials and has been developed in collaboration with the All India Radio, State Institute of Education and H.M. Patel Institute of English. In Kerala, the SIE has been engaged since 1975 in organizing radio-cum-correspondence teacher training programmes in collaboration with the All India Radio and other State agencies. The experience of these programmes led the State Education Departments to realise the need for establishing a special agency like the Educational Technology Cell for operating such programmes.

Problems

The Working Group noted that he progress of the Educational Technology Programmes had been hindered by certain factors. Some of these are listed below:

Lack of Adequate Staff: The scheme provided for the officer-incharge of the ET Cell and two programmes-cum-scriptwriters with some supporting staff. Inadequate as this provision was, it was often not respected. There were frequent changes which undermined smooth operation and development of the programme. Most of the staff members were hot trained, not even exposed to orientation programmes. The suggestion made to the States to amalgamate the Audio-Visual units with the ET Cell to improve the staff situation was not implemented for various reasons. Moreover, the scheme did not provide for staff with managerial and technical skills which are necessary for an educational technology programme.

Inadequacy of Physical Facilities: The physical facilities were also unsatisfactory. The accommodation of an Educational Technology Cell is usually a room or two which is barely adequate for seating arrangements of the three officers and their supporting staff. The offices are often in depressing and slum-like conditions, exposed to dust, wind and rain and variations in temperature altogether altogether inadequate for a technology programme. The equipment made available is lying unused partly for lack of space and partly for lack of technical staff.

Absence of Coordinating Mechanism: While the implementation of an educational technology programme depended on the close collaboration between media agencies and departments of education, appropriate mechanisms for coordinating their efforts were generally not established or where established were show to develop.

Unsatisfactory Pattern of Assistance: The piece-meal manner of assistance and uncertainty about the period for which it would be available has discouraged several States from taking advantage of the 100 per cent offer of Central assistance. This has led to the under-utilization of budgeted funds and uneven development of the programme. States which wanted a clear assurance of five years of such assistance have so far remained outside the scheme.

Lack of Acceptance: Educational Technology is new discipline. In India it has been in operation for a very short period and its methods and concept have not been fully understood by all concerned. This has resulted in slow acceptance of the Educational Technology Programme.

2. Concept of Educational Technology

Education involves the transfer or communication of information, knowledge and skills from one point (the source) to another (the receiver). Until recently this process depended on the spoken word (through the medium of the teacher), supplemented by printed material and occasionally facilitated by the use of audio-visual aids.

The development of the technology of communication has placed at our disposal the means to transfer knowledge more effectively to larger number of receivers at multiple points irrespective of the distance between the source and the receivers.

Educational Technology implies the full deployment for education of the new means of communication and would thus embrace all educational methods and media offered by communication technology for dissemination of information and knowledge. This would require identification of media, selection of educational content with best lend themselves to treatment by these media, and the best methods which can be adopted for the purpose.

In the Indian context, the media presently best capable of serving the national priorities in education and should be selected.

3. Guidelines for Developing Educational Technology Programmes

The major thrust of Educational Technology programmes should be to promote the universalisation of elementary and adult education and enlargement of opportunities for secondary education.

The Educational Technology programmes should make widespread use of radio, television and printed media with a view to reaching out to the largest possible numbers in the different groups. Television is an effective and persuasive medium for education. In anticipation of the nationwise television coverage with INSAT by 1981, more emphasis should be given to the development of this medium as an important part of Educational Technology programmes.

It is imperative that the Educational Technology programmes should be conceived for development and operation on a massive scale to make it possible for them to contribute to the national goal of achieving universalisation of education in the next five years.

The Educational Technology programmes must develop fundamentally new approaches to make education accessible to all, especially to the deprived sections of the population and thereby supplement in a massive way the formal system of education which cannot expand rapidly enough to meet socio-economic aspirations of the people. Appropriate organisational and production structure would be required to support these programmes.

The Educational Technology programmes must develop new contents and methods leading to new learning outcomes which should facilitate the change in the educational system to make it more relevant and functional.

The Educational Technology programmes have to be directed towards arousing motivation for learning and for activising self-instruction among the recipients.

The Educational Technology programmes have to be geared to creating awareness among the people of their rights as human beings and to help them attain those rights. They should also arouse a keen interest in the environment. These programmes should generate salutary pressures.

The Educational Technology programmes will require the support of all development agencies, namely planning, education, health, agriculture, etc., to make an impact on social and economic development.

The Educational Technology programmes must be constantly evaluated, reviewed and modified to make them as effective as possible.

4. Role of Educational Technology

The main function of education is communication of knowledge, skills and attitudes. The mass media have great potential in communicating them effectively. Much greater use of these media for education especially for non-formal education, will make it possible to promote universalisation of elementary and adult education and programmes of educational expansion at other levels as well.

Television

Research studies have indicated that television, if properly used, has great potential for education and training of all types of personnel. Therefore, wherever available, telecast facilitates should be exploited fully. A beginning could be made almost immediately in the SITE States where TV facilities are directed to rural audiences. Intensive utilisation of existing facilities will provide the much needed experience in the management of large scale operations involving the use of a sophisticated, complex and capital intensive medium. It would also involve coming to grips with problems concerned with the planning and production of TV programmes, training of technical personnel, maintenance and repair of hardware, utilization of TV programmes, linking TV programmes with development activities and activising the ET Cells and other educational institutions. All this experience will in turn prove invaluable for making better use of the INSAT in 1981.

Television has a definite role to play in the eradication of illiteracy. It is the only medium which can reach out to the large number of illiterates in a persuasive and readily understandable form of communication. Television also lends itself to non-formal methods of communication which have proved quite effective with adults.

In the area of teacher education, there is an urgent and persistent need to improve the quality of teachers both in content and methodology. Here also television can play an important role by utilising such techniques as micro-teaching, CCTV and supplementing the correspondence courses for teachers.

Since most of the under qualified teachers come from single teachers schools, generally located in rural areas, they cannot be removed from their respective schools for the purpose of training. Instructional TV can play a vital role in their training *in situ*.

Universalization of elementary education has the highest priority in educational plans. This would involve additional enrolment of 30 million children during the next five years, as against the normal addition of one million children per year. It will be difficult to achieve this target unless television is used on a massive scale both inside and outside the formal system.

Radio

Although radio does not have as powerful an impact as TV, it does offer the possibility of extensive development in education because of the infrastructure available, the comparatively low cost of receiving sets and our long experience with this medium. If supported by printed and visual materials, the potential of radio becomes enormously high for educating all kinds of groups including children. Its special appeal would be in establishing contact with specific groups in hilly, snowbound or otherwise inaccessible areas where the isolation of the community needs to be broken before any change can be brought about. Radio communication, specially for these areas, would prove to be the cheapest means of establishing contact on a continuing basis. In course of time, it would become a two-way system of communication in India as in other countries.

Print

TV and radio are ephemeral media of communication. For educational purpose, where storage and retrieval of information is an essential feature, both these media will have to be supplemented by various kinds of print materials. If radio and TV are to be used for providing fresh approaches to the transfer of knowledge, the supplementary print materials should be an essential and integral part of the Educational Technology Programmes. These materials should be workbooks, reading materials, notes and guidebooks for instructors, time tables and schedules, etc.

Other forms such as newspaper and printed publicity will be needed to create the motivation and environment for change. New kinds of newspapers will have to be developed to satisfy the needs of neoliterates, to provide a regular flow of information and to consolidate their newly acquired abilities.

5. Priorities for Educational Technology

Educational Technology programmes should accord priority to areas of education and learner groups as follows:

I. *Elementary Education*

(i) *Children in elementary schools:* A non-formal approach will be adopted, aimed at releasing the young from the boredom and tedium of classroom confinement, rigidly spelt out curricula and unimaginative text books. It is hoped that the enrichment of the learning situation through such programmes will motivate the children to continue school and also effect improvement in the teaching methods prevailing in elementary schools, especially those in the rural and tribal areas.

(ii) *Out-of-school children:* The programmes for these children will aim at arousing their interest in learning, conveying general education and motivating them for further learning. In the process, these children will feel encouraged to attend schools for formal education or centres for non-formal education.

(iii) *Elementary school teachers and supervisors:* Every educational system is confronted with the difficult problem of maintaining contact with teachers and upgrading them through inservice training. All efforts to this effect (sponsored training, short-term refresher courses, summer schools, etc.) have generally fallen short of the targets. Educational Technology provides an opportunity for the first time to reach large number of teachers simultaneously, to maintain continuing contact with them, to disseminate knowledge in systematic and programmed manner and to provide inservice training *in situ.*

II. *Adult Education*

(i) *Adult population:* The national programme for adult education, which aims at making 100 million adults literate during the next five years, make it imperative that all mass communication media (TV, film, radio and print) be fully exploited. The use of these media will create a climate of change besides aiding directly the instructional processes.

(ii) *Instructors and supervisors for adult education:* They very large number of instructors required for effective and expeditious implementation of the adult education programme could be trained by using methods similar to those suggested for elementary school teachers with suitable modifications.

III. *Secondary Education*

Secondary Education groups: It is well realized that the formal school system with its limited resources may not be able to cope with the rising demand for secondary education. Necessary efforts will therefore, have to be made to provide secondary education through non-formal channels to as vast a population as possible, particularly to disadvantaged group like backward classes and girls. Already there is a proposal to set-up Open Schools for extending facilities for secondary education. In this system educational technology can play an important role.

6. Organisational Set-up

The planning, development and execution of the Educational Technology programme will require concerted action by a large number of organisations at the national and state levels. The major organisations are identified and their roles defined as follows:

(i) *Ministry of Education:* The major responsibility of the Ministry of Education would be in the area of policy formulation, financing the Educational Technology programme and overseeing its implementation. The specific functions would be—

— to lay down the broad policy, to determine its emphasis, oversee implementation and make periodical appraisals;
— to provide funds and ensure other support for the programme;
— to sponsor, assist, in and stimulate research;
— to coordinate the work of governmental and non-governmental agencies at the national and states levels; and
— to assist in the formulation of state work plans.

In order to carry out these functions, the Ministry of Education should have a full-fledged Division of Educational Technology, which should be headed by a specialists in Educational Technology and should be adequately staffed and provided with supporting services.

(ii) *National Council of Educational Research and Training/Centre for Educational Technology:* They should provide professional support for the Educational Technology programme within the policy framework laid down by the Ministry of Education. More specifically—

— to apply educational technology in the areas of universalization of elementary education and adult education;
— to function as a service organisation for all States in matters pertaining to identification of needs, training of personnel, production of prototype materials and evaluation;
— to establish facilities of educational technology in Headquarters (CET) and in Regional Colleges of Education;
— to promote an awareness of the role of educational technology in education and to develop expertise;
— to revise the existing courses in teacher education/training so as to incorporate educational technology as a subject of study;
— to produce books and materials for the teacher training courses at different levels;
— to introduce appropriate changes in the system of evaluation

— to foster and undertake research in different aspects of educational technology; and
— to provide orientation for producers of educational broadcasts in All India Radio and Doordarshan.

(iii) *State Departments or Department of Education/Educational Technology Cells:* The (D/E) should take the full responsibility for the planning and execution of the Educational Technology programmes and to this end it should—

— establish the necessary machinery for the implementation of the programme;
— appraise its functioning particularly to ensure high standard;
— take such steps as are necessary to expand the areas of its application;
— ensure coordination with all departments concerned with development;
— take over the financial responsibility of the programme in due course of time;
— develop the infrastructure for the organisation and implementation of the programme; and
— obtain participation of state educational institutions, universities, training colleges and correspondence institutions and other allied agencies.

A centrally sponsored scheme for the establishment of a full-fledged Institute of Educational Technology in each State/Union territory has been recommended (see Section 7). Till these State Institutes of Educational Technology are established, Educational Technology Cells should continue to perform the following functions:

— to mobilise public opinion and community support for the programme;
— to coordinate with state educational agencies and others concerned with development at local levels;
— to collaborate with media agencies in the planning and production of programmes and research on them;
— to produce support materials and ensure their distribution and utilisation;
— to ensure provision of equipment and its maintenance;

— to undertake training of teachers in collaboration with concerned institutions;
— to identify areas of specific concern and develop programmes for action;
— to assist in developing curricula in collaboration with the State Institute of Education; and
— to act as secretariat to the State Council of Educational Technology recommended in section 9 *Coordinational and Linkages.*

(iv) *Ministry of Information and Broadcasting:* The Ministry of Information and Broadcasting will be closely associated with the Educational Technology programme and its media organizations will play an active role in its implementation. The functions of some of these organisations are indicated below:

(a) *All India Radio and Doordarshan*

— production and transmission of Educational Technology programmes to be prepared in collaboration with the educational authorities;
— provision of information and motivation for programmes of educational development;
— provision of adequate resources to support the technical aspects of the Educational Technology programme; and
— decentralisation of programme operations to the State/Centre level.

(b) *Directorate of Audio-Visual Publicity and Field Publicity Organisation*

— publicity for motivation through nationwide campaigns; and
— provision of supporting services in the field.

(c) *Films Division*

— to produce films which are suitable for non-formal education, much on the lines it is doing for the Ministry of Agriculture through its special unit for production of agricultural films, the budget for which is provided by the Ministry of Agriculture

— to make available the vast resources of its stock shot library for production of educational films at no or nominal cost

— to prepare catalogue of stock shot in greater detail than at present in accordance with established practice for film clip libraries.

(d) *Indian Institute of Mass Communication*

— to organise on a regular basis short-term basic courses in mass communication for those working in Educational Technology establishments;

— to familiarise them with the potential, problems and limitations of the mass media and their techniques;

— to admit personnel from educational institutions to its specialized courses in photography, operation and maintenance of equipment, research methodology, etc.; and

— to undertake research in media with special reference to education as well.

(e) *Film and Television Institute, Pune*

— to provide training in educational television films; and

— to encourage prototype production and formative research in educational television

(v) *Indian Space Research Organisation/Space Application Centre*

— to design low cost studios;

— to provide training in the use of 1/2 inch video technology;

— to train personnel for formative research; and

— to provide orientation in team modes of production and evolving scientific approach to programming

(vi) *University Grants Commission and Educational Institutions*

(a) *University Grants Commission*

— to provide financial support to universities and other

educational institutions which offer courses in mass communication and allied field or set up departments of educational technology;

- to support the establishment of educational technology centres at selected educational institutions which could ask for Franchise to broadcast educational and extension programme;
- to provide funds for extension work by universities and colleges; and
- to support intensive utilization of educational technology programmes for farmers' training and functional literacy, specially by the agricultural universities.

(b) *Universities*

- to offer courses in mass communication in order to meet the manpower needs resulting from the expansion of broadcasting facilities;
- to undertake extension work directly in cooperation with other bodies;
- to train personnel in various levels for the educational technology programme;
- to undertake experimentation and research in this area;
- to produce programmes;
- to create their own broadcasting facilities in order to accelerate the expansion of educational facilities and extension work through programmes of distance learning; and
- to support programme of farmers' training and functional literacy.

(c) *Educational Training Institutes*

- to offer a compulsory course in educational technology with particular reference to broadcasting;
- to undertake research in suitable areas of educational technology;
- to produce programmes directly or in collaboration with production agencies; and
- adopt modern methods of training teachers and other educational personnel such as managerial cadres, super-

visors, administrators, etc.

(d) *Institutes of Technology and those for Technical Teacher Training*

— to undertake training of technical personnel at various levels for maintenance and operation of equipment;
— to undertake research and experimentation for further development of the educational technology programme;
— to introduce courses in script writing, particularly for television; and
— to produce appropriate programmes.

(vii) *Non-governmental Organisations*

The non-governmental organisations have an important role to play in promoting educational technology. Their capabilities in this field should be extensively utilized and supported where necessary. Such organisations should be encouraged to undertake innovative micro-level projects which have a demonstration value.

7. State Institute of Educational Technology (SIET)

State Institutes of Educational Technology should be established along the following lines:

(i) *Overall Objectives*

The main objective of the SIET is to develop appropriate programmes to promote the spread of education to improve its quality at all levels through all means of instructional technology, including the mass media. To begin with, the SIET will concentrate on the universalisation of elementary and adult education, and will make intensive use of radio, television and print media. The SIET will also be expected to provide support to other high priority educational programmes, such as expansion of educational opportunities at the secondary level though radio-cum-correspondence courses.

(ii) *Conceptual Framework*

The Educational Technology programme is conceived to overcome the drawbacks of the traditional system of education, such as inappropriate content and inability to reach the large numbers in need of education and training. The Educational Technology programmes will make use of non-formal methods of education designed to develop new approaches and new means to cater to the needs of in-school and out-of-school groups. The Educational Technology programme has the potential to achieve high quality as it is possible to deploy the best talent available for producing well-researched programmes to large audiences without the vagaries of individual teachers coming into play. The high quality is all the more important for motivating the learners and also for developing self-instruction habits.

The Educational Technology programmes will be so designed as to supplement the work of teachers. Besides enriching the learning situations these programmes will expose the teachers to innovative methods employed by these programmes, in itself a form of training and will ensure the support of the teachers for the Educational Technology programmes.

In view of the diverse languages and the varying educational needs of groups in different areas, it is essential to have a network of institutes and centres of Educational Technology to cover the whole country. An Institute of Educational Technology in each State and Union Territory is an essential part of this network.

(iii) *Organisational Set-up*

The SIET should be set-up as a distinct institute by the State Department of Education, outside its existing formal structure because none of the existing institutions is equipped to take on the Educational Technology functions. The SIET should have functional autonomy to enable it to attract talent and to have freedom in programme operations.

Since the SIET will need special care during its formative years, it should be provided with all the resources necessary for experimentation and launching of large scale programmes. The cooperation and support of the Education of the Education Department and the Directorate of Education is essential for its successful and smooth working.

The SIET will work in close collaboration with the SIE, SISE, SCERT, Teacher Training Institutes and other agencies and draw upon the talents in various disciplines available with them. The SIET will absorb the existing audio-visual and other facilities coming within its purview.

In the large perspective, educational technology is part of the total system and as such any institutional arrangements that may be visualised will have to keep in view the need for a very close and constant interaction between the SIE/SCERT and the SIET. While, ultimately, these two may have to be merged, educational technology will require a certain focusing over the next five years. In this context the Working Group took note of the way in which the Centre for Educational Technology was established as a separate institution initially but was later merged with the NCERT. Some such pattern is visualized with respect of the SIET as well.

On the programme production and transmission side, the SIET will work in close cooperation with the Akashvani and Doordarshan Centres where programme generation will take place. This means that the SIET will have to decentralize programme planning and production.

(4) *Functions*

— to advise the State Department of Education in the formulation of educational technology policy which is specifically aimed at the exploitation of mass media in spreading and improving educational norms;
— to carry out survey of target groups to assess their educational needs;
— to supervise the working of reception centres to be set up, equipped and staffed by the State Department of Education;
— to develop programmes aimed a removing the drawbacks of the educational system whether in the content or the methods of teaching in both the formal and non-formal structures;
— to evaluate the programmes on a continuous basis;
— to develop in collaboration with other concerned agencies, special courses of content and related scripts for radio and TV broadcasting paying particular attention to the preparation of support materials for radio and television broadcasts;

— to select personnel and arrange for their training in local, Indian and overseas contexts; and
— to act as the secretariat to the State Council for Educational Technology.

(v) *Physical Facilities*

It is absolutely necessary for SIET to have a functionally designed building with an appropriate campus of some amplitude for the development and operation of its programmes. This requirements has not been fulfilled and it would be disastrous for the educational technology programme if the authorities concerned continue to ignore this basic need.

The spaciousness of the campus is emphasized because a basic function of the SIET is experimentation and innovation. The testing and carrying out of pilot projects in the fields of agriculture, handicrafts, art design, etc., demands more space and appropriate functional structures.

Whereas the administrative areas and the educational and technical areas inclusive of hostels, auditorium and staff quarters can fit into a compact area of 5 acres or so, the project and extension work will need mobile space with only temporary structures which could be frequently refurbished to suit various types of experimental and pilot projects. It is expected that another 10 acres will be required for this purpose. The details of the space required for technical areas and auditorium are given in Appendix IV.

A list of the equipment is at Appendix V. The radio and TV component of the equipment is the basic minimum requirement for training prototype production. The actual production of programmes will be carried out at the Akashvani and Doordarshan Kendras. The question of providing animation equipment needs to be gone into carefully. In any case, the indigenous development of appropriate animation equipment should be encouraged and a provision made for that purpose. Appropriate amounts of foreign exchange should be provided for importing essential equipment not being manufactured in the country. In order to achieve economy, the equipment for all SIETs should be purchased in bulk by a Central agency.

(vi) *Manpower Requirements*

The first and foremost task is the identification of leadership talent for the development of new educational programmes by the SIET. The education specialists will need exposure to communication theory and practice and the communication experts will require an understanding of the processes of education. The SIET has to become a bridge where education and communication must meet to develop educational technology for resolving and enormous educational problems. In course of time, specialists well-versed both in education and communication will emerge. In the meanwhile specially designed programmes of training will need to be organised to equip the SIET personnel to perform the Educational Technology functions.

The Ministry of Education should sponsor a training opportunity of three months' duration for the future personnel of the SIET who will have to combine in themselves communication articulation and educational sensibility to put through the programmes. As this is the first time, anywhere in the world, that such a massive effort is being planned to reach people educationally through radio and television, it is very important that the selection and training of the personnel is done with great care and by people who already have some experience in educational innovation through the use of television, radio, film, video cassettes, etc. The services of outstanding innovators and specialists who have made notable contributions in the area of Educational Technology should be mobilised for this training programme. It must be noted that no existing formal institution of education can provide this kind of training.

The staff requirements are given in Appendix VI. The SIET will have a core faculty, as it is expected to draw upon the pool of expertise available in the State complex of educational and other development agencies. While the job descriptions and detailed qualifications will need to be worked out, it is important that the selected and trained staff should be retained for a sufficiently long period (say a minimum of five years) in the SIET.

The actual production of radio and television programmes will be undertaken by the Akashvani and Doordarshan Centres in collaboration with the State Institutes of Educational Technology which will be responsible for planning programmes, training and prototype production. In the area of print media, the SIET will be fully responsible for all work, including support material for radio and television programmes, corresponding courses, teacher training courses and material, etc. Staff requirements have been worked out in the light of these consideration.

(vii) *Cost Estimates*

The vast scope of the Educational Technology Programmes, the multiplication of educational programmes to cater to different groups and use of specialised technology, will call for substantial investment if results are to be achieved. The detailed costing, both for non-recurring and recurring components will need to be worked out, taking into consideration that the cost of equipment is escalating day by day.

The entire non-recurring and recurring costs of the SIET should be met by the Centre for a full five-year period. The provision of ground network for the utilisation of the Educational Technology Programmes, including the personnel, hardware, i.e., television and radio sets, film and filmstrip projectors, etc., will be the responsibility of State Governments. The State Governments, will, therefore, have to develop a phased programme to cover the entire State with the required network in five years.

8. *Financial Support*

After considering various approaches, the Working Group came to the firm conclusion that the Educational Technology Programme should be wholly financed by the Centre for the following:

— the development of mass media techniques for education is a new area;
— the specialised and technical nature of Educational Technology requires concentration of efforts and resources which cannot be secured by individual State Governments; and
— the States will be hard put to share the heavy financial resources for the Educational Technology Programmes in preference to other compelling demands.

The minimum period for Central assistance should be five years. By that time the basic infrastructure should come into being and operations started. At the end of five years a review should be undertaken to assess the progress made and to consider whether further extension of Central assistance is justified.

The on-going Educational Technology Programmes for establishment and operation of Educational Technology Cells in the States should continue to receive 100 per cent Central assistance till these are absorbed by the SIETs.

Educational Technology is a new sub-system of education. Therefore it would be advisable to develop it fully before making it an integral part of the system of education.

It is necessary for all institutions to undertake work in the development of the Educational Technology Programme in their own areas of competence and to provide the requisite funds in their own budgets. However, under the Educational Technology Programme of the Ministry of Education, funds should be provided for specific jobs that these institutions may be contracted to undertake. A block grant of say Rs. 5 lakhs, may also be given to each institution which sets up an Educational Technology Centre.

A suitable policy should be evolved for giving financial support to non-governmental agencies working in this field in order to utilise their capabilities extensively. The recommended forms of assistance are:

— provision of resource persons for designing a project and its evaluation;
— commodity assistance and out of pocket expenditure on project activity;
— grant for publication of reports; and
— facility for import of equipment for production of material.

Since radio sets are of crucial importance, they should be provided by the State Government where possible with the support of the community. There could be two approaches for the provision of radio sets:

— to cover the entire State with radio sets as has been done in Tamil Nadu; and
— to provide radio sets to schools or centres which are included in a special project built around a radio station in those States which cannot immediately provide radio sets to all schools or centres.

Specific projects at the micro-level covering the schools in the transmission area of the radio station or part of such area could be considered for funding from Central sources or the Plan allocation earmarked for educational technology. An intensive development strategy could thus be considered for selected areas. Such a project should cover all aspects of Educational Technology and identify the resources available and the extent of support necessary from the State and Central Governments.

The Planning Commission is providing Rs. 7 crores for software for radio, of which Rs. 2 crores are allocated for Research and Development in radio broadcasting and television. Unless appropriate measures are taken, it would be difficult to utilise fully the provision for Research and Development in this area.

9. Coordination and Linkages

Perhaps the major weakness of SITE was that the linkage between ministries, departments, institutions, voluntary organisations, field agencies and personnel were not strong enough. It is recommended that appropriate structural arrangements should be made to ensure a high degree of coordination between all agencies concerned. There must be perfect coordination between the SIETs and the Akashvani and Doordarshan Centres. The coordination mechanism suggested for the purpose should be at three levels—Station, State and Central—as follows:

(i) *Station Level Committee*

An Advisory Committee at the station level is necessary in view of the considerable amount of work relating to planning and programme generation involved. This Committee should be headed by Station Director, TV/AIR and may include representatives of beneficiary groups, etc., teachers, leaders of public opinion, teacher training institutions in the areas, women workers in touch with women's groups, parents, extension training institutions, writers of children's literature, State Department of Education, State Institutes of Educational Technology/Educational Technology Cell and broadcasting stations. The terms of reference of this Committee may be:

— to mobilise support and participation of community in programmes of educational development;

— to create in the community an understanding of the role of media in development;
— to assist in preparing broadcasting plan with support material; and
— to ensure constant evaluation, supervision and improvement of the quality of broadcasts.

The Station Director will be responsible also for convening the meetings of the Committee.

(ii) *State Level Committee*

This Committee should comprise representatives of the Akashvani and Doordarshan as well as all State-level agencies concerned with development and education *e.g.* department of education, rural development and panchayats, social welfare, tribal welfare, agriculture, health, universities, etc. This Committee should serve as the State Educational Technology Council, with the following functions:

— to lay down policy and guidelines for statewise programmes;
— to coordinate functioning of local station committees (All India Radio/Doordarshan) and to lay down broad guidelines for their work;
— to ensure that a judicious balance is maintained between needs of the different communities, groups and regions;
— to ensue technical and other inputs for proper development of need based programmes; and
— to evaluate effectiveness of programmes.

The Head of the State Institute of Educational Technology will be responsible for convening the meetings of the Council.

(iii) *Central Level Committee*

The Committee at the Central level may include representatives of the following:

— Doordarshan
— Akashvani
— Ministry of Information and Broadcasting

— Indian Institute of Mass Communication
— NCERT
— National Staff College
— Directorate of Adult Education
— Ministry of Education (Education, Culture, Technical Education)
— Non-governmental agencies engaged in areas of relevance of educational technology
— University Grants Commission
— National Book Trust
— Planning Commission.

A provision should be made to coopt representatives from other Ministries such as Social Welfare, Agriculture, Health and Rural Development for programmes in their areas of work.

Education Secretary will be Chairman of this Committee and the concerned Joint Secretary its convener. The Committee would meet at least twice a year. Its terms of reference would be to adopt the policies and programmes, to coordinate activities of various ministries, State Governments, agencies and institutions concerned and to oversee implementation of the Educational Technology programme. A small group may be set-up to monitor the programme.

The Working Group also recommends that Standing Committee may be constituted to oversee the Educational Technology Programme and to assist the Ministry of Education in the formulation of a policy for educational technology. It should have both official and non-official members.

10. Hardware: Manufacture and Maintenance

Production Equipment

Efforts should be made to encourage indigenisation of hardware with a view to developing inexpensive, compact, light weight and highly reliable equipment that would help universities, programme producers and programme receiving agencies to participate in programme production. This would not only decentralise programme production but would also enable the user agencies to mould the medium for their own purposes.

The Working Group felt that there was a need for the qualitative assessment of the technology available and that required for the Educational Technology Programme.

Radio

In view of the emphasis on the use of radio for universalisation of elementary education and non-formal education which will involve a very large number of radio sets, the Government should ensure that radio sets are manufactured and supplied to educational institutions at a very low cost.

Maintenance

For proper maintenance of Radio and Television receivers, the following steps are recommend:

— The Division of Educational Technology of the Ministry of Education should commission a workbook on making low cost radio receivers and maintenance of commonly available radio receivers. Such a workbook will enable a local enthusiast in the rural areas to make a low cost radio receiver and/or maintain available radio receivers; and

— Similarly a workbook on maintenance of television receivers may be commissioned to Space Application Centre who have gained experience in this field.

Films

Films are an important component of educational technology particularly for non-formal education. Though there are about 15,000 working 16 mm projects in the country and about thousand 16 mm projectors are being manufactured annually, their utilisation is extremely poor.

Apart from the state film libraries, an important source of film lending is the Central Film Library under the NCERT in New Delhi. It has about 8,000 titles and about 4,000 members. But regular borrowers are few. This is because of the dearth of educational films that would meet the needs of Indian school children. Therefore, it is high time that efforts should begin to capitalise on the investments we have already made on the hardware. It is obvious that for better utilisation of projection facilities, production of effective educational films should be a given a high priority. To specific recommendations in this areas are that —

— a study group should be set up to review the development and utilisation of educational and children's films in India; and
— a joint Working Group of the Ministries of Education and Information and Broadcasting should be set up to study the feasibility of the film resources of the Films Division for educational films.

11. Model Projects

One of the major tasks of Sub-group I was the development of a few proposals for research and action which would give concrete expression to the thinking and recommendations of the Working Group. A number of agencies (Planning Commission, Centre for Educational Technology, CENDIT, DG(AIR), Ministry of Education) were involved in preparing such proposals. These provide new approaches and cover all priority programme areas making use of all media, either individually or in combination of two or more. While most of these proposals will need to be developed into detailed projects, all of them emphasis a need-based approach, non-formal methods, and continuing evaluation. A list of these projects is given in Appendix VII and the detailed projects form its Annexures.

In submitting these proposals, the Working Group underlines the fact that Educational technology is a new multi-disciplinary approach which should be applied on a massive scale in order to help in the expansion and improvement of education in the country. At the same time, there are as yet no established and proven forms and strategies for exploiting educational technology. These must be developed through considerable research and investigations and tested for their relevance to Indian conditions. This in itself is a huge task. Therefore, the Government would be well advised to set-up a Committee or Group not only to assist in the planning and coordination of research projects but also to supervise their actual execution as well as to evaluate their results.

53

WORKING GROUP ON VOCATIONALISATION, 1977 – REPORT[1]

Chairman Shri P. Sabanayagam

Members Dr. Ajit Mazumdar; Shri K.P.A. Menon; Dr. Shib K. Mitra; Dr. M.S. Swaminathan; Shri S. Loveraj; Dr. P.P. Goel; Dr., S.N. Saraf; Shri J.N. Tewari; Shri P.R. Nayak; Dr. R.P. Singhal; Dr. (Smt.) Rajammal P. Devadas; Dr. C.R. Mitra; Dr. G.S. Laddha; Prof. Rais Ahmed; Shri S.L. Kirloskar; Shri I.K. Gupta; Shri B.P. Poddar; Shri Narendra Kalantri; Prof. P.S. Mani Sundaram; Shri Inder Malhotra

M. Secy. Smt. J. Anjani Dayanand

Spl. Invitees Shri I.P. Anand; Shri R.N. Azad; Prof. C.V. Govinda Rao

Appointment

The Ministry of Education and Social Welfare (Department of Education) in consultation with the Planning Commission set up a working Group on Vocationalisation of Education in 1977).

Terms of Reference

(a) to review the developments in the field;
(b) to advise on the approach and priorities for the Sixth Plan;
(c) to formulate concrete proposals indicating financial implications and structural arrangements; and
(d) to apportion the areas of responsibility among the Centre, State and Voluntary Agencies.

---

1. New Delhi, Ministry of Education and Social Welfare, 1978, 35 p.

Contents

Introduction; Historical Background; Existing Facilities and Present Position; Scheme of Implementation; Financial Estimates; Summary of Recommendations; Annexures I to V.

Recommendations

6.01 To identify the vocations having good employment potential, to locate good schools where the new vocational courses can be introduced and to assess the local assistance for on-the-job training, vocational surveys should be conducted, in a phased manner before introducing Vocational Courses and only those courses which have good employment potential should be started. (Paras 4.04 to 4.08)

6.02 Such vocational surveys should be conducted at regular intervals to evaluate the on-going vocational programmes, to suggest modifications or improvement of curricula and recommend new vocations for which courses have to be designed. (Para 4.09)

6.03 During the next 5 years, vocational facilities should be provided in a minimum of 2000 schools/colleges in a phased manner of which 500 should be new ones. (Para 4.15)

6.04 Since almost all the Vocational/Technical institutions are located in the urban or semi-urban centres, the new schools for vocational studies should be constructed in the rural areas and they should be well-equipped. (Para 4.13)

6.05 All the existing Technical and Vocational schools at the secondary stage should be revitalized by providing appropriate inputs and new courses should be added to ensure optimum use of the existing facilities. (Paras 4.12, 4.16, 4.17 and 4.19)

6.06 Adequate incentives in the form of scholarship should be offered to the students of vocational streams at the secondary stage. (Para 4.19)

6.07 Adequate number of vocational teachers should be appointed and trained both on regular and part-time basis on suitable remunerations. Periodical in-service training should also be arranged for the regular staff for updating their knowledge and skills. (Para 4.20, 4.21 and 4.22)

6.08 In all vocational schools/colleges where vocational studies are offered, either the Head of the School/College or the Deputy Head should possess vocational qualifications in at least one major vocation, to look after the proper implementation. (Para 4.23)

6.09 Preparation of curricula centrally should be done away with. Curriculum Committees consisting of professional experts, future employers and academics should be set up for each region and should be entrusted with the task of preparing curricula relevant to the region or the district. The accent should be more on preparing students for self-employment than wage employment. (Para 4.25)

6.10 All vocational courses should be offered in terms of well connected, self-contained units or modules and the students achievement should be evaluated at the completion of each module. A Certificate of completion of the module satisfactorily should be issued to the student. (Para 4.26)

6.11 Good textbooks, teaching aids and teacher guides have to be ready before the vocational courses are launched. At the initial stages, foreign publications should be procured and made available. Local authors and publishers should be encouraged to produce suitable books in simple language and with adequate practical details. (Paras 4.28, 4.29 and 4.30)

6.12 The programmes of vocationalisation in rural areas should be linked with various programmes of rural development. (Paras 4.30, 4.31 to 4.37 and 4.43)

6.13 In the urban sector, more stress should be laid on the courses in the areas of commerce and trade, textiles, para-medical, electrical and other technical subjects. (Para 4.30, 4.38 to 4.43)

6.14 Vocational courses should be designed to inculcate the capacity of combine intellectual knowledge with skill training in the selected vocations. (Para 4.43)

6.15 Opportunities of vertical and horizontal mobility for vocationally qualified students should be provided in ample measure to encourage a sizeable section of students to pursue vocational studies. Specialised courses in the lines of occupation should be offered in professional institutions to help students claim superior positions of employment. (Para 4.45 and 4.46)

6.16 There should be flexibility in the duration of vocational courses according to the needs of students, the required levels of competency and proficiency. Rigidity of duration of courses is hardly conducive to the vocational courses and may tend to become disincentive to the aspiring students. (Para 4.47)

6.17 For updating and improving skills and knowledge, advanced specialised courses of varying durations should be planned through part-time, correspondence, sandwich and short-time intensive courses. (Para 4.48 and 4.49)

6.18 Socially Useful Productive Work should be integrated with general education in the academic stream to equip all the students with certain elementary skills. (Para 4.50)

6.19 Creative Work Centres/Hobby Centres should be established in the centrally located situations to encourage creative faculties of the youngsters and to promote productive impulses. (Para 4.51)

6.20 Apprenticeship facilities should be extended to all the students who complete vocational courses so that good on-the-job training is available for further improvement of competencies. (Para 4.52)

6.21 Steps should be taken to provide guidance and counselling facilities for careers and courses to all the students. (Para 4.53)

6.22 The recruitment policy of the Governments and public sector undertakings should be revised and job requirements should replace the academic qualifications as *essential qualifications* for selection. Where graduates and vocationally qualified persons appear for tests/interview, other things being equal or nearly equal, preference should be given to vocationally qualified persons. (Para 4.54)

6.23 The National Council of Vocational Education and State Councils of Vocational Education should be set up without delay and their spheres of action, composition and functions to be performed should be defined. These Councils should ensure, quality and standard of vocational education, co-ordination and cooperation among all agencies which are at present offering vocational education and those connected with employment. (Para 4.55)

6.24 Since Vocationalisation of Education falls into the purview of 12-year school education it is necessary that it remains under the administrative control of a Senior Officer, at least of the rank of a Bureau Head, whose staffs should be adequately strengthened to enable the Bureau Head to discharge his responsibilities effectively and expeditiously. He shall be responsible for implementing all the decisions of the N.C.V.E. (Para 4.56)

6.25 The private organisations and individuals should be encouraged to participate in the programme by providing incentives to start new schools and ensure autonomy to run them. Incentives may also be provided by allowing certain tax exemptions in lieu of training facilities provided to the students of vocational streams. (Para 4.57)

54

WORKING GROUP ON ORGANISATION OF VOCATIONAL EDUCATION, 1977 – REPORT[1]

Chairman Shri V.R. Reddy

Members Shri B.K. Singh; Prof. C.V. Govinda Rao; Dr. R.P. Singhal; Shri B.N. Chaturvedi

Appointment

The new pattern of Secondary Education 10+2 had been introduced in the Union Territory of Delhi in 1976 as a sequal to the reorganised of Higher Secondary Education. The first batch of students was admitted to 9th standard in the new pattern in June, 1975. This batch will complete their 10 years of general education in April/May 1977. Facilities for 2 years of Higher Secondary Education will, therefore, have to be provided in June 1977 all over the Union Territory.

Since the characteristic feature of the two-year higher secondary education is diversification which aims at offering students opportunities to choose programmes of study in a much wider field of education in keeping with their aptitudes, interests and abilities with a view to increasing their employability, adequate facilities should be provided not only for the academic stream but also for a large number of vocational streams which would generally be terminal in character. In organising vocational programmes considerable thought has to be given to the vocations for which facilities have to be provided and to selecting the schools where these courses should be offered. Efforts should be made to utilise the available facilities of equipment and teachers in the existing educational and training institutions and other agencies as far as possible.

In view of the fact that the vocationalisation programmes should

---

1. Programmes at Plus 2 Stage in the Union Territory of Delhi, New Delhi, Ministry of Education and Social Welfare, 1977, 57 p.

be introduced in Delhi from the academic year beginning from July 1977 and there is an urgent need for making necessary preparations which include among other identification and organisation of the courses, and associating the existing technical and professional institutions the Government of India in the Ministry of Education and Social Welfare have set up a Working Group on Organisation of Vocational Education in 1977.

Terms of Reference

(a) Identification of institutions and industries where the existing facilities can be utilised for developing programmes of vocational education in selected higher secondary schools;

(b) Selection of higher secondary schools to be associated with this project;

(c) Identification of subjects/courses for which such facilities can be utilised;

(d) Determination of the extent to which such facilities could be utilised in terms of student numbers, hours of work, etc.;

(e) Financial implications, if any, of implementing this project;

(f) Suggestions for a suitable administrative and organisational mechanism to ensure maximum co-operation between participating institutions and to develop the project as an essentially collaborative one between the concerned authorities; and

(g) Any other matter relevant to the effective implementation of this project.

Content

Introduction; Economic Development—A Background; Educational Facilities; Identification of Vocational Courses; Selection of Schools; Organisation of Courses; Financial Implications; Summary of Recommendations; Acknowledgement; Annexures I to VII.

Recommendations

1. Scientific socio-economic survey and area skill survey of the Union Territory in cooperation with industry, trade and commerce should be carried out periodically to identify the occupations in demand and to estimate the numbers required. Such surveys should

be updated continuously. (Para 4.20)

2. Job analysis of activity analysis of occupations in demand should also be carried out to delineate the precise functions, to determine the knowledge, skills and competences needed to perform the functions and to design the courses which will best serve the purpose. Para 4.21)

3. Students in vocational education should be motivated for self-employment and entrepreneurship. A course of training in this aspect should be made compulsory to all the students taking up vocational education. A systematic and organised training in self-employment and entrepreneurship right from the beginning will go a long way in changing their outlook and building confidence in them to be self-reliant. (Para 6.2)

4. Vocational guidance and career counselling should be given to all children from the age of 14 in the schools by organising career talks by people from industry, professional institutions and other experts. (Para 5.5)

5. Vocational education facilities should be provided for 5000 students at +2 level in 1977-78 in the Union Territory of Delhi. (Para 5.5)

6. The vocational programmes should be organised in 50 schools selected by the Group at the rate of 100 students in each school. (Para 5.6)

7. The selection of schools in future, should be based on industrial and other economic activities in the area and the availability of training facilities in the existing industry and educational institutions. (Para 5.6)

8. Four vocational courses out of those recommended against each selected school may be offered in 1977-78 depending upon the demand from the students. (Para 6.2)

9. The technical higher secondary schools at Okhla and Kashmere Gate should be converted into vocational schools. (Para 6.3)

10. The State Vocational Education Board should be set up under the Chairmanship of the Chief Executive Councillor with 25 members representing various production activities and services, trade and commerce, administration, planning and educational institutions to advise the Delhi Administration on the planning, organisation, coordination and development of vocational education in the Territory. (Para 6.4)

11. A vocational education unit should be set up in the Direc-

torate of Education with full-time officers and supporting staff to work as the secretariat to the Board and to monitor and administer the vocational education programmes. (Para 6.5 and 6.6)

12. As soon as the syllabus and the curriculum for the courses proposed are ready, arrangements should be worked out for the staff and training facilities on a part-time basis from the existing institutions and industry. (Para 7.6)

13. Pre-service and in-service training for teachers of vocational education should be organised. (Para 7.3)

14. The total non-recurring provision required for equipment and library for all the 50 schools put together is Rs. 30 lakhs. The recurring expenditure on salaries, materials and contingencies including the staff required for the units in Directorate of Education is estimated to be Rs. 60 lakhs per annum. (Para 7.3)

55

WORKING GROUP ON ADULT EDUCATION FOR MEDIUM TERM PLAN 1978-83, 1977 – REPORT[1]

Chairman Shri P. Sabanayagam

Official Members Dr. Ajit Mazumdar; Dr. B.D. Sharma; Smt. P. Ramachandran, Dr. Ishwar Das; O.P. Gautam; Shri C.G. Rangbhashyam; Shri C.S. Shastry; Shri M.P. Baizbarua; Prof. Satya Bhushan; Dr. S.N. Saraf

Non-official Members Dr. Ramlal Parikh; Dr. Malcolm S. Adiseshiah; Shri Kishore Saint; Shri K.S. Radhakrishnan; Dr. (Smt.) Chitra Naik; Shri S.N. Maitra; Dr. T.A. Koshy; Smt. Elaben Bhatt; Shri Mushtaq Ahmed; Father Gjousalves; Dr. Anil Sadgopal; Shri G.K. Gaokar

M. Secy. Shri Anil Bordia.

Appointment

The Working Group on Adult Education appointed by the Ministry of Education and Social Welfare, Government of India in 1977.

Terms of Reference

(a) To review the developments in the field of adult education;

(b) To advise on the approach and priorities for the Sixth Plan 1978-83;

(c) To formulate concrete proposals indicating financial implications and structural arrangements; and

(d) To apportion the areas of responsibility among the Centre, States and voluntary agencies.

---

1. New Delhi, Ministry of Education and Social Welfare, 1978, 30p (Summary)

Contents

Adult Education and Development; The Perspective and Strategy; Special Priority; The Organisational and Promotional Agencies; The Instructional Agencies; Resource Development; Post-literacy and Follow-up Programmes; Monitoring, Evaluation and Research; Planning and Administrative Structures; Programme Planning; Financial Arrangements and Phasing; The International Dimension; Appendices from I to V.

Recommendations

The Perspective and the Strategy

1. The attention paid in the successive five-year plans in the past has shown a declining awareness towards this sector of education.

2. *The Literacy Scene:* An analysis of the literacy scene for age-group above 14 years shows that while the percentage of literacy has increased in 1951, 1961, 1971 and 1977 from 19.26, 27.76, 34.08 to 38.00 the number of illiterate persons has also increased during this period from 17.39, 18.70, 20.95 to 22.66 crores. The segmental dimension of the problem is even more serious. In 15—35 age-group, out of a total of 9.71 crores of illiterate persons the rate of literacy among rural females is only 18.80 per cent and there are vast variations between rural and urban and between scheduled castes and scheduled tribes on the one hand and the remaining population on the other. These disparities will continue to rise unless arrangements are made to bridge this gap.

3. *The Operational Strategy:* The National Adult Education Programme recognises the importance of giving special priority to these segments of society, and lays importance on the 15—35 age-group because it is during this phase in life that people make families and have to upgrade their skills and understanding in the socio-economic perspective. In the first couple of years, rather than organising programmes on a massive scale, programmes of smaller size which are carefully planned would be taken up. Adult education programmes would be implemented through a network of projects. Every agency intending to take up the programme would determine the area which would be covered by it. As far as possible the project

area would coincide with CD blocks, or in tribal areas with integrated tribal development projects. The effort would be to take up a contagious compact area and to organise as many adult education centres as feasible.

Special Priority

4. *Women:* Women form a substantial and integral segment of the labour force. An understanding about the role and status of women in society will, therefore, be an essential part of all programmes organised under NAEP. Adult education programmes for women may also have to be separately organised and, as a part of the post-literacy and follow-up programme, they may have to be encouraged to form their own groups for learning and to strengthen their participation and voice in the developmental process. As far as instructional responsibility is concerned it shall have to be borne be women teachers and other educated women in rural areas. A large programmes of condensed courses and training shall have to be organised.

5. *Scheduled Tribes:* Elimination of exploitation of the tribal people is an important task of development and this can be achieved only by building up the inner strength of those communities. Only education can provide this crucial inputs. In the organisation of adult education programmes for the tribals, the special characteristic of their society must be kept in mind. These programmes should (a) help them to acquire skills so that they may be able to negotiate effectively with the world around them and compete with outsiders in job situation and business dealings; (b) it should assist them in acquiring appreciation of their vibrant culture and conserve their environment; and (c) be interwoven with the rest of the development programmes being organised through integrated tribal development projects. Within the vast tribal areas there are some to which higher priority needs to be given: the regions where industrial and mining activity is increasing, the pockets of particularly low levels of illiteracy and areas with large population of landless labourers.

6. *Scheduled Castes:* Persons belonging to the scheduled castes are scattered through the length and breadth of the country. Some of the issues in connection with organisation of adult education programmes are as follows:

(a) Though not desirable, it may be necessary to organise separate classes for these persons;
(b) As far as possible, if there is only one adult education centre in a village, it should be for persons belonging to the Scheduled Castes;
(c) Even if the enrolment in a Scheduled Caste centre is thin, a centre should be organised for them making an effort to bring enrolment to an optimum levels as soon as possible;
(d) Efforts should be made to improve their skills and techniques and if possible enable them to rise above their traditional occupations;
(e) Programmes of occupational diversification should be organised, such as poultry farming, plantation of fruit tees, animal and sheep husbandry, khadi and village industries;
(f) In the course of the adult education programmes as well as follow-up, organisations with fair representation of persons belonging to Scheduled Castes should be created. Where mixed organisations are not feasible, separate organisations should be set-up; and
(g) In regions where organisations of persons belonging to Scheduled Castes can lead to serious social tensions, the district authorities should be kept well informed about it so that creation of such organisations may not lead to conflicts resulting in further deterioration of the condition of these people.

The Organisational and Promotional Agencies

7. *The Central Government:* As a part of its responsibility for social and economic planning the Central Government has naturally to provide leadership in NAEP. It should have special responsibility for involvement of the various agencies, particularly the voluntary organisations and universities/colleges, and taking up of programmes such as training, production of teaching and learning materials and evaluation. The Ministries and the Departments of the Central Government, as well as their various autonomous organisations and other agencies, should explore ways to relate their programmes with NAEP.

8. *The State Governments:* In planning and implementation of NAEP the States have a pivotal role to play. Integration of adult education with development can take place only by a firm resolve of

the State Governments. The State Governments will also have to take responsibility for identification of various agencies and creation of appropriate administrative and managerial structures. As in the case of Central Government, NAEP in the States also cannot be the concern only of one department : all departments who organise programmes in which the involvement of beneficiaries is crucial to the success of the programme ought to look upon adult education as a method for such involvement.

9. *Political Parties and other Associations:* No account of promotional agencies can be complete without a mention of the importance of

— the leadership of political parties and their mass organisations of women, youth, workers and peasants;
— all-India cultural, religious and youth organisations;
— federations/associations of teachers, employees and of trade and industry:

These agencies can help in transforming of NAEP into a mass programme and they can also create the environment which would motivate the functionaries as well as the learners. The role expected from these agencies is to catalyse their members and affiliates, rather than taking up the field programmes themselves.

10. *Voluntary Organisations:* They have a place of precedence among the organisational agencies. These agencies should organise field adult education programmes, including post-literacy and follow-up programmes. Voluntary agencies also have special responsibility in resource development, particularly training, production of teaching and learning materials and evaluation. The all-India voluntary organisations should be encouraged to organise orientation programmes for voluntary agencies. Agencies entering the field of adult education for the first time should ordinarily begin with a small programme which might be enlarged after an evaluation of their work. The Government must also replace the mechanisms which obstruct involvement of voluntary agencies by enabling mechanisms. Voluntary organisations should be non-political and non-communal in nature in order to become eligible for assistance to implement programmes.

11. *Educational Institutions:* Introduction of national and social service at all stages of education is now the accepted policy. Involve-

ment of educational institutions in NAEP would provide to them a well-defined means to interest students in service; it would also provide to NAEP a large number of dedicated workers. Although it needs to be emphasised that educational institutions should organise field adult education including literacy programmes, there are a large number of other things which also they can do. These would include:

(a) creation of an environment;
(b) surveys;
(c) preparation of curriculum, teaching/learning materials and organisation of training, etc.;
(d) supplemental programmes of instruction through audio-visual means, cultural programmes, sports and games, etc.;
(e) facilitating women participants by taking care of their children;
(f) post-literacy and follow-up programmes;
(g) construction of adult education huts in villages where facilities for organisation of adult education activities are not enough; and
(h) evaluation and research.

12. *The Employers:* In respect of all their employees all employers should be expected to organise adult education programmes including literacy, skill training, etc., Government being the biggest employer has a special responsibility. In large construction works, such as railways, irrigation dams, scarcity relief operations, roads, etc., arrangements of adult education should be provided for the workers. Apart from Government, the organised sector including factories, mines, plantation, etc., engage very large sized work-force. It should be the responsibility of the employers, in cooperation with the Central Board of Workers Education or other concerned agencies of labour welfare, to organise adult education and literacy programmes. Employers in the semi-organised sector also should be encouraged to organise such programmes.

13. *The Local Bodies:* Municipalities and the Panchayati Raj Institutions can also play an important role in the organisation of adult education programmes in their areas. In particular the municipalities will have to take full responsibility for post-literacy and follow-up programmes in cities.

The Instructional Agencies

14. *Considerations in Selection:* In the past there has been excessive reliance on elementary school teachers to function as instructors in adult education centres. This happened not because there was a deliberate decision regarding their suitability but by a force of habit. This uncritical method must be replaced by well-considered decisions, keeping in view the various possibilities and considerations, which would include:

— *voluntariness:* all persons to be involved as instructional agencies should participate on a purely voluntary basis;
— *motivation:* motivation among the instructors is a precondition of motivation among the learners;
— *communication:* the potential instructors should have the linguistic capability to communicate as well as an attitude of equality towards the learners.

15. *Village Youth:* Owing to the possibility of natural communication, existence of unemployment and under-employment among the villagers and the possibility of creation of a new kind of rural leadership, the village youth need to be preferred as the instructional agents. A majority of the village youth would prefer to work on full-time basis, it would be worth while to continue the part-time adult education work with either the non-formal elementary education work or as a part of the various programmes of rural development.

16. *School Teachers:* Although school teachers have some advantages, such as being accustomed to organisation of educational programmes and their training in handling of teaching and learning materials, the formal system of education has become a part of their lives. They tend to be authoritarian and rigid and are seldom able to deal with villagers in a spirit of equality. Yet, such of the teachers as volunteer to participate in the programme should be welcomed. Besides, it should be possible to appoint unemployed persons who have had teacher training. They could be paid a meagre subsistence allowance, and can be entrusted responsibility for organisation of non-formal educational programmes for children and for adults for a well defined community.

17. *Students:* Students at +2 stage and in institutions of higher

education should be encouraged to take responsibility for organisation of adult education centres, including literacy. This would necessitate continuous work for 200 to 350 hours a year, depending on the type of programme organised. It would be necessary for teachers to involve themselves in NAEP if students are to be so involved. Representative organisations of students can also play a vital role in this connection.

18. *Developmental Functionaries:* It would be of immense advantage if village level developmental functionaries could take responsibility for organisation of adult education programme. While this would be good for adult education, it would also facilitate the work of those functionaries. Even when development functionaries do not themselves organise adult education centers they should contribute to the programme as a part of a team. Keeping in view the importance of village revenue record keepers (Patwari, Lekhpal) and their role inland reforms, their participation in the programme would be of immense value.

19. *Retired personnel:* A large number of ex-servicemen are discharged every year and can function as adult education instructors. In addition to ex-servicemen there are several other categories of retired personnel who can take instructional responsibility.

Resource Development

20. In the context of NAEP, resource development is intended to mean the instrumentality for transforming the concept and the objectives of the Programmes into a learning system. Its elements include curriculum development, preparation of teaching/learning materials, training, and evaluation. Resource methodology has to be based on the principles of:

— flexibility and openness;
— devolution; and
— efficiency.

21. *Curriculum development:* Curriculum in NAEP has to be related to the identifiable needs of the groups of learners, and, therefore, would ordinarily be preceded by a survey of such needs. The curriculum:

— should enable the learners to get a basic understanding of the social and physical environment in which they live,
— should develop an attitude of self-reliance and initiative,
— should encourage them to constructive action,
— should prepare them for parenthood and family life,
— should enable them to realise their rights and responsibilities, and
— should impart skills in literacy and numeracy so that self-reliant learning may take place. The duration of the adult education programmes, including literacy, should be of 300 to 350 hours.

22. *Teaching/learning material and training:* Teaching and learning materials, based on the curriculum, should help participants in entering into dialogue and mutual communication. The language to be used in the materials should be the spoken language of the participants and special material should be prepared for linguistic minorities. The size and diversity of NAEP will necessitate well-organised training for all functionaries. The training of instructors should be organised by the project agency using locally available resource persons. Training of district adult education officers, project officers and supervisors should be the responsibility of a specially designated training institution, which would generally be established with a voluntary agency or an autonomous organisation. The training of State-level functionaries, heads of major voluntary agencies and other key personnel would be the responsibility of the Directorate of Adult Education.

23. *The Resource Structure:* At the apex of the resource structure is the Directorate of Adult Education, the National Resource Centre. In each State there is to be a State Resource Centre, which is critical level in resource development. A SRC is not expected to be a large unwieldy institute, it should use available resources within the State and make effort to devolutionise resource capability at the district and project levels. A district resource consortium should be organised to support the project agencies, which themselves would have substantial resource capability. Ultimately each village where there is to be an adult education centre will have to develop its resource system, so that the programmes are related to the local needs and problems.

Post-Literacy and Follow-up Programmes

24. *The Educational Continuum:* If adult education and literacy have to play a germinal role, then the programme cannot be a one-time programme of 8 or 10 months, or 300 or 350 hours. It must be a part of a continuous process of education leading to action and action needing further education. The post-literacy and follow-up programmes will mean that the learners will reinforce their literacy, will gain a more critical understanding of the environment and will become more aware of the impediments which are blocking their way. At the same time they will have a clearer idea about what economic programmes can be taken up, how to utilise different Government and non-government schemes, how to grasp effectively the facilities which are provided by banks and other institutions, how to organise cooperative societies and how to form and upgrade relevant skills.

25. *Organisation of Continuing Education Centres:* The responsibility of organisation of post-literacy and follow-up programmes will rest with the project agency. Each project will have a Project Library Centre and a network of village continuing education centres would be created. In the urban areas the responsibility for organisation of continuing education would rest with municipalities and educational institutions. A continuing education centre would also serve as the focus for creation of village organisations. Besides, short duration training courses and condensed courses could be organised to raise understanding and levels of skills in regard to the occupational, health and civic issues. Mass media and folk culture can provide valuable means of recreation and learning.

Monitoring, Evaluation and Research

26. *Central level:* The past experience leads us to the realisation that the system of monitoring, evaluation and applied research should aim at improvement of the management of the programme at all levels. Besides, evaluation of training outcomes, monitoring of progress and impact studies are special areas to which all exercises at evaluation must apply themselves. In organisation of evaluation and monitoring, the Directorate of Adult Education will play an important role, on the one hand establishing cooperative relationship with a number of appropriate management and research agencies as well

as institutions of higher education and on the other hand preparing agencies in the States and districts to develop capability for evaluation and applied research.

27. *Field level:* It is important that the progress of the programme, with reference to specific determinant points, is regularly and systematically reported. This shall be the responsibility of the adult education instructor and the project agency. The second aspect of monitoring and evaluation would be a system of data audit, through creation of parties in practically every district who would draw samples in a prescribed manner and would undertake a check of the information furnished. The district parties could comprise teachers in universities, colleges and higher secondary schools or research workers. The third aspect is an examination regarding the extent to which the programme conforms to the objectives, its impact in the field and the reaction among the participants and other members of the community. Finally, on the basis of study of impact, measures for improvement of the programmes will have to be identified and disseminated to the implementation agencies.

Planning and Administrative Structures

28. *Project level:* NAEP is to be implemented through projects, which are visualised as the key unit for planning and implementation of the Programme. Ordinarily the area of a project would be coterminous with one or two CD blocks and the number of adult education centres to be organised per project would vary from 100 to 500. Agencies taking up the programme for the first time could take up smaller projects also, but generally not less than 30 centres. There should be close and dynamic link between the project and the various development programmes in a project area. A project is visualised in a spirit of autonomy, and the project administration should have not only sufficient financial powers and power to appoint instructors, but it should also organise training of instructors, prepare or moderate teaching/learning materials and organise evaluation and monitoring Post-literacy and follow-up activities would be an essential part of the project activity. The administrative structure of a project would comprise a project office, in the case of large project generally assisted by an assistant project officer and a continuing education organiser, a certain number of supervisors and instructors.

29. *District level:* At the district level the primary responsibility

for the programme shall rest with the Collector/Chief Executive Officer. The Government project agencies would be supervised by the district Collector and he would also organise coordination, monitoring and general supervision over all agencies in the district. The Collector/CEO would be assisted by a district adult education officer. There would be a district adult education board/committee, presided over by the district Collector/CEO, of which all project officers would be members, in addition to district-level development officers, public workers, etc. The district level agency would normally examine the proposal of a voluntary agency and would make suitable recommendation to the State Government. The committee would also oversee the work of all project running in the district.

30. *State level:* At the apex in each State would be the State Board of Adult Education, presided over by the Chief Minister or the Education Minister. The State Board would provide policy guidelines and would periodically appraise the progress of implementation. For ensuring coordination between the development programmes and adult education, to oversee programme formulation and to receive periodic reports regarding implementation, a Steering Committee would be set up under the Chairmanship of the Chief Secretary. A State adult education office shall have to be set up in each State. The office would be headed by a senior official who should be a head of the department, either working under the director of the department dealing with adult education or independently.

31. *Personnel policy:* In appointment of personnel at various levels—project, district and State—certain general considerations should be kept in view. The scales of pay of staff working in adult education should normally be comparable with appropriate levels in education or development departments. Rather than appointing persons by routine promotions or non-selective transfer, suitable selection should be made from any department the staff of which can have experience or expertise in the field of adult education. Preference in appointment should be given to women and to person belonging to Scheduled Castes and Scheduled Tribes. Arrangements should be made to retain good workers, and when promotions become due to them, they should be provided opportunity within the sphere of adult education.

Programme Planning

32. *Objective:* The ultimate aim of programme planning process

is to create village and mohalla adult education units which would take their own decisions regarding duration of programmes, persons, to be entrusted instructional responsibility, teaching/learning material to be used, post-literacy and follow-up programmes, etc. Right from the beginning, effort should be made to create such units.

33. *Project as the level of programme planning:* The vital level of programme planning would be the project level. The programme planning at this level can be divided into (i) preparation for starting of the programme, (ii) organisation of adult education centres, and (iii) post-literacy and follow-up activities.

34. *Preparatory action:* Preparatory action should begin with appointment of project officers and supervisors, which would take place about three months before the centres are to be established. Their first month would be spent in training. The instructors would ordinarily be appointed a month after the appointment of project officers and supervisors and a training would be organised for them in the second month. The third month, which would be the month preceding establishment of adult education centres, would be spent on survey, identification of places for establishment of adult education centres, securing of supplies including teaching/learning materials, creation of environment and establishing communication with the people of the community where the centres are to be established.

35. *Implementation stage:* With the starting of the adult education centre, systematic enrolment of learners should be made and no adult, whatever his age, who wishes to participate in the programme, should be refused enrolment. Simultaneous steps should be taken to involve the development and revenue functionaries and a beginning should be made with discussion around problems of land, production programmes, health and child-care, etc. There is need to create a special consciousness among the instructors and supervisors regarding the measures to be taken to sustain the interest of the learners. Accurate progress reporting measures of self-evaluation in which learners might also be involved, and systematic supervision have to be ensured. Preparatory action for the next batch should start a couple of months before conclusion of a particular batch.

36. *Follow-up: concurrent action:* Action for post-literacy and follow-up programmes should also start before conclusion of the first batch. This would involve establishment of a village Continuing Education Centre, identification and training of continuing education

worker and involvement of a large number of agencies for organisation of short-duration training programmes, cultural and recreational activities and formation and strengthening of village organisations.

Financial Arrangements and Phasing

37. *Central responsibility:* The responsibility of the Central Government in financing of NAEP should be for involvement of voluntary agencies and youth, taking up of model pace-setter projects (the on-going Farmers' Functional Literacy Programme and Non-formal Education for 15-35 age-group to be merged from 1979-80) and for establishment of institutional structures for training and resource development. Besides, funds for strengthening of planning and administrative structures may also be provided by the Central Government. The rest of the financial responsibility must rest with the State Government and, speaking of the overall five year outlays, the expenditure to be incurred through the States should match the expenditure to be incurred by the Central Government.

38. *Costing:* The cost per person enrolled in adult education programme has been calculated at the rate of Rs. 60. Since approximately one-third of the participants may drop out, the effective cost per learner comes to Rs. 90. However, as the duration of some of the programmes may be shorter, and some voluntary contribution may also be made, the effective cost per learner has been assumed at Rs. 80. This, however, does not include the expenditure on planning and administrative structure, on evaluation and monitoring and on post-literacy and follow-up activities. Assuming that the effective target for the Five Year Plan period would be 650 lakhs, as indicated in the Draft Five Year Plan document, the requirement of funds for the period 1978-83 would work out as follows:

6.50 crores X Rs. 80.00	Rs.	520	crores
Add 10% (Administrative cost)	Rs.	52	crores
TOTAL	Rs.	572	crores
Add 20% (follow-up cost)	Rs.	114.4	crores
GRAND TOTAL:	Rs.	686.4	crores
		or	say
	Rs.	686	crores

The Yearwise Phasing of the Target would be as follows:

Year	Annual coverage (in millions)	Cumulative coverage (in millions)	Cost (Rupees in crores)
1978-79 (year of preparation)	1.5	1.5	15.84
1979-80	4.5	6.0	48.52
1980-81	9.0	15.0	95.04
1981-82	18.0	33.0	190.05
1982-83	32.0	65.0	336.95
	Total Cost:		Rs. 686.40 crores or say Rs. 686 crores

39. *Multiple agency funding:* Only Rs. 200 crores have been provided for this programme in the Five Year Plan 1978—83. In this contest, it may be mentioned that the Planning Commission has observed that this provision is only one source of funds for programme of adult education and that funds for this purpose would also become available in other developmental sectors such as tribal development plans, rural development programmes and programmes of agricultural development. The Planning Commission has also stated that the present outlay indicated will be stepped up if necessary on the basis of the experience gained in the year to year implementation of the programme.

The International Dimension

40. *The International Dimension:* Keen interest has been evinced by a number of international agencies and other countries in supporting NAEP as well as in obtaining the services of Indian experts in the programmes, being organised by other developing countries. While appreciating the offers made in this behalf, it would be advisable to base NAEP on country's own financial resources. Some of the areas in which the Indian search and experimentation needs to be supplemented include (i) integration of adult education and development; (ii) functionality of adult literacy; (iii) problems of linguistics; (iv) the manner in which programmes oriented towards liberation of the illiterate and poor persons are to be organised; and (v) evaluation and applied research. The countries from which we should seek short-

duration experts would be mostly developing countries. It might be of greater advantage for Indian field workers and experts to visit foreign countries and observe their experiences and learn from them. There may be need to secure support from international agencies or on bilateral basis for training and audio-visual equipment and paper. At the initial stage it would be desirable to channelise international cooperation through UN agencies. Close contact should also be established with international and regional non-government organisations such as the International Council of Adult Education, directly by Government as well as through all-India voluntary agencies.

APPENDIX II

Functional Chart I

National Adult Education Programme
National Board of Adult Education

Ministry of Education and Social Welfare, Directorate of Adult Education, U.G.C., Shramik Vidyapeeths, Nehru Yuvak Kendras, N.S.S., Voluntary Organisations

State Board of Adult Education

Dev. Ministries/ Departments Agriculture, Labour, Information and Broadcasting, Cooperation, Industry, Home (Tribal Dev.), etc.

State Deptts. of Education (or Deptt. Dealing with Adult Education), Directorate of Edu./Adult Education, State Resource Centre, Universities, Voluntary Organisations

State Development Deptts., Agriculture, Animal Husbandry, Dairy, Labour, In-
dustry, Information
and Publicity, Cooperation, Tribal and Harijan Welfare, Community Development, etc.

District Adult Education Committee

Distt. Edu./Adult Education Office

Distt. Offices of Dev. Deptts.

Project Officer

Supervisors
Instructors

Field Functionaries

APPENDIX III

Functional Chart II

State Level Agencies

1. **State Board of Adult Education**

(a) Laying down of policy guidelines.
(b) Certain of Environment.
(c) Periodic appraisal of the Programme.

2. **Steering Committee**

(a) Plan formulation.
(b) Coordination between adult education and various sectors of development.
(c) Coordination among various implementation agencies — Government, voluntary agencies, educational institutions, employers, etc.
(d) Monitoring of the programme.
(e) Advising the State Board.

3. **Education Department or any other Department dealing with Adult Education in Secretariat**

(a) Establishment of management system.
(b) Laying down of financial pattern—delegation of financial powers.
(c) Coordination between adult education and formal system of education—involvement of universities, colleges and schools.

4. **State Adult Education Office**

(a) Preparation of plans, project formats, methodological guidelines.
(b) Encouraging voluntary agencies to participate.
(c) Direction and overall supervision over Government programmes.

(d) Overseeing and coordination of programmes taken up by various agencies other than Government.
(e) Selection and placement of personnel.
(f) Monitoring and evaluation.

5. **State Resource Centre**

(a) Organisation of seminars, symposia, etc., for wide understanding of the concept and objectives of NAEP.
(b) Development of methodological guidelines for curriculum preparation.
(c) Preparation of teaching/learning materials, and devolution of this capability.
(d) Training support to the Programme.
(e) Preparation of guidelines for post-literacy and follow-up action, production or material for neo-literates.
(f) Evaluation, research and innovation.
(g) Publications.

APPENDIX IV

Functional Chart III

District Level Agencies
Collector/Chief Executive Officer

:
:
:

District Adult
Education Committee/Board

:
:

District Adult
Education Officer

(a) **Coordination**

(i) between adult education and development agencies,
(ii) between adult education and formal system of education,
(iii) between adult education and revenue and law and order agencies,
(iv) among various adult education agencies—earmarking of area of operation and creating a consortium for resource development.

(b) **Training**

(i) training of instructors—in projects where the project officer and supervisor need supplementation of their capability,
(ii) inter-learning among project officers and supervisors of various agencies in the district through seminars, workshops.

(c) Control over Government agencies—allowing as much autonomy to them as feasible.
(d) Processing of the applications of voluntary agencies for financial assistance, periodic appraisal of the progress of their work.
(e) Monitoring and evaluation.
(f) Conduct of enquiries necessitated by the direction of State-level or national-level agencies.

APPENDIX V

Functional Chart IV

Project Level

1. **Project Officer**

(With the assistance of Assistance Project Officer and Community Education Organiser)

(a) Identification and appointment of instructors.
(b) Training of instructors.
(c) Securing supplies for instructional arrangements.
(d) Preparatory action for starting of adult education centres curriculum, teaching/learning materials.
(e) Establishment of contact with the field.
(f) Supervision over and guidance to supervisors, and instructors wherever possible.
(g) Contact with district level agencies.
(h) Contact and liaison with block level development revenue and law and order functionaries.
(i) Management of office, maintenance of accounts, etc.
(j) Monitoring and evaluation.
(k) Planning and organisation of post-literacy and follow-up activities, including setting up of a project library centre.
(l) Preparation of periodical project reports.

2. **Supervisors**

(a) Assistance of project officer in resource development, particularly training—recurrent training of instructors in monthly meetings.
(b) Supervision over and guidance to instructors.
(c) Establishing a living rapport with the people of the area where adult education centres are being run.
(d) Liaison with local development functionaries extension officers—and institutional structures such as youth clubs, Mahila Mandals, cooperative societies, panchayats, schools, etc.
(e) Ensuring payment to instructors and availability of supplies.
(f) Ensuring that timely returns are submitted by instructors.
(g) Post-literacy and follow-up activities.

WORKING GROUP ON SCHEDULED CASTES AND OTHER BACKWARD CLASSES DURING MEDIUM TERM PLAN, 1978-83, 1977 – REPORT[1]

Appointment

The Ministry of Home Affairs appointed a Working Group on 8th December, 1977 for the formulation of strategy and programme priorities for the welfare of scheduled castes and other backward classes during the Medium Term Plan, 1978-83.

Terms of Reference

(a) to review the programmes in respect of Scheduled Castes and other Backward Classes;
(b) to advise on the approach, strategies and programme priorities in the next five years; and
(c) to formulate concrete proposals and suggest phasing of the programmes indicating financial and other requirements.

Recommendations

Economic Development

Landless Agricultural Labourers/Marginal Farmers: Special provisions should be made in the land laws of the States to regulate transfer of land and to ensure continued possession of land belonging or assigned to members of the Scheduled Castes.

The State should become a necessary party in all cases of illegal alienation, tresspass and obstructions to taking of possession in cases of assigned land.

---

1. New Delhi, Ministry of Home Affairs, 1978, 106 p.

Special summary procedure should be prescribed under the law for dealing with the cases in which one of the parties is a member of Scheduled Castes.

Penal provisions, of a sufficiently effective and deterrent nature, may be made in the existing land laws to deal with those who, after any land is allotted to the Scheduled Castes, occupy or reoccupy it. These provisions may provide for graded punishment for each repetition of the offence.

All share croppers should be recorded according to a time bound programme in all the States and rights as envisaged in the legislations are made available to them.

The definition of personal cultivation should be amended so as to make absentee landlordism illegal facilitating the transfer of land in favour of actual tillers.

In categories of public services connected with land recording like village office, survey departments, etc., reservations should be fully and quickly implemented.

Implementation of ceiling laws be expedited.

Fifty per cent of the allottees of the surplus land may be chosen from the landless members of Scheduled Castes and Scheduled Tribes.

Minimum wages for agricultural labourers should be strictly enforced and the implementing machinery adequately strengthened in the quantity and quality.

The food for work programme of labour mobilisation, rural works programme and similar other activities including the programme of integrated rural development should also be planned so as to provide alternative and additional employment opportunities to the agricultural labourers throughout the year or for as large part of the year as possible, necessarily including the agricultural labourers bargaining position, at present hopelessly adverse to them, may be improved in their favour and they may be able to be bargain for better wages and their income may be maximised. Such measures should be taken in a planned manner with priority for chronically low agricultural wage and high unemployment and under-employment areas.

Similarly, the non-agricultural occupations should also be taken up on an extensive scale in such areas with accent on Scheduled Castes, through various possible agencies like the I.R.Ds., Scheduled Castes Development Corporations and other organisations as they will also help to improve the bargaining power of the agricultural labourers as well as increasing their income, purchasing power and consumption of wage goods.

All the blocks with more than 20 per cent Scheduled Castes population should be covered under the Intensified Integrated Rural Development Programme within the next two years at the latest.

The benefits in the Integrated Development Programmes should be earmarked to the extent of the proportion of Scheduled Castes amongst the largest groups in each case and till such figures are not available it should be 50 per cent on the total benefits.

The various economic programmes should be reviewed with a view to adopt them to enable the members of scheduled castes become eligible for those programmes and partake in their benefits to the desired extent.

The quantum of subsidy may be suitably revised in all programmes keeping in view the sub-marginal land and weak economic conditions of the members of Scheduled Castes.

The condition of minimum holding for small irrigation wells should be removed and all those members of Scheduled Castes who want to have a well should be provided on priority basis.

A separate chapter in all Rural Development Projects should deal with the development of Scheduled Castes, especially, highlighting the adaptation of the programmes; relaxation of norms and arrangements for review of accrual of benefits and taking up timely review wherever necessary.

There should be a programme to cover all the holdings of Scheduled Castes landholders, most of whom are marginal farmers, with irrigation wells to the fullest possible extent.

Groundwater Irrigation units, which should be self-contained, including specialists from the fields of geology, hydrology, drilling, etc., should be created to provide organisational support for quickly identifying and exploiting the groundwater resources. These units should be adequate in a number to exploit the entire groundwater potential in areas where there is a fair amount of landholding by Scheduled Castes in a time bound programme of three years. Such units should be provided with sufficient physical and financial resources including drills, etc.

Similarly, in respect of surface water irrigation, it should be ensured that the Scheduled Castes landholdings in the command areas are fully covered through channels and necessary physical and financial support is made available.

An Integrated project for development of land held by Scheduled Castes, whether by distribution of ceiling surplus lands or by assignment or by long-term base of temple land, etc., should be formulated so that the grant of land and its development are simultaneous.

The various sectoral programmes particularly in animal husbandry and fisheries should be family oriented. The individual family should be helped to acquire command over the land or the water resources which forms basis of his economic activity. While drawing up these programmes the required inputs and other facilities like fodder and milk collection and marketing arrangements for animal husbandry schemes, should be tied up, so that Scheduled Castes beneficiaries of this sectoral programme may not be handicapped.

All assignments of lands for cultivation in future by corporate bodies of any description should be favour of the Scheduled Castes and other weaker sections of the community. A suitable legislation, if necessary may be brought for this purpose.

All forest waste-lands should be allotted to Scheduled Castes/Scheduled Tribes staying in the vicinity for growing fruit trees with usufructory rights trying the programmes with the food for work programmes.

Artisan Group: Comprehensive programmes may be prepared for those occupational groups in which a large number of participants are members of the Scheduled Castes covering all phases including possessing, manufacture and sale. These programmes should have the primary producer at the centre, and should have as their objectives maximisation of the share of the primary producer in the net proceeds of the sale of the products.

In the light of the above the concerned ministries may prepared a broad frame for development of the relevant occupations as a part of the general sector plans within the next three to six months to effectively cover all the participants therein within the medium term plan 1978-83. These programmes should become operational with effect from 1979-80.

Wherever the demand pattern warrants training up of new entrants into any such occupation take carpet weaving, cane and ban book-based crafts, crafts based on palm leaf, grass, reeds and making of matches at cottage industry level, atleast 50 per cent of the candidates for training should be selected from among the Scheduled Castes. In the District Industries Centres (DICs) which have become the main agency for the development of small, cottage, and village industries especially in rural areas, and in which there is one manager designated to look after the cottage and village industries, the entire organisation should be oriented to the philosophy of not permitting any modern sector industry which will adversely affect the traditional sectors or the existing employment, and should positively give first priority to further increasing the scope for traditional artisans and employment in this sector. This approach should also be enjoined upon the various coordination groups of the state, regional and national level dealing with the guidance as well as monitoring of DICs.

Since a large proportion of Scheduled Castes are engaged in occupations based on leather, it will be useful to have a leather development corporation in the states which will look after the occupations based on leather from the raw material point to the final processing and marketing stage, geared towards maximizing the income of the primary producers and craftsmen.

Organising the Rural Poor

The strategies and programmes of assisting the creation of sound organisations of the poor should be devised keeping in view the objective of enabling the poor, through their organised pressure, to counteract the inadequacies of administration and opposition of vested interests and claim as a right the benefits that should accrue to them.

The process initiated by the Ministry of Labour for organising the rural poor should be further intensified and effective programmes chalked out in the light of the above.

The programmes for bonded labour undertaken by the Ministry of Labour should be intensified, covering the process of identification, release from bond and simultaneous rehabilitation by providing an economic programme along with organisation.

Legislation should be undertaken to make rickshaw-pullers and cart-pullers, etc., owners of their means of livelihood and to prohibit others from owning or plying rickshaws, carts, etc.

Research and development should be required to undertake studies to being technical improvement which will reduce the physical strain of these occupations.

Modern Sectors

Adequate opportunities should be made available and wherever necessary reservations made for members of the Scheduled Castes in all spheres of economic life to promote professionals diversification and vertical mobility. Reservation should also be made in the governing bodies of institutions which will promote and facilitate professional diversification and mobility such as elective posts in cooperatives, particularly including their President; Board of Directors of Banks and other credit financial institutions; Board of Directors of various promotional organisations; bodies governing education such as university senates; Boards of Intermediate Education; Boards of Secondary Education; Board of Technical Education. Elective posts in institutions of local self-government including posts of Chairman/ President of Panchayat Raj Institutions, at the district, block and village level and municipal Chairman.

The steps taken in the government and public sector services need to be fully consolidated and extended to any branch of government and public services to which they do not apply now, closely monitored and remedial measures suggested promptly. The Bureau of Public Enterprises should be responsible for overseeing and coordinating for all industries under their purview. Other Ministries and departments in the Centre and States should similarly be responsible organisations under their jurisdictions. The Department of Personnel should oversee the reservations in services in the Centre, States and public sectors.

Acceptance of a suitable employment policy in consonance with the national objective should be a precondition for all advances and other facilities and assistance of the private sector for business, trade and industry.

The Department of Banking and the Ministry of Industrial Development together may be responsible for ensuring observance of compliance by the private sectors of the employment conditions.

Suitable reservations in all licences, quotas and permits including fair price shops, milk vending shops, coal depots, kerosene shops, etc., for member of the Scheduled Castes be ensured. This should be tied up with suitable assistance programmes suggested elsewhere.

Special efforts should be made to bring about vertical mobility through intensive training and professional guidance. In order to make it effective, employers in the public sector as well as private sector should be required to make advance identification of job opportunities in their organisations, so that suitable candidates for training may be selected jointly by the potential employer, the Education Department and the Harijan Welfare Development and such candidates put through an appropriate course of training with pre-identified employment being made available at the end of the training.

The members of the Scheduled Castes who are nominated to posts like directors, members of governing bodies, etc., and also Scheduled Castes representatives on D.P.Cs. and selection committee, etc., should be given orientation courses in order to enable their to effectively play their role in channelising the benefits of development as well as employment within the sphere of their respective organisations and bodies.

Self-employment schemes should be so devised by every Departments incharge of it so that reasonable participation of not less than their percentage in the population, should to members of Scheduled Castes who are capable of undertaking such schemes.

The Constitution should be amended by the abolition of clause 4 of Article 16 and the introduction of a new Article overriding all other provisions making it mandatory for the State to provide for reservation in employment or appointment to posts and promotion for Scheduled Castes in services under the state, public sector and the those sections of private employment where reservation can be enforced and monitored, provide for reducing the backlog over a period of time and provide for carrying forward vacancies from year to year it qualified candidates are not available at a particular selection. This should be followed by a comprehensive legislation.

The children of marriages where one of the spouses belongs to Scheduled Castes should be entitled to the same benefit of reservation as provided for the Scheduled Castes.

Where one of the spouses of a marriage belongs to the Scheduled Castes, each spouse may be given the highest priority in employment in the quota/category to which he/she will be ordinarily entitled so long as there is no separation or divorce.

The Government of India should prepare a package of guidelines regarding reservations in services, training for eligible candidates to fill the reserved posts, etc., along the above lines and implement it.

Government of India should advise the State Governments to follow the guidelines and provide an attractive incentive in the allocation of Plan resources, for State Governments which will follow it.

When approving any large project it should be ensured that it contains a component for the economic rehabilitation of the small and marginal farmers and agricultural labourers with priority to Scheduled Castes who are dislocated by the location of the project.

There should be a review and revision of fiscal laws especially income tax exemption for depreciation which till the balance against labour intensive technology where it is otherwise viable.

To the extent such exemptions for the capital intensive sector are found to be necessary, countervailing benefits will have to be provided in the fiscal law for the labour intensive sector.

Research and development should be directed towards evolving new appropriate technologies which will make labour intensive projects viable, wherever they are not viable.

Financial Corporations for Development of Scheduled Castes

Corporations for the development of Scheduled Castes should be established in all States which should function as guaranteers and promoters and also provide missing inputs wherever necessary. They should operate through the sectoral authorities and other organisations providing the necessary backup for the programme.

The Corporation should have branches upto district level to begin with in the first phase to be extended as its functions expand. The district branch should be headed by the Collector with district heads of concerned departments, financial institutions as the members and official of the corporation as the secretary. The Managing Director of the State Corporation should have a suitable secretariat status.

At least 50 per cent of the Scheduled Castes families should be covered by some economic development programmes by the end of the medium term plan 1978-83, by the active initiative of the corporation of locate suitable beneficiaries, with a reasonable proportion of women, who can be linked with appropriate schemes through concerned sectorial organisations and financial institutions, as done by the SFDAs.

The Central Government should help the Corporations suitably through participation in their financial structure along with the State Government. The participation of Central Government and State Government should both have a share capital component and a grant-in-aid component to respectively cover commercially viable operations and essential promotional activities like surveys, subsidies for electricity and managerial assistance which may not be viable in commercial terms.

Reorientation of Backward Classes Sector Programme

All Substantive programmes under the backward classes sectors should be taken over by the concerned sectoral authorities in their new plans.

In order that the above goal clearly laid down by the Planning Commission is achieved, the Planning Commission can effectively help by laying down that every sectoral plan including Area Plans should have an optimal special component plan for the Scheduled Castes and should earmark a substantial share of their plan provisions therefor; wherever the pattern off expenditure is not amenable to such allocation they should contain a specific optional share for the Scheduled Castes in the resultant employment, training and other benefits of such plan schemes; the special component plan should also have an adequate in built mechanism of concurrent monitoring and evaluation; and make the above measures a pre-condition for the Planning Commission's consideration and acceptance of sectorial plans of all Central Ministries. A similar approach should also be adopted as a condition for the release of share-capital to co-operative Financial Institutions and other public sector organisations. Such funds should be non-divertible and their satisfactory utilisation should be made an condition for further allocation of resources. In the case of the State plans, the Planning Commission can help by providings, for attractive incentives in the allocation of plan resources for states which accept and implement this approach of an optimal special component plan for Scheduled Castes. The Planning Commission may also insist on a concurrent monitoring and evaluation system being part of the special component plan every sectorial plan as a pre-condition.

The outlays under the backward classes sectors should be used for adapting all going programmes suitably which may include relaxation of the norms liberalising subsidy, providing nucleus money, etc.

It should be ensured that outlays under the backward classes sector have a substantial multiplier effect, their use is made extremely flexible and any scheme of direct relevant to the Scheduled Castes and immediate concern should quality for accommodation therein.

Blocks with Predominant Scheduled Castes Population

Special comprehensive Integrated Development Programmes may be prepared for those blocks where the Scheduled Castes population is more than 50 per cent.

The Ministry of Agriculture may step up as-istance to these blocks if considered necessary and this assistance may be allowed to be used more flexible.

A Committee may be set up comprising representatives of Ministry of Agriculture, Home and Planning Commission which may consider these projects and provide guidelines for their development. The Committee may co-opt members from other Ministries also.

Credits

Where the Financial Institutions disburse credit directly to Scheduled Castes, third party surety for immovable property other than the assets created with the finance assistance should not be asked for.

All banks, Financial Institutions and cooperatives must segregate and disclose in their annual reports and quantum of credit that has gone to Scheduled Castes in each category of loan in the year.

A certain percentage of cooperative credit should be earmarked for the weaker sections including Scheduled Castes and their needs should be met fully and on priority basis.

Weaker sections including Scheduled Castes should be effectively represented on the Boards of Directors, Executive Committees, etc., of Banks, Cooperatives and other Financial Institutions.

In the case of cooperatives the majority of members of the Managing Committee should be from small farmers and those who are below economically and reasonable proportion of this should be reserved for Scheduled Castes by rotation.

The credit needs of agricultural labourers should be studied comprehensively and credit programmes mounted to enable them to organise additional means of livelihood and improve their income.

Consumption credit should be given to borrowers of weaker sections as an essential component of the credit given to them for economic development.

The Ministry of Cooperation, the State Governments and Reserve Bank of India should draw up programmes for the coverage of all weaker sections specially Scheduled Castes bearing these factors in mind.

Arrangements should be made whereby credit will become available for economically weak members of the Scheduled Castes at D.R.J.

Educational Development and Social Services

Education in the case of Scheduled Castes should be accepted as an essential input for social and economic development as also for providing them effective production against exploitation.

The cost of education of a child in the elementary school should be borne by the State by providing midday meal, uniform, text-books and if possible suitable scholarship and stipend.

The assistance programmes should begin with the communities and areas at the lowest level in literacy in case there is a constraint of resources.

The Central Government in the Ministry of Education should give assistance to the States for providing these facilities to the Scheduled Castes children particularly in those States where their level of literacy is extremely low.

The village panchayat and the teacher at the village level, the block level committee and the district level committee at those levels should be given special responsibility for the desired level of enrolment of Scheduled Castes children in the school. This should be especially reviewed by the visiting officials and the committees periodically.

These should be an incentive to the institution or teachers in charge of those schools in case they are able to contain wastage and stagnation for Scheduled Castes and Scheduled Tribes within a permissible limit.

In the Harijan hamlets with population of 50 or more these should be a sub-school catering to the children in the age group 6-9 which should be a branch of the primary school in the main village.

All new educational institutions that may be started in future, other than those referred above may be institutions common to all communities including Scheduled Castes but should be located in the Scheduled Castes localities.

The talented Scheduled Castes Children may be selected at the end of class V on the basis of competitive examination who may be admitted as resident scholars in selected high schools in the district, the cost of which may be borne by the State. The Ministry of Education may modify their existing scheme so as to include two Scheduled Castes Children from each block.

A continuous assessment should be made of those opportunities where adequate numbers Scheduled Castes entrants is not available and suitable occupational guidance should be given to the student coming from schools to enter relevant courses.

The rate of scholarships for all technical and professional courses at all levels including industrial training institutes should be revised so as to cover the entire cost of the resident scholars.

For all professional and technical courses spread over four to five years, a preparatory year may be added for Scheduled Castes students attaining a minimum standard but not the desired standard for entry into the regular course. This year should be treated as a part of the technical education for the purpose of scholarships and stipend.

The anamoly, because of big difference in the policy relating to pre-matric scholarship and post-matric scholarships should be examined quickly particularly taking note of the fact that in the coming years bulk of the expenditure on the post matric scholarships will be borne by the States non-plan outlays.

The rates of scientific, technical and professional courses at the middle and lower level including I.T.Is. may be revised so as to provide fully for resident scholars.

The disbursement of post-matric scholarships should be done through the banks on the production of entitlement card endorsed by the principal of the college.

The administration of the post-matric scholarship schemes may be streamlined and strengthened. The system of random check of scholars may be introduced the administration should be apart of the post-matric scholarship scheme.

Adult Education

Members of the Scheduled Castes should be given the highest priority in the adult education programme. They should be included to the maximum extent in the earlier phase of the movement.

In every village the adult education programme should begin with the Harijan hamlets localities in suitable cases the sub-schools, which we have pressed elsewhere, should also become the centre of adult education.

Adult education should be recognised as an important instrument for eradication of untouchability and the message relating to thereto should be carried to all sections of the society through this medium.

Health Services

The medical department should take special measures to acquaint themselves with the health conditions prevalent in the helmets inhabited by Scheduled Castes.

The duties of the community workers should be so organised that visit to Harijan Hamlets are ensured and they get reflected in the reporting system. The extent of assistance given to individuals belonging to Scheduled Castes should also get reflected in their report.

The doctors at the P.H.C. and district level should specially visit Harijan Hamlets while touring in the rural areas and personally assess the health conditions, therein. Special surveys may also be undertaken in the known pockets of high incidence of general or special diseases.

Traditional Dais

The existing isolation between the modern mother and child care system and the traditional system service by dais should be removed so that the benefit of the former can reach the lowest strata of society through the traditional network.

The services of dais should be 'municipalised' under the aegis of the panchayats, each dai being paid minimum fee of Rs. 25 for each delivery performed by her. The expenditure on this service of the panchayat should be fully reimbursed by the State being suitably shared between the Government of India in the Ministry of Health and the State Governments. The total expenditure on these schemes would come to roughly Rs. 25 crores per annum.

All dais within the jurisdiction of primary sub-centre should undergo intensive/refresher training periodically. They should also be provided scientific instruments and first-aid medicines for prenatal and post-natal services.

Drinking Water Wells

The availability of drinking water sources in the Harijan basties should be separately assessed treating the hamlet as a unit in all the villages.

The Harijan *basties* which have no source of drinking water should be provided drinking water wells on a priority basis, the numbers allocated for them each year should be in the same proposition as the number of Harijan hamlets without drinking water sources in the total number of villages in the States.

Common wells for all including Scheduled Castes may be dug wherever the scope and the need exist for a single common well, but such common wells should be located in the Scheduled Castes localities.

Housing

A strategy for a massive programme of house building for rural poor including members of the Scheduled Castes should be evolved to improve the housing condition according to a phase programme.

This programme should be based on local designs, local material and local skills. The contractor should not be allowed to come into the picture.

The State would give assistance for enabling the landless persons to construct their own house with their own labour thus capitalising it in the process.

This programme should be taken up on a cluster basis, so as to bring about social cohesion and optimal services.

No Housing Cooperatives will be registered unless they have 15 per cent of the members from the Scheduled Castes communities, except if, and to the extent exempted with the approval of the Social Welfare department for want of members of Scheduled Castes interested in joining. The societies including those already registered, which do not follow these instructions and also do not provide for the needs of the Scheduled Castes members should not be given financial or other assistance by the Government or any financial or promotional institutions.

While the massive housing programmes is in progress according to its time schedule, simultaneously as a short-term measures, an operation "house sites for all houseless poor" should be undertaken to provide house sites for all houseless poor persons and implemented through teams of officers, with emphasis on Scheduled Castes, moving from village to village and solving the problems in totality within two years.

Wherever member of the Scheduled Castes and other houseless poor are in occupation of Government land and other public land, ownership rights be conferred on them immediately.

All vaccant land in the main village site area should be allocated to such persons including Scheduled Castes.

In addition, suitable public land adjoining the village site should be earmarked, or private land acquired, and developed plots allotted to houseless poor persons who are not in occupation of any unobjectionable land already.

While making land allotments, land acquisition, etc., care should be taken to see that these policy of segregation and isolation should be avoided and wherever lands are available, Scheduled Castes are brought into the main village and where no such land in available in the village, land adjacent to the main village of the area should be allotted acquired.

In all the above new housing areas and existing residential areas of the Scheduled Castes, all the living and social amenities like safe drinking water, electricity, drainage and convenient access to the main road, to burial/cremation grounds and to educational and medical institutions should be provided.

All house site areas allotted for houses to poor persons including Scheduled Castes should be covered with housing programmes as far as possible.

Wherever electricity has reached the main village it should be extended to the Scheduled Castes locality.

In future electrification of a village should first start with the electrification of the Scheduled Castes localities of the village.

All works of above types may be allotted to Labour Cooperative Societies of the beneficiaries.

Urban Housing

In slums, which do not have to be re-located, the living conditions should be upgraded to acceptable levels by providing municipal and social amenities like protected drinking water, drainage, electricity, internal roads connected with the main road, fair supply shops of essential commodities, educational and medical facilities and community halls with radio, library and recreation arrangements.

In order to accommodate surplus residents of the above type of slums and residents of slums which are beyond repair and have to be relocated, 50 per cent of surplus land under urban ceiling legislation may be earmarked for Scheduled Castes.

Social and municipal facilities as prescribed above may be provided in re-located slums and also in localities other than slums which have a concentration of Scheduled Castes.

Ownership rights on the sites in slums and other localities with Scheduled Castes concentration should be vested in genuine and deserving residents, wherever their huts or houses are located on unobjectionable public land, wherever they are located private land, ownership rights be given to them.

Work relating to slum improvement, slum re-location should be allotted to labour cooperatives of beneficiaries.

The above task should be taken as the priority task of urban local bodies, Central and State Level urban development and housing finance bodies, urban development authorities and State Housing Boards and these should be reflected in the physical programmes as well as in the allocation of resources.

Professionalisation of Unclean Occupations

The delinking of the occupation from the caste and improving the methods of working in these occupations. So far some efforts have been made in relation to the second aspect only with limited success.

We would like to shift this emphasis to the first part so that the occupation gets professionalised. The problems of the working condition of the occupation are not relatable to a caste but to that profession and can be dealt within ordinary course similar to those in any other modern profession.

Scavenging

The occupation of scavenging of dry latrines should be professionalised of within a period of four years in all the municipalities throughout the country. The Ministry of Works and Housing should provide necessary funds say Rs. 25 crores to States within their Budget for this purpose.

The working life of the persons engaged in scavenging of dry latrines should be completely segregated from their personal and social life.

The wage of scavenger of dry latrines should be sufficiently high and not lower than that of a class III employee. He should be given a suitable occupation allowance for this purpose. A phased programme of conversion of dry latrines should be undertaking, taking care that those who are engaged in cleaning dry latrines are simultaneously found attractive employment.

Employment of the children below the age of 16 in this direction should be made illegal.

The localities inhabited by scavengers should be made liveable forth with. Each family engaged in this occupation should be provided adequate loan and grant for residential house to be constructed in general localities. The grant portion should be met by the Central Government, the State Government and the voluntary share of large industries, who should be persuaded to associated themselves with this. The loan and grant element should be so proportioned as to fit it with the realistic repaying capacity of the family.

All the children in the age group 6 to 14 should be provided education compulsorily in residential schools to be fully subsidised by the State. There should be Balwaris for all children belonging to these families. The Central Scheme of pre-matric scholarship should be suitably expanded.

Professionalisation of this occupation should be taken as a National Programme for which Government of India should assume the responsibility by providing funds and directions wherever necessary. An outlay of Rs. 20 crores may be made for this scheme in the Central Plan for the next medium term plan.

Strong social reform measures should also be initiated through voluntary effort for improving the social conditions of the communities.

Flayers and Tanners

The entire spectrum of activities from lifting of the animal to the final stage of bones collected and processed skin should be appropriately organised by KVIC under the aegis of the Ministry of Industrial Development.

The field level support for this organisation will be provided by the State Board and the concerned State Departments.

A quick study should be made of practices adopted by the flayers and tanners and their remuneration by way of conventional payments or commercial value of products in different parts of the country.

A suitable scheme should be prepared to ensure minimum return to the flayer for each animal flaying either through a system of purchasing the skin at a support price or paying him fees for flaying the animal. Similar approach may be adopted for other processes also.

Tanning should be organised in villages on modern lines throughout the country.

The Indian Veterinary Research Institute should study the traditional techniques of flaying and work out a package of transferable technology to individual flayers dispersed in the villages.

A time-bound programme should be prepared for professionalising this occupation on the lines suggested above within the next four years for which adequate financial provision should be made.

Development of Denotified, Nomadic and Semi-Nomadic Communities

A substantial programme for the development of Nomadic and semi-Nomadic and Denotified communities should be taken up in the medium-term plan 1978-83 jointly by the Central and State Government special financial provisions being made under their respective plans.

That the programmes for development of Denotified Nomadic and Semi-Nomadic communities should be group oriented addressed to the problems identified for each specific group.

Since it will be difficult to trace and tie up the flow of benefits from general sector programmes to each tiny group, their contribution may not be insisted upon in the case of similar groups and in the earlier phase of developmental programme of even the bigger groups.

Each State should make an overall assessment of the situations relating to Denotified, Nomadic and Semi-Nomadic Communities by a general enumeration of these communities; a detailed but rough documentation of their present condition, mode of living, etc., based on information already available and detailed study commissioned for specific groups.

Programmes should be prepared immediately for such of these groups as are enlisted as Scheduled Tribes as a part of the tribal development programme on a model similar to that for the primitive groups.

Programmes should also be prepared for those groups which are enlisted as Scheduled Castes drawing upon the funds available under the Backward Classes Sector and the special allocations for Denotified, Nomadic and Semi-Nomadic Communities recommended by us earlier.

Programmes for identified groups may be taken up for others also based on reconnoital survey of each group identified.

The programmes for Denotified, Nomadic and Semi-Nomadic Communities should be comprehensive in coverage and no aspects of their social and economic life should be outside its ambit.

In the case of Denotified Communities, if will be necessary to immunise them from harassment on mere suspicion and instant help in distress should be built into programmes if the group agrees to follow the path of honest living, forgetting its past.

In the case of Nomadic and Semi-Nomadic Communities their adjustment to the new economic forces and provision of social services should be given priority.

Flexibility and problem solving should be the by words in the programmes of Denotified Nomadic and Semi-Nomadic Communities.

Time Bound Programme for Eradication of Untouchability

Stamping out of dissemination or disability, in all forms in relation to access to pubic places and social and religious and economic services.

Professionalising those occupations which are treated as unclean with a view to delink the occupation from the caste.

An effective programme of social and economic development, particularly for the weakest sections amongst the Scheduled Castes with clear targets for the next four years.

A national endeavour to bring about an order eliminating discrimination on caste considerations. All organisation must accept this responsibility as their legitimate tasks.

Creation of general consciousness amongst all sections of society to treat the practice of untouchability in all forms as an evil and eliminate it.

Free access to all public and religious places as also availability of professional services should be ensured forthwith to all sections of our society. Virulent pockets in the district and blocks may be identified for intensive work. Broad-based committees may be set up at these levels whose members should assume direct responsibility for intensive work in assigned villages. All these pockets should be covered within three years according to a clear time-schedule. Economic programmes should get highest priorities in the development project programmes covering that area.

Professionalisation and municipalisation of scavenging of dry latrines should be taken up immediately with a view to effectively delink this occupation from the caste and social life of the workers. A package of programmes should be drawn up for them to be funded by the Municipal Communities, Central Government and the State Governments. This task should be completed within a period of three years.

Intensive economic development programmes should be taken up which may broadly include the following.

(a) These should be earmarking of outlays in all economic programmes which should be in proportion to the number of Scheduled Castes in the target groups with some weightage in their favour and relaxation of the norms;
(b) At least 50 per cent of the landless labourers and agricultural farmers should be covered under these programmes within the next four years;
(c) Comprehensive programmes should be prepared for identified professions in which bulk of the workers belongs to Scheduled Castes. These Programmes should aim at ensuring accrual of benefit of higher technology, better marketing credit, etc., to traditional Scheduled Caste workers; and
(d) Scheduled Castes Development Corporations should be established with adequate financial support by the State and the Centre.

Each Ministry/Department should draw up suitable schemes for implementing the action plan urgently. Committees may be set up in the Centre as also in the States which may clear these plans to be incorporated in the annual plans of concerned Ministries.

The Ministry of Home Affairs in the Centre and the Scheduled Castes Development Departments in the States should have a nuclus fund for supporting priority schemes under Eradication of Untouchability Programme to be taken over by the concerned Ministries/Departments in the subsequent years.

Arrangements should be made for effective implementation of Civil Rights Act for which cells should be created in the Centre and the State.

High level broad-based committees may be set up at the Centre and the State with representatives of the political parties, social worker, voluntary organisations which may give the entire programme the form of a National Movement.

There should also be a special cell to review the progress of steps along the above lines. It will help to impart the requisite urgency and priority if the highest authority of the State, namely the Chief Minister, makes it convenient to have the Cell functioning under his direct guidance.

Implementation and Administration

A national consensus should be evolved about action programme for development of Scheduled Castes and eradication of untouchability so that (a) sporadic resistance to its implementation can be effective over come; (b) the programme does not run into controversies political or otherwise, and (c) its implementation can be seen through to a successful finale by single minded administrative action.

Social service and voluntary organisations should have a very special position in the programme of removal of untouchability and development of the Scheduled Castes particularly in creating the right social environment for the implementation of these programmes. Financial resources should not be constraint in expanding their programmes provided the services of dedicated persons can be obtained for this work.

The entire curriculum of elementary and secondary schools should be reviewed by top sociologists and educationists under the aegies of the NCERT with a view to inculcate an attitude against social discrimination and at the same time, developing egalitarian outlook.

As an immediate step, the NCERT, Ministry of Education and State Education Departments should undertake the introduction of one lesson in all text-books dealing with subjects like Social Studies, History, etc., bringing out the anti-rational, anti-national, in human and unscientific nature of untouchability.

On the front page of all other text-books, four or five sentences should be prominently printed stating that (a) untouchability is a sin;

(b) untouchability is a crime; (c) untouchability in inhuman; (d) untouchability is unconstitutional, etc.

The representatives of various media particularly newspapers, films, radio, T.V., theatrical groups should come together and evolve a strategy for internationalising the message against social discrimination particularly untouchability, into their general programmes on continuing basis. The Ministry of Information and Broadcasting should take the lead in this and be the nodal point for this purpose.

The various media should be used for carrying the messages of social reformers of the past. Special films may be commissioned and their teaching should be given a place in the school and college texts and reading material for the adult.

The teachings of social reformers against the caste system, untouchability and inequality should also be widely publicised by being affixed inside buses, trains and publicised on hoardings and posters in public places and in schools, libraries, etc.

Films already taken in different languages dealing with the subject may be exhibited widely and doubled in other Indian languages.

Classics dealings with the subject should be translated in other Indian languages.

The most radical structuring may be needed in the field of agriculture and rural development administration covering not only State service but all wings of public service including the servants of Banking Institution and other Financial Institutions, etc. The personnel of all categories dealing with development projects in the State have to be persuaded to a system of values where service in rural areas and work with rural agencies is regarded as more important than other fields of work which, in the past, have carried greater prestige. A revised structure of rewards by way of recognition and preferment would be helpful in achieving this.

Each organisation should be fully responsible for implementing the developmental programmes relating to scheduled castes in their respective sectors. They should have a senior officer exclusively for attending to this task in their departments.

Development of weaker sections should be an essential part of all re-orientation, entry point and in-service training programmes. Special re-orientation programmes may also be taken up wherever necessary under the overall guidance of the Department of Personnel.

The Harijan Welfare Department in the States should be re-orgnised and they should be placed under a senior officer of standing. He should exclusively attend to the development of Scheduled Castes except where he may also be in charge of Scheduled Tribes in all those state where their population is very small.

A senior officer should be appointed in each district as Scheduled Caste Development Officer who should be of the rank of Additional District Magistrate and should be given a place next only to the Deputy Commissioner.

There should be a Committee for Scheduled Castes Development which may be constituted at the district level under the Chairmanship of the Collector with heads of departments as members and the Scheduled Castes Development Officers as the convener, for reviewing the implementation of programmes by the respective departments whose directions in this regard should be binding on all departments.

The officers working in the Scheduled Castes Development should be handpicked and their services should be specially recognized.

A new personnel policy will have to be formulated and implemented immediately covering all public services including State service and the service of our public agencies like Banks, etc. It should consider aspects such as additional allowances which should be fully compensatory as also an incentive, weightage in the calculation of level of service for the purpose of promotion, accepting the extent of benefits to weaker sections as the basic criterion for the assessment of the officers and making service in this priority sector the route to the international assignments and other such advantages which are in practice generally held in value and esteem.

An effective high level committee in the Government of India with the powers and competence to give mandatory directions should be set up in order to ensure that the requisite steps are fully, promptly and competently taken by the various Central Ministries and other Central Agencies.

A provision of Rs. 500 crores be provided in the plan for special programmes for Scheduled Castes.

The requisite human infrastructure be built up.

The procedure for creating the human infrastructure and releasing the special Central Assistance be efficient and free from bottleneck.

CHAIRMAN INDEX OF COMMITTEES & COMMISSIONS IN INDIA 1947-77 Volumes 1 to 15

APPENDIX

CONTENTS SURVEY OF COMMITTEES & COMMISSIONS IN INDIA 1947-77 Volumes 1 to 15